Translation Practices Explained

Translation Practices Explained is a series of coursebooks designed to help self-learners and teachers of translation. Each volume focuses on a specific aspect of professional translation practice, in many cases corresponding to actual courses available in translator-training institutions. Special volumes are devoted to well consolidated professional areas, such as legal translation or European Union texts; to areas where labour-market demands are currently undergoing considerable growth, such as screen translation in its different forms; and to specific aspects of professional practices on which little teaching and learning material is available, the case of editing and revising, or electronic tools. The authors are practising translators or translator trainers in the fields concerned. Although specialists, they explain their professional insights in a manner accessible to the wider learning public.

These books start from the recognition that professional translation practices require something more than elaborate abstraction or fixed methodologies. They are located close to work on authentic texts, and encourage learners to proceed inductively, solving problems as they arise from examples and case studies.

Each volume includes activities and exercises designed to help self-learners consolidate their knowledge; teachers may also find these useful for direct application in class, or alternatively as the basis for the design and preparation of their own material. Updated reading lists and website addresses will also help individual learners gain further insight into the realities of professional practice.

Sara Laviosa
Sharon O'Brien
Kelly Washbourne
Series Editors

Supplementary Resources Disclaimer

Additional resources were previously made available for this title on DVD. However, as DVD has become a less accessible format, all resources have been moved to a more convenient online download option.

You can find these resources available here: www.routledge.com/9781905763290

Please note: Where this title mentions the associated disc, please use the downloadable resources instead.

Translation-Driven Corpora

Corpus Resources for Descriptive and Applied Translation Studies

Federico Zanettin

Routledge
Taylor & Francis Group
LONDON AND NEW YORK

First published 2012 by St. Jerome Publishing

Published 2014 by Routledge
2 Park Square, Milton Park, Abingdon, Oxfordshire OX14 4RN
605 Third Avenue, New York, NY 10017

Routledge is an imprint of the Taylor and Francis Group, an informa business

First issued in hardback 2015

Typeset by
Delta Typesetters, Cairo, Egypt

British Library Cataloguing in Publication Data
A catalogue record of this book is available from the British Library

Library of Congress Cataloging-in-Publication Data
Zanettin, Federico.
Translation-driven corpora corpus resources for descriptive and applied translation studies / Federico Zanettin.
p. cm. -- (Translation practices explained)
Includes bibliographical references and index.

ISBN 978-1-138-13722-6 (hbk)
ISBN 978-1-905763-29-0 (pbk)

1. Translating and interpreting--Study and teaching--Data processing. I. Title.
P306.5.Z36 2012
418'.02--dc23

2011038436

This book is dedicated to my mother, and to the memory of my father

Table of Contents

List of figures and tables

Acknowledgements

I would like to thank the Series Editors, Sara Laviosa, Sharon O'Brien and Kelly Washbourne, for their careful reading, critical comments and helpful suggestions; Guy Aston, Silvia Bernardini and Dominic Stewart for reading and commenting on various draft chapters; and Federico Gaspari for a detailed reading of a first version of the whole manuscript. All remaining errors are of course mine.

Federico Zanettin
July 2011

1. Introduction

Electronic texts and text analysis tools have opened up a wealth of opportunities to higher education and language services providers, but learning to use these resources continues to pose challenges to scholars and professionals alike. This book is concerned with the creation of electronic text corpora and their exploitation in descriptive and applied translation research. As such, it takes a broad perspective on the use of technologies for analyzing texts, ranging from the applications of corpus linguistics to translation studies to the use of corpora in translator training as well as the use of corpus resources by translators, language services providers and computational linguists.

Almost 20 years have passed since Mona Baker's (1993) seminal article on the application of insights from corpus linguistics to translation studies. Since then, corpus methodologies have become almost mainstream in descriptive translation studies, and corpus-based language instruction has become a standard component in many translator training university courses. Concurrently, computational applications increasingly based on corpora such as translation memories (TMs) and machine translation (MT) systems have become part of life for all language services providers, not only for specialized and technical translators. Monographs and collected volumes have appeared on both theoretical and descriptive aspects (e.g. Laviosa 2002; Olohan 2004; Anderman and Rogers 2008) and pedagogical applications (e.g. Bowker and Pearson 2002; Zanettin *et al.* 2003; Beeby *et al.* 2009; Tengku Mahadi *et al.* 2010), and monographs on corpus linguistics often include sections on translation and contrastive linguistics (e.g. Tognini-Bonelli 2001; Meyer 2002; Hunston 2002). The online Translation Studies Abstracts database (TSA Online) lists over 800 entries in the Corpus-Based Studies category.

In this volume, corpus creation and use are illustrated through practical examples and case studies, with each chapter outlining a set of tasks aimed at guiding researchers, students and translators to practise some of the methods, and use some of the resources discussed. These tasks are meant as hands-on activities to be carried out using the materials and links available in the accompanying DVD. Suggested texts for further reading at the end of each chapter are complemented by an extensive bibliography at the end of the volume.

The main focus is on the creation and use of corpus resources by researchers and scholars as well as university students following advanced translator training and translation studies courses. However, the volume may prove of interest not only in translation-oriented academic settings but also to language and translation professionals. While some familiarity with translation studies research may be helpful, it is not taken for granted. No knowledge of corpus linguistics is assumed.

1.1 Book outline

Following this Introduction, the book is divided into six main chapters, each focusing on specific aspects of corpus creation and use, and containing a number of practical tasks and a list of suggested further reading and links to online corpus resources. The book can be read sequentially and basic concepts are defined as they are encountered. However, each chapter has an autonomous structure and some topics, tools and methods are discussed or mentioned in more than one place. In these cases, the reader is consistently referred to the other places in the volume where these aspects are discussed. All chapters include a Tasks section inviting researchers, students and translators to practise some of the methods discussed and use the materials. The tasks are related to the examples presented in each chapter, and they are meant as hands-on activities to be carried out on the accompanying DVD (see section below). Practical activities are reproduced in print for the reader's convenience and ease of reference, and it is assumed that users will have access to online computing facilities in order to carry out (part of) the tasks.

Chapter 2 offers an introduction to corpora and applications of corpus linguistics methodologies to translation studies. The various types of corpora used in descriptive and applied translation research are presented, and examples from a number of corpus-based projects are surveyed and discussed. A typology of corpus-driven corpora is sketched out, starting from a variety of corpora used in descriptive research. These usually contain two or more subcorpora which are compared in order to find similarities and differences between source and target texts or languages, to isolate potential distinguishing features of translated texts or languages, or to study translation styles and genres. Some studies investigate varieties of translated language produced by specific types of language users such as interpreters, translation trainees or language learners. There follows a brief overview of the types of corpora typically used in translation teaching and learning, namely large monolingual corpora and small, *ad hoc*, disposable do-it-yourself (DIY) corpora, either monolingual or bilingual. This general introduction to translation-related corpus typology and corpus-based research ends with a short overview of the use of corpora in machine-assisted translation and computational linguistics.

Three different tasks are proposed as a way to practise the research methodologies discussed. The first consists in replicating a piece of research using the *Translational English Corpus* (*TEC*) hosted at the University of Manchester and accessible online. In the second, the same techniques and procedures are employed to compare research findings with those obtained from *COMPARA*, a bilingual, bidirectional parallel Portuguese-English corpus hosted in Lisbon and also accessible online. In this experiment, only the English language components (both translations and non-translations) of the corpus are selected and used. Finally, the online interface of the *Learner Translation Corpus* (*LTC*) is examined. This contains original and translated texts in many European languages, produced by both translation trainees and professional translators.

Chapter 3 deals with corpus design and acquisition. After the main phases of corpus construction are introduced, various issues regarding the size and composition of corpora are discussed. The evaluation of the internal composition of a corpus in relation to its size is required when assessing representativeness and comparability. This is especially relevant for studies based on translation-driven corpora, which usually involve a comparison of findings derived from subcorpora in the same and different languages. To exemplify the implications of decisions that can be taken when designing a corpus, a detailed case study is presented. This concerns the design of *CEXI*, an Italian-English bilingual bidirectional parallel and translation-driven corpus.

Ideal criteria for corpus design often need to be adjusted to practical constraints such as project funding, copyright restrictions or lack of appropriate corpus material or tools. These considerations lead to and examination of the implications of creating corpora from the Web, which contains enormous quantities of textual material already available in electronic format. First, the Web is examined as a 'surrogate corpus' with respect to issues of size and representativeness. The tools available to use it as a language rather than a content resource are also discussed.

This is followed by an analysis of the Web as a source of corpus data. Corpus linguists and translation researchers, as well as translation practitioners, can in fact create monolingual corpora as well as bi- and multilingual comparable ones, both general and specialized, by downloading and processing Web documents retrieved using Internet search engines and directories. Such corpora can also be created through semi-automatic routines implemented by *ad hoc* programs and online services. Further issues concerning the design and acquisition of bilingual and multilingual corpora, both parallel and comparable, are explored in relation to corpus alignment and processing in Chapter 6.

The tasks presented in Chapter 3 involve the drafting of a corpus creation project, and the design of two DIY Web corpora. It is up to the individual reader to decide upon the precise nature of the project. A grid for outlining a corpus building project is provided to guide the prospective corpus developer through all the main stages. This task is followed up in Chapter 6 where the reader will be asked to reconsider some of the issues addressed, with a focus on the construction of multilingual corpora. The two DIY corpora will be created in one case by manually sifting results from Internet searches (in English), in the other by semi-automatically compiling a bilingual comparable corpus.

Chapter 4 goes through the different stages of corpus compilation and use, from corpus encoding and annotation to indexing and data retrieval, focusing on methods and standards for the annotation of robust corpora to be used in descriptive translation studies. It is suggested that common encoding standards should be adopted by the research community, and that a modular approach accommodating different layers of annotation can be used to encode different textual features. This approach is illustrated by a short introduction to some existing standards for corpus annotation, i.e. the Text Encoding Initiative (TEI) guidelines and the XML Corpus Encoding Standard (XCES). A model header is presented, followed by a summary introduction to how structural and linguistic annotation can be recorded in an XML TEI conformant document. Different layers of annotation can also be stored by implementing a model in which annotation is kept separate from the running text. This is illustrated through examples of annotation from the *Learner Translation Corpus* (*LTC*), first introduced in Chapter 2.

The practical tasks designed for this chapter allow the user to create and search a single-document corpus. First, an XML TEI conformant document is created from a source PDF file by manually marking up documentary and structural information in the text. The document is then linguistically annotated, validated and indexed, and finally the very small corpus created is explored through a couple of sample searches. The different pieces of software used to process the text at various stages (text conversion, manual and automatic annotation, indexing, text retrieval) are freely available on the Web and partly included on the accompanying DVD.

Chapter 5 offers an overview of software tools which can be used to create, manage and analyze corpora, and describes methods and techniques which allow end users to make sense of corpus data. After a discussion of the hardware and software requirements which have to be met in order to successfully carry out the various stages of corpus construction, the chapter focuses on corpus analysis. Basic corpus analysis tools and techniques as well as more advanced ones are presented and illustrated through practical examples, in order to show how they can be used to investigate lexical patterning. The concepts of collocation, colligation, semantic preference and semantic prosody are also introduced and briefly discussed. Like Chapter 3, this chapter focusses on monolingual corpora and subcorpora. The tools and techniques described provide the background for a more detailed discussion on the construction and analysis of multilingual corpora in the following two chapters.

Practical examples of how to investigate phenomena such as collocation and semantic preference using corpus analysis software are provided in the Tasks section. The reader will be shown how to create, manipulate and explore wordlists and concordances using as data the bilingual comparable corpus created in Chapter 3, and a text-only version of the *Open American National Corpus (OANC)* (provided on the DVD). These tasks can be carried out using freely available text analysis software (copies on the DVD) or commercial software. More advanced computational tools are tried out in order to investigate lexicogrammatical relations through the analysis of word clusters and word profiles.

Chapter 6 focusses on the creation and use of bilingual parallel corpora. After a discussion of the terms and concepts of comparable and parallel corpora, it provides a survey of procedures and tools for the alignment of parallel corpora at 'sentence' level, which illustrates issues in parallel corpus processing. Various aspects are exemplified through reference to the creation of various parallel corpora. The *OPUS* collection of parallel multilingual corpora is presented as a case study of tools and procedures that can be used to build an aligned version of parallel corpora. There follows an examination of the difference between parallel corpora and translation memories, and a discussion of 'word alignment' in both comparable and parallel corpora.

The tasks in this chapter include the alignment of a parallel corpus using texts provided on the DVD and already partially processed in a previous task. Two different alignment programs (both available on the DVD) are used to align three text pairs of different length and processing ease. The alignment of the three parallel texts involves different approaches to automatic alignment and different degrees of interaction between the user and the alignment application. Readers may either start the process from scratch, after selecting parallel texts of their choice and performing basic preparatory processing, or use the files in plain text format available on the DVD, and to which the activities described refer. A further task consists in revising the corpus building project outlined in Chapter 3, in light of the information acquired in the following chapters and using the checklist provided.

Chapter 7 deals with tools and techniques for using multilingual corpora in descriptive and applied translation studies. It also addresses issues concerning the display and analysis of parallel concordances. After an overview of some of the tools which can be used to search parallel corpora and retrieve parallel concordances, two case studies are presented to illustrate the types of analysis which can be carried out with parallel corpora, depending on the level of annotation and on the software used for retrieving and displaying parallel concordances. First, the methodologies that can be adopted for investigating the descriptive features of translated texts are illustrated through examples from a parallel corpus comprising some novels of Salman Rushdie and their Italian translations. These are analyzed using the *ParaConc* parallel concordancer. Then, a contrastive analysis of the words 'eye' and *occhio* is carried out using the search interface to the *OPUS Multilingual Word Alignment Database*. Finally, the use of multilingual corpora as resources for professional translators is briefly examined. It is argued that comparable and parallel corpora can help translators deal with translation problems for which they may not find a solution elsewhere.

The tasks for this chapter include hands-on explorations of two different parallel corpora: the small literary English-Italian parallel corpus created and aligned in the Tasks section of Chapter 6, and the multilingual parallel corpus *Europarl*, which contains several hundred million words of the EU parliamentary proceedings from 1996 onwards in 20 languages. The corpus of literary texts is searched using the Demo version of *ParaConc* included on the DVD, while the *Europarl* corpus is searched using the online *OPUS* online multilingual search interface.

The concluding chapter looks at foreseeable developments of applications of computer technology to the retrieval of textual and linguistic information in electronic texts of relevance for descriptive and applied translation studies. Some recommendations are also made as to possible future developments of corpus-based projects in translation research. A reference section and a names and subjects index are appended at the end of the volume.

1.2 How to use the DVD

The DVD is divided into three main sections:

Tasks
Software
Texts and corpora

Each *Tasks* section contains directions on how to carry out the activities and links to the software applications, online services, texts and corpora needed. Hands-on activities can be done individually or in pairs. It is advisable to open external links in separate tabs or pages, so as to always keep directions in view. Users should also save their texts and working files in a personal folder (and subfolders if necessary) on their computer or on a server.

The *Software* section contains an index to the programs which are needed to carry out the activities in the Tasks sections. Copies of these programs, on which the activities proposed in the Tasks sections have been tested, are stored on the DVD. These programs are available as either freeware, shareware or demo copies, and links to the sites from which the programs were downloaded are provided, together with further links to other corpus tools discussed. The versions of the programs available on the DVD run on a standard PC with a Windows operating system. However, most applications have also been developed for use under other operating systems, and are available at the respective Web sites.

The *Text and corpora* section contains the textual material needed for some of the activities. The files should be copied into a working folder. The texts used are taken from the Web and presented at different stages of processing. They serve as backup and reference texts to be compared with the materials processed by the user while carrying out the tasks. Corpora have either been created by myself from available sources and services, or taken from online repositories in the public domain.

Computer programs and websites often have a short lifespan, and it is inevitable that some of the links to online texts and resources will become obsolete, and some services and pages will be no longer available. With time, improved versions of some of the software included on the DVD will be produced, while some will disappear, and new and better programs will be developed. However, most of the resources linked to and listed have proved to be resistant, as they have existed in one version or another over a number of years. Research teams and corpus projects may undergo institutional changes, but if well grounded they are usually maintained and funded, and broken links may often be easily found and replaced using an Internet search engine. More and better corpora are being made available online as corpus-based translation research and practice become more widespread. It is hoped that the book and accompanying DVD may serve as a springboard for further experimentation and autonomous use.

2. Corpus linguistics and translation studies

In general language, the word 'corpus' simply means a collection of texts put together according to some informed criteria, for example the works by one particular author (e.g. all of Shakespeare's plays), or the writings on a particular subject produced within an institution (e.g. the entire body of the European legislation). In the field of corpus linguistics, a corpus is by default assumed to be a collection of texts in electronic format which are processed and analyzed using software specifically created for linguistic research. Corpus linguistics has in fact been made possible by the advent of computers, and, while progress has not been due only to technological advancements, its present developments rest largely on increasing computational power and availability of electronic texts.

The first electronic text corpus dates back to the 1960s, when the *Brown Corpus* was created at Brown University in the USA (Kučera and Francis 1967). The corpus itself is about one million words, and contains random samples of texts selected from the Brown University Library catalogue. While the stated aim was to represent contemporary written American English, it seems clear that the corpus could at most aspire to representing a "published", learned variety of it. The application of computer technologies to the study of language continued, for instance with the *Lancaster-Oslo-Bergen (LOB) Corpus* (Johansson *et al.* 1978), created on the model of the Brown corpus and used, among other things, to investigate variation between American and British written English.

Developments in corpus linguistics were initially slowed down by technological constraints but also because a mentalist approach to the study of language largely prevailed over a social one in the second half of the Twentieth century. According to Robert de Beaugrande (1994, 1997, 1998), the adoption of corpus linguistics as a methodology for the study of language is based on the idea that language is a social phenomenon and as such it must be investigated starting from actual data. Hence the use of corpora entails a "functionalist" approach to linguistic meaning as opposed to a "formalist" one. Stubbs (1996) equates this functional approach mainly with the "British tradition", which goes back to the work of J.R. Firth of the 1930s and was further developed by M.A.K. Halliday and John Sinclair. This approach is in opposition to the "American tradition" as represented mainly by the ideas of Noam Chomsky. Indeed, Chomsky has been regarded as the main person responsible for the discredit of corpus linguistics until the field's return to favour not long ago (McEnery and Wilson 1996:4ff).

The use of corpora in linguistics remained largely marginal until the 1980s, when the first corpus-based dictionary was published (COBUILD, Sinclair 1987). Nowadays most dictionaries claim to be based on a corpus, and corpus linguistics has become mainstream as a methodology if not a theoretical approach in the academic study of language. The 1990s saw the establishment of second-generation, 'general, national, reference' corpora which, in the wake of the 100-million-word *British National Corpus* (Burnard 1995), were created in various Western countries, including Spain, the Czech Republic, Germany, Slovenia, France, and Italy. During this time, corpus linguistics informed other fields of linguistic research besides lexicography and language theory, reviving applied research areas such as machine translation and computational linguistics as well as discourse studies and language variation. Corpus linguistics has also influenced related fields such as language pedagogy and translator training, multilingual terminology, tools for professional translators, contrastive linguistics, and descriptive translation studies.

Third-generation 'mega-corpora' now run in the many hundred million words for many languages, and, even more importantly, many corpora of various size and description are available to the larger public, often on the Internet. The availability of large quantities of text in computer-readable form over the Internet has had important consequences for corpus linguistics, leading, for instance, to a reappraisal of the criteria used to define corpora. Corpus design and construction issues will be addressed in Chapter 3 and Chapter 6, but it is important to stress that a corpus is not simply a collection of electronic texts. In order to have a corpus we need a purpose for collecting and analyzing them, and a set of criteria for selecting and describing them.

The purpose of building and/or using a corpus varies of course according to the research or professional project. This book is especially concerned with "translation-driven" corpora, i.e. those which are created and/or used for some translation-related purpose. Like other types of corpora, they can be described using general criteria such as medium (written, spoken, or both), date, language, author and translation status of the texts. A corpus can be synchronic or diachronic, depending on whether the texts were produced in a fixed span of time or over a period, and its composition is usually dictated by the type of language which it aims to represent. General monolingual, synchronic corpora may only contain a typewritten electronic version of printed texts (for example the *Brown* and *LOB* corpora) or, like the *BNC*, they may also include transcriptions of spoken language (10% of the corpus). The internal categories of the *Brown Corpus* mirror the bibliographic descriptions of a 1960s US college library, whereas the *BNC* was designed according to more "democratic" criteria. Both textual production and textual reception were considered, and texts were drawn from a number of sources (book catalogues, best-seller lists, lists of magazines, library lending statistics and periodical circulation figures) as well as a smaller percentage of unpublished texts (Burnard 1995). Translation-driven corpora can be monolingual, i.e. contain only texts in one language, or bi-/multilingual, i.e. contain texts in two or more languages.

It is now often the case that source texts for corpora are already available to the corpus compiler in 'native' electronic format rather than having to be typed or scanned in. But in order to be profitably used in a corpus they must usually undergo some sort of conversion from one file type or format to another. Also, they have to be standardized according to the specifications of the corpus project and the software used to create and analyze the corpus. Such specification may entail not only issues of character encoding and file format, but also the processing of the texts in order to enrich them with documentary and linguistic annotation. Issues of corpus annotation will be taken up in Chapter 4, but a first distinction which can be introduced here is that between 'plain text' and 'annotated' corpora. The former contain only running text, encoded as an ordered sequence of characters. The latter are collections of texts to which explicit interpretative annotation has been added to the words in the texts in order, for example, to distinguish between instances of the word 'run' as a verb and the same word used as a noun, or to group together 'run' and 'runs' as two forms of the same verb.

After a corpus has been compiled, it can be subjected to analysis. The primary data used in corpus-based investigations are wordlists and concordances. Figure 2.1 shows the top head of a wordlist (the first 25 'words', including punctuation) from a corpus of English academic texts (selected from the *British National Corpus*), ordered according to their frequency in the corpus.

word	Freq
the	429343
,	391643
.	313580
of	270136
and	207623
to	188666
in	137911
a	125736
is	110721
)	91843
(	90538
that	78781
-	72584
The	62638
as	62128
be	58053
for	54827
''	47283
:	47060
are	42545
with	40947
it	39044
by	38772
on	38754
was	36764

Figure 2.1. A wordlist

A concordance is basically an index of all the instances of specific words or phrases in a corpus, along with their contexts (usually one line). Figure 2.2 shows a concordance for the word 'translation' in the same corpus. Concordance lines are ordered according to the first word to the left of the search word (the line containing 'brand-name translation' comes before the one containing 'broken translation').

SS	foreign market. E.g. Dong and Helms brand-name	translation	model aids the 'Language' dimension. </p>
AH	translation in the play, Hugh's static and broken	translation	of Virgil's fated fall of Carthage, is
SS	influencing the decisions of publishers buying	translation	rights. Sales volumes depend on the type
LS	like GLP-1 implies regulation perhaps by	translation	control, or protein stability. POS-1 seems
AH	see communication everywhere, whether by	translation	, signs or systems; not perfectly, but successfully
LS	covalently attached to the 5' end which causes	translation	to switch to cap independent translation
AH	our interpretation on something. A correct	translation	or interpretation is a translation which
AH	what, when, where etc'. To make a correct	translation	we need to rely on understanding of the
SS	awarding contributions destined to cover	translation	costs. </p><p> Storia and Missione, pages
PS	income statement. Examples - foreign currency	translations	risks, fixed asset revaluations, actuarial
AH	accepted that what he means is a direct	translation	to 'compassion', or more accurately 'suffering
AH	demanded what amounted to an incorrect direct	translation	for American scholars in the 1880's, who
AH	language. For example, 'The first Dutch	translation	of the Institutes appeared in Emdem in
AH	Frankfurt: Verlag der Autoren, 1988 (English	translation	by Michael Hoffman, London: Faber and Faber
AH	Association of Shinto Shrines), English	translation	of this pages available, however, as the
SS	In England' 1969 (original 1845, English	translation	1887) London, Panther Books </p> <p> Giddens
AH	more recently Vasunia. </p><p> An English	translation	was provided in 1988. </p><p> Froidefond
SS	from the Man Booker prize if an English	translation	is not available or gone out of print.
AH	with a dialogue which included the English	translation	below it. Vocabulary was presented in lists
SS	omitted from the process causing the entire	translation	of bases into different codons, or amino

Figure 2.2. A concordance of the word 'translation' in the BNC

Issues concerning processing, display and analysis of corpus data will be dealt with in Chapter 5 and Chapter 7.

2.1 A typology of translation-driven corpora

Corpora used in descriptive and applied translation studies usually involve the comparison of at least two main sets of data, which can be called corpus components or subcorpora. These can be texts belonging to different varieties in the same language (e.g. translations vs non-translations), or texts in different languages. These in turn can be translations, together with their respective original texts, or only texts originally produced in different languages. If translated texts are included in the corpus, these can all be translations of different texts from one language to the other, or multiple translations of the same text, in one or more directions of translation. The authors of the translations (or of the source texts) may be native speakers of the source or target language, language learners, trainee or professional translators.

Using the number of languages involved as the main classification criterion, a first type of corpus is the *monolingual comparable corpus*, in which two varieties of the same language, in translated and non-translated texts, are compared. A second type of corpus is the *bilingual corpus*, which can come in two varieties: a) the parallel corpus (sometimes also called translation corpus, e.g. Johansson and Hofland 1994; Altenberg and Granger 2002), in which source and target texts are paired; b) comparable corpora, in which two (sub)corpora, paired on the basis of textual similarity, are compared (see Chapter 6 for further discussion). A third type of corpus is the *multilingual corpus*, in which more than two languages are involved. This too can be either parallel or comparable. Bi- and multilingual corpora in which both directions of translation are accounted for (thus generating four corpus components for each pair of languages) are sometimes also called *'reciprocal' corpora* (Teubert 1996). Translation-driven corpora may contain published translations or unpublished texts produced by professional translators, as well as translations (and their sources) produced by trainee translators and language learners. A learner translation corpus, like corpora produced by other kinds of language users, may come in all the flavours described above (monolingual and bi- or multilingual, comparable and parallel). Finally, while not specifically created for translation research or practice, general reference corpora in one or more languages can also be used as control data for comparison purposes. Reference corpora are simply corpora which are taken as a point of reference for standard usage. They are designed in order to be maximally representative of a language or language variety (see discussion in § 3.1.3).

It is important to distinguish clearly between comparable and parallel corpora. Comparable corpora can be monolingual, bilingual or multilingual, and are composed of texts which have no direct translational relationship, i.e. they are not translations of each other. In contrast, parallel corpora (bilingual or multilingual) have a translation relationship. This defining relationship can be either unidirectional, going from one source to a target language, or bidirectional, going both ways.

The following diagram summarizes the main types of mono- and bilingual translation-driven corpora described in the literature.

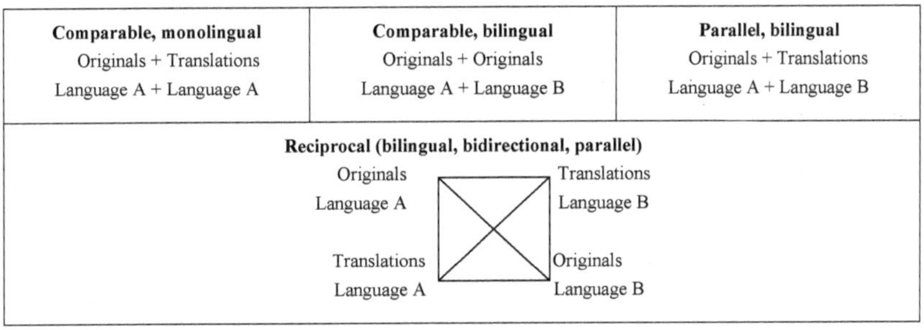

A bilingual, reciprocal corpus may be graphically represented as a square cut across by diagonal lines, in which the different subcorpora stand at the corners. Multilingual, reciprocal parallel corpora may generate complex models which can be described as star and diamond configurations (Johansson 2003:139-142). In a star model there are multiple translations of the same texts in different languages. The diamond model includes source texts in more than two languages as well as their translations in all the other languages.

2.2 Corpus-based translation research

This section provides an overview of a range of corpus types and methodologies which have been used in descriptive translation studies. It first considers research into regular patterns of behaviour which characterize the language of translated texts, often referred to as 'translation universals'. The discussion is illustrated through case studies involving the use of monolingual comparable corpora and bilingual corpora, both parallel and comparable. This is followed by a discussion of how translation-driven corpora have been employed for research into regular patterns of translator behaviour, and to compare different languages. Each line of research is illustrated through examples of research hypotheses, methodologies and findings.

It is suggested that corpus-based translation studies seem to profit most not only from the comparison of different corpus components but also from the triangulation of data, and the combinations of different components of multilingual corpora as well as of reference corpora not originally created for translation-oriented purposes. Finally, a brief description is provided of learner corpora, that is databases containing translations by trainee translators or language learners, and of interpreting corpora, containing the transcriptions of spoken translations, possibly together with the audio/visual recordings.

2.2.1 *Regularities of translations*

The word 'translationese' is often used in connection with translation as "a fairly colloquial designation for any characteristics of a text that indicate that it has been translated from another language" (Graubart Champe 2000:1421). The term has often been used pejoratively to indicate "awkward, overly literal language that clearly shows the translator's incompetence" (Wechsler 1998:270) or "literal translation that makes little sense or is unnatural" (Newmark 1991:106). The term, however, has also been used in a more neutral sense, meaning simply that the language of translated texts may differ from that of other texts produced in the same language. One of the first corpus-based studies investigating the language of translations as a specific variety in itself was in fact Martin Gellerstam's (1986) research on 'Swedish translationese'. Gellerstam used a corpus of English fiction translated into Swedish and a comparable corpus of original Swedish novels in search of 'translation fingerprints', that is "all forms of translation which can in some form be viewed as having been influenced by the original text, without the term implying any value judgement" (Gellerstam 2005:202). The research demonstrated clear statistical differences in the use of certain Swedish structures and expressions between translated and non-translated fiction. Gellerstam's 'fingerprints' metaphor is helpful in distinguishing this type of linguistic interference from translationese as odd and unnatural language, and provides evidence of the influence that the source language exerts on translation.

The idea that a corpus of translations may be compared with a similar corpus of comparable texts originally written in the target language to isolate descriptive features of translations was also put forward by Mona Baker (1993), who suggested that a comparison of linguistic data in a comparable monolingual corpus of translated and non-translated texts could unveil some regular patterns of behaviour common to all translated texts, from all languages and into all languages. Such features would be the result of the process of translation, and could be used to confirm or disconfirm given hypotheses about the properties of translated texts.

Baker brought together two research strands, descriptive translation studies and corpus linguistics. From the so-called descriptive branch of translation studies (Holmes 1972; Toury 1995) came the suggestion that translations should be studied in their own right as facts of the target language (Toury 1995) and as a 'system' in the 'polysystem' (Even-Zohar 1979) of the culture and language into which the texts are translated. Like descriptive translation studies, corpus linguistics is deeply committed to a grounding in empirical data. It subscribes to the view that language should be studied in actual texts and described for what it is rather than for what it should be. Monolingual comparable corpora seemed ideal to test theories that had hitherto been posited but not demonstrated by empirical data on a large scale.

Baker (1993, 1995, 1996) proposed that monolingual comparable corpora could be used to study universal features of translation, some of which were derived from previous studies suggesting that translated texts may have their own distinctive linguistic profile (Blum-Kulka 1986; Frawley 2000; Toury 1995). The hypothesized universals were *simplification*, *explicitation*, *normalization* or *conservatism*, and *levelling out*, which together can be seen as pointing to a general process by which translation as a specific type of writing activity involves the 'de-complexification' of language. It is assumed that translators simplify the source texts, by cutting on the fringes of more creative uses and conforming more closely to typical patterns of language, while at the same time adding supplementary information where a need is perceived. In this area of study, the task of corpus-based translation studies is to identify the linguistic features which may provide evidence of such regular patterns of behaviour, and to examine such features by means of corpus methodologies.

As in corpus linguistics, the application of corpus-based methodologies to translation research was largely made possible by the availability of corpora of translated texts. One of the first corpus projects created for research purposes was the *Translational English Corpus* (*TEC*), which has been developed since the mid-1990s under the direction of Mona Baker at the University of Manchester, UK, and is currently available online. The *TEC* model was followed by other research projects, and more monolingual comparable corpora were created for languages such as Finnish, Swedish and Brazilian Portuguese, among others.

Research into the so-called 'translation universals', a term which has been questioned by Mauranen and Kujamäki (2004) and Baker herself (2007), has widened to include other linguistic features investigated through monolingual comparable and parallel corpora. Translation universals were originally defined by Baker as "features that typically occur in translated texts rather than original utterances and which are not the result of interference from specific linguistic systems" (Baker 1993:243). As suggested by Gideon Toury (2004), 'universals' should be taken to mean universal tendencies, that is linguistic behaviour generally occurring in translated texts rather than in non-translated texts, a behaviour governed by probabilistic laws rather than by cognitive necessity.

While the inclusion of translations from many languages in corpora such as the *TEC* may go some way towards preventing a source language bias, it remains unclear to what extent features of, for instance, explicitation are due to contrasting linguistic systems and to what extent they are due to the process of translation. This is why, as Maeve Olohan (2004:43) suggests, findings from comparable monolingual corpora should be supplemented with findings from parallel corpora. In this respect, Andrew Chesterman (2004) proposes a distinction between T-Universals (where T is for Target), which are "characteristics of the way translators use the target language" (Chesterman 2004:39) and S-Universals (where S is for Source), which are "characteristics of the way in which translators process the source text" (*ibid.*). Thus we may distinguish between 'explicitness' and 'explicitation', where the first term refers to a characteristic of translation products, as compared to non-translated texts in the same language (T-Universal), and the second refers to a characteristic of the translation process, to be investigated using translations and source texts (S-Universal).

Studies investigating universal features of translation appear to focus on both the T- and S- types, and examine categories such as simplification, explicitation, standardization, translation unique items, untypical collocations, and interference (Mauranen 2008). In what follows, I present some examples of research hypotheses, methodologies and findings concerning translation universals as investigated in both monolingual comparable and bilingual parallel corpora. Most examples are taken from research carried out with well-known corpora such as the *TEC*, the *Corpus of Translated Finnish* (*CTF*) and the *English-Norwegian Parallel Corpus* (*ENPC*), of which more will be said in section 2.3.2 on contrastive studies.

2.2.1.1 Simplification

Sara Laviosa used the *TEC* to try to isolate linguistic indicators of the hypothesized phenomenon of simplification (Laviosa 1996, 1997, 1998b, 1998c), defined by Baker (1996:176) as "the idea that translators subconsciously simplify the language or message or both". Laviosa adopted a target perspective, comparing two English monolingual subcorpora, the first being a subset from the *TEC* and the second a subset from the *BNC* (together making the *ECC*, *English Comparable Corpus*). One investigation involved the comparison of two small subcorpora of newspaper texts (each between 75,000 and 100,000 words); a second one compared two subcorpora of fiction (each between 750,000 and 1,000,000 words). The 'news' *TEC* subcorpus contained translations from *The European* and *The Guardian* newspapers, while the 'fiction' subcorpus contained 14 translated narrative texts. The research methodology was the same in both cases, and consisted of deriving indicators of lexical simplification from word count statistics. The software used in the research was *WordSmith Tools* (Scott 1996-2011), and the statistical data on the texts in the two subcorpora were used as a basis for comparison.

A first simple measure included a comparison of standardized type/token ratio, or the ratio between the number of unique word forms (types) and the number of running words (tokens) in the corpus. The higher the number of different, non-repeated words in a (sub)corpus, the more varied the language variety represented by it. A lower type/token ratio in translated texts would point to a variety of language resulting from a process of simplification. The type/token ratio is standardized in the sense that it is computed not on the whole corpus, nor on individual texts, but on fixed intervals set by the researcher (by default the type/token ratio is computed by *WordSmith Tools* for every 1,000 words) to prevent the skewing of data which would result from having texts of different lengths. Both *BNC* subcorpora proved to have a higher lexical variety than the subcorpora of translated texts, thus confirming the simplification hypothesis.

A second feature of simplification considered was lexical density. This was measured by computing information load as a function of the ratio of lexical (content) words to grammatical (function) words (Stubbs 1996:172), and by looking at the percentage of the corpus taken up by 'list-heads', that is to say by the words which are repeated more often. Translated texts are hypothesized to have a higher ratio of grammatical words and more repetition, and thus a simplified lexicon. Findings consistently pointed to a higher lexical density in non-translated texts, i.e. grammatical and most frequent words take up a larger share in the corpus of translations vis-à-vis the corpus of non-translations.

Other indicators of lexical simplification were also considered, and not all statistics were in agreement, for example a comparison of the average sentence length for all subcorpora offered contradictory results. However, the data seemed to be good evidence that the lexicon of translated texts is less varied and less dense compared with non-translations.

Laviosa's findings concerning lexical variety have been replicated by other studies, for instance by Xiao *et al.* (2010) whose data, a monolingual comparable corpus of Mandarin Chinese, confirmed a tendency for lexical simplification in translated texts. While in this study the source language of the translational component was almost exclusively English (99%), rather than a range of languages, the typological distance between the two languages provides important support for the supposed universality of simplification.

Other researchers have attempted to look at other measures of simplification, starting from the analysis of concordances rather than from word count statistics. The lexical, collocational and syntactical behaviour and frequency of features such as connectors, synonymous quantifiers, and infinitive *that*-constructions were for instance investigated for translated Finnish. In her study of lexical patterns, Mauranen (2000) compared the linguistic behaviour of a number of 'metatextual' connectors (expressions referring to the text, text-internal connectors, discourse labels and addresses to the reader) in a subset of the *Corpus of Translated Finnish* (*CTF*) in conjunction with Finnish non-translated academic texts. Jantunen (2004) investigated the behaviour of a group of nearly synonymous Finnish degree modifiers (roughly meaning 'very') in a corpus of fiction translated into Finnish, both in comparison with a comparable target Finnish corpus and with the corpus of source texts. Findings from these and other similar case studies are contradictory and do not point to a single tendency. Rather, they show much variation according to text type and source language influence. While not entirely contradicting the results of other studies of lexical simplification, research into translated Finnish warns that some caution should be taken before claiming conclusive evidence for the simplification hypothesis. Cross-validation should be conducted on a large scale by comparing research findings in different corpus types (both comparable monolingual and multilingual parallel), different languages and text types, and by using both quantitative and qualitative methodologies.

It should also be noted that, if a parallel corpus is needed in order to control the source language variable in a corpus of translations as opposed to a comparable corpus of non-translations, monolingual reference corpora for both languages are needed for a study of simplification which involves parallel corpora. In an exploratory investigation of lexical simplification in a small English-Italian parallel corpus containing six novels and one short story by Salman Rushdie, Zanettin (2000, 2001a, 2001b) carried out a comparison of the standardized type/token ratio for the two components. The results apparently seemed to provide evidence against lexical simplification in translation, since the Italian translations had a higher type/token ratio than the English source texts. However, parallel texts are clearly not directly comparable, since they are written in different languages. Thus, statistics for each corpus component need to be gauged against a standard measure of lexical variety in comparable, reference corpora, one for each of the two languages involved. This was done by first comparing the statistics of the target corpus with those from a reference corpus of about the same size (1 million words) containing 17 novels originally written in Italian. A comparison was then drawn between the source corpus and a reference corpus containing an equal size subset of fictional text extracts from the *BNC*. Finally, as in Laviosa's research, figures for the findings were subjected to a test to establish the statistical significance of the results. These showed that both original and translated novels are more lexically varied than the average for each language, as would be expected in linguistically creative works such as those by Salman Rushdie. However, the standardized type/token ratio of the corpus of translations was closer to the Italian average than that of the source text corpus was to the average for English. In other words, these translations can be claimed to have a lower lexical variation than their source texts.

2.2.1.2 Explicitation

The second presumed universal of translation derives from Shoshana Blum-Kulka's general Explicitation Hypothesis, which states that explicitation may be "a universal strategy inherent in the process of language mediation, as practiced by language learners, non-professional translators and professional translators alike" (Blum-Kulka 1986:21). More specifically, Baker (1996:176) refers to it as "the tendency to spell things out in translation, including, in its simplest form, the practice of adding background information". Like simplification, explicitation has also been investigated both from a monolingual and a bilingual perspective, using monolingual comparable corpora as well as bilingual and multilingual parallel corpora. One well-known example of research concerning explicitation as a

T-Universal is a study on the use of the optional reporting *that* in the *TEC* corpus (at the time consisting of 3.5 million words) in comparison with a subset of the *BNC* (Olohan and Baker 2000). This study, described by Olohan (2004:94-97) as "one of the first large-scale empirical studies to compare language patterning in a corpus of translations with that of a corpus of non-translations", focuses on lexicogrammatical relations, and the methodology implies manipulating and looking at concordance lines retrieved by regular search patterns. The assumption is that the optional reporting *that* in English is an indicator of explicitation, and translators use it more often than do writers of original texts. To test this hypothesis, it is first necessary to isolate instances of the optional reporting *that* in both subcorpora, translated and non-translated. To establish how many occurrences of the optional *that* are omitted, it is necessary to establish how many occurrences could have been used but were not. This is something which cannot be done by using the word *that* as a search term, since such a search would not only not retrieve the contexts in which the optional *that* was not used, but it would also retrieve those instances in which *that* was not optional or was not used in a reporting structure.[1] Furthermore, the search would generate a very large number of concordances, possibly too many to handle. To restrict the sample and to circumvent the 'missing option' problem, the technique used was that of retrieving contexts which may require the use of the optional *that*, and counting the instances where this was used or not. The context is evoked by using the forms of the reporting verbs *say* and *tell*. After weeding out unwanted occurrences (the vast majority), the percentage of omissions of the optional *that* in the translated texts was compared to that of the non-translational component. The results support "the claim that translators make syntactic relations more explicit by using the optional 'that' more frequently than is typical of non-translated language" (Olohan 2004:71). The methodology used in this case study will be partly replicated in the first practical task at the end of this chapter using the *TEC* corpus, freely available online.

Like simplification, explicitation has also been investigated as an S-Universal. A first indicator of explicitation could be the longer textual extent of translations as compared to their source texts. The explanation would be that translators resort to more words in their effort to explain culturally or linguistically distant features of the source texts. This suggestion, which prior to corpus studies was an often stated but unproved hypothesis, seems to find partial confirmation in some studies involving different languages and translation directions, including translations (of literary texts) from Brazilian Portuguese into English (Maia 1998), Spanish into English (Munday 1998:545), and from English into Italian (Zanettin 2001b). Frankenberg-Garcia (2009a) found that this was true for translations into both English and Portuguese in the *COMPARA* parallel corpus. Word counts for the two subcorpora were not directly comparable, since different languages have different structural features. For example, a nominal group in which the head is premodified by a noun in English (computer screen) is usually translated

[1] This is the problem known in information retrieval as 'noise' (see § 5.2.2).

in romance languages as a noun group postmodified by a prepositional phrase (Italian *schermo del computer*, French *écran d'ordinateur*, Spanish *pantalla de la computadora*), which requires more words. In order to filter out language-dependent biases, Frankenberg-Garcia (2009a) carried out a combined analysis of word counts on the basis of a carefully balanced sample of source texts and translations, whose statistical significance was tested using a paired T-test (see §5.2.3). She suggests that (*ibid.*:57) "the overall increase in the number of words observed in the translations is more likely to be due to differences between source texts and translations than due to lexico-grammatical differences between Portuguese and English".

Linn Øverås (1998) studied explicitating and implicitating shifts in the *ENPC*, in both directions of translation. The study required the manual inspection of the first 50 sentences of each of the 20 paired novel fragments, or 1,000 sentences altogether. The grammatical and lexical devices used to make texts more explicit were noted and counted for both English and Norwegian. Both grammatical and lexical shifts were classified as instances of either 'addition' or 'specification'. Instances of over- and under-specification were also accounted for. An example of addition is the translation of "halvlukkete eller halvåpne øine" (lit. "half-closed or half-open eyes") with "half-closed eyes or half-open eyes", thus replacing an ellipsis by a noun head. Specification includes shifts resulting from either expansion, as when "Nå er St. Patric den største helgenen I hele Ireland" (lit. is the greatest saint) is translated as "Now Saint Patrick is regarded as the greatest saint in all of Ireland", or substitution, as when "Jeg er ingen lommetyv, ingen Veskenapper" (Literally: I'm no pickpocket, no purse snatcher) is translated as "I'm neither a pickpocket nor a purse snatcher". Shifts were counted only if considered to be the result of optional, stylistic choices rather than being due to structural differences between the two languages. About one shift every two sentences was detected in the translations from English to Norwegian, about one in three sentences for the translations in the opposite direction. Of these, the majority consisted in explicitation rather than implicitation shifts. The findings thus appear to substantiate the claim that translated texts, independently of the target language, are rendered more explicit through the insertion of grammatical and lexical items which are added to or specify some item in the source text.

However, there seems to be some variation in the results concerning the explicitation hypothesis (Mauranen 2008:39). While a number of studies for other languages, including research carried out on parallel corpora of Hungarian and English (Pápai 2004; Klaudy and Károly 2005) and German and Czech (Konšalová 2007) have claimed that their results support this universal, others have provided different results, including Puurtinen's (2003) study of connectors in translated and non-translated Finnish children's fiction. Other investigations (e.g. Saldanha 2008; Becher 2010a, 2010b; Musacchio and Palumbo 2010) question the interpretation of the higher frequency of features such as connectors or optional reporting *that* in English as indications of explicitation, arguing that these may also be explained in terms of standardization or source language inference. Becher (2010a) even advocates for the dismissal of the explicitation hypothesis, arguing that it is not formulated and testable with enough rigour.

2.2.1.3 STANDARDIZATION

A third posited translation universal has been variously called standardization, normalization, conventionalization or conservatism. It is related to the idea that in translation, source textual relations are often modified "in favour of [more] habitual options offered by a target repertoire" (Toury 1995:268). The hypothesis is that the language of translation tends to conform to typical patterns of the target language, and that translators tend to adhere to conventional expressions at the expense of more creative ones. A case study of standardization as a T-Universal is Olohan's (2004) study of the derivational suffix *–ish* in the *TEC* corpus. The *–ish* suffix is used to modify both adjectives and nouns (especially colours and numbers), usually rendering them fuzzier or less precise, or functioning as quantifying edges in conversation. Olohan sifted through all instances of words ending in *–ish* in the *TEC* fiction subcorpus, and in a comparable subcorpus from the *BNC*. She found that creative uses of *–ish* were more frequent in translations than non-translations, although modified *–ish* forms for colours, especially basic colours, were more frequent in the *BNC* texts. The study was then followed up by an investigation which tested the hypothesis that translators resort to *–ish* forms because of "the difficulties of mapping source colour terms for non-basic colours onto a target language colour system" (Olohan 2004:116). Lists of colour synonyms for the colours brown, red and blue were extracted from *Roget's Interactive Thesaurus* (for instance, synonyms of blue included azure, beryl, cerulean, cobalt, indigo, navy, royal, sapphire, teal, turquoise and ultramarine), and used as search words. Unwanted concordance lines were weeded out, while relevant instances were counted and added up for each subcorpus. The final frequency counts showed that colour synonyms have a significantly higher overall incidence in non-translated texts. This finding may explain the higher incidence of colour *–ish* forms in translated texts, and be considered as an indicator of higher lexical variety in non-translations.

Since Olohan's case study was based on a monolingual comparable corpus, it was not possible to ascertain whether there was a relationship between the use of colour *–ish* forms in translated texts and the use of a more diversified lexis for colours in source texts. A study of the translation of lexical creativity as an indicator of standardization/normalization from an S-Universal perspective was carried out by Dorothy Kenny (1997, 1998, 2000), using a parallel corpus of contemporary German fiction translated into English. Kenny's methodology consists in identifying instances of idiosyncratic lexis in the source texts by starting from a list of hapax legomena, i.e. word forms that only occur once in the corpus. The initial list was cleared of unwanted items such as non-standard orthographic variations and filtered through a wordlist obtained from a reference German corpus, in order to obtain only words that are unique to the particular works in the corpus. The results of the study show that writer-specific words were normalized, i.e. translated by using more common target text words of phrases in almost half of the cases (Kenny 2000:142-88). Kenny also identified a number of unusual collocations, mostly around the German word *'auge'* (eye). She then looked at how these collocates were translated, finding evidence of normalization in this case as well. Collocation and related lexicogrammatical relations will be discussed in Chapter 5. In Sinclair's words (1991:170) a collocation can be simply defined as "the occurrence of two or more words within a short space of each other in a text", and the unusuality of a collocation may be derived by contrasting it with more typical collocations for that word. A statistical measure of collocation strength can be obtained through corpus analysis software.

2.2.1.4 Translation of unique items

While levelling out, the fourth universal tendency of translation originally proposed by Baker and defined as "the tendency of translated text to gravitate around the centre of any continuum rather than move towards the fringes" (Baker 1996:177) has never been empirically investigated, other candidates for universality have been proposed. Sonja Tirkkonen-Condit (2002, 2004) first put forward the suggestion that target-language specific lexical items, that is words which tend to be "untranslatable" because they lack a straightforward lexicalized equivalent in other languages, are proportionally under-represented in translation. Examples of such items are Finnish clitics and Finnish verbs containing language-specific semantic features such as those of 'sufficiency' (e.g. *uskaltaa*, 'has enough courage' and *malttaa*, 'is patient enough'). Using the *CTF* she found that these 'translation unique' lexical items are indeed significantly less frequent in translated compared to non-translated texts.

Tirkkonen-Kondit's research into lexical T-Universals was built on by other studies using the *CFT*, including investigations of other linguistic indicators such as syntactic and pragmatic features. Sari Eskola (2004), for instance, investigated Finnish-specific syntactical constructions in two subsets of the *CFT*, consisting of translations from English and from Russian. The aim was to examine the possible impact of the source language. The unique items investigated, which have no or rarely used straightforward equivalents in either English or Russian, were less frequent in the translations from both English and Russian, though the latter differed more from original Finnish than the translations from English.

2.2.1.5 Untypical collocations

Another area of corpus-based descriptive research is the investigation of collocational relations in monolingual comparable corpora. A tendency towards untypical collocations was proposed as a T-Universal by Anna Mauranen (2000), who found that translations tend to favour word combinations that "although possible in the target language system, were rare or absent from actual target language texts" (Mauranen 2008:44). Like Mauranen, Jarmo Jantunen (2001) analyzed collocations in translated Finnish, and found that translations display collocational patterns that differ from those found in non-translations.

The methodology used in the study of collocations relies on both manual and automatic techniques. Marco Baroni and Silvia Bernardini (2003), for instance, conducted a preliminary study of collocational patterns in two monolingual comparable corpora, one in English and one in Italian. The English corpus contained both translated and non-translated official reports submitted by different EU countries to the EU Commission, while the Italian corpus contained a collection of articles from the Italian geopolitics journal *Limes*, featuring a large amount of texts translated from a number of languages. In this study, collocations were selected and compared across original and translated texts by computing the relative frequencies of any pair of adjacent words that were made up of words that occurred at least twice in all the subcorpora and at least three times in the relevant subcorpus. The results concerning the *Limes* corpus showed a small but clear tendency for the translated texts to contain a larger number of collocations with stronger association scores (see § 5.2.3). No clear tendency was discerned in the other, much smaller corpus.

A methodology for comparing quantitative aspects of collocational patterning was also proposed by Carmen Dayrell (2007), who analyzed a comparable corpus of translated and non-translated texts in Brazilian Portuguese (*BPCC*). Dayrell selected, through semi-automatic procedures, 10 nouns with a minimum frequency of 200 occurrences in both the translated and the non-translated subcorpora. The frequencies in the two subcorpora were as similar as possible. The collocates were then automatically computed using statistical techniques and retrieved for analysis. The results indicated that collocational patterns tend to be less diverse (i.e. reduced in range) in translated than non-translated texts, that is, translated texts display "a stronger tendency to draw heavily on a small number of collocates" (Dayrell 2007:377) in comparison with non-translated texts.

2.2.1.6 Interference

Finally, some studies claim to provide empirical support for the universal of interference which was proposed as a 'general law' of translation by Toury (1995), and postulates that features of the source language are transferred to the target texts in the process of translation. This hypothesis can be tested by comparing texts translated from one or more languages versus a comparable corpus in the target language. For example, using fairly complex statistical techniques, Baroni and Bernardini (2006b) found that the distribution of non-clitic personal pronouns and adverbs can be used to discriminate between translations and non-translations. Mauranen (2008) presents evidence from some case studies carried out with mono-source language subsets of the *TCF* in conjunction with comparable corpora of non-translational Finnish showing, for instance, that translations tend to over-represent features that have straightforward translation equivalents in the source language.

The case studies described so far provide a non-exhaustive survey of research questions, methodologies and findings, and offer a partial exemplification of what is involved in doing translation research using corpora. The debate is still open on whether the regularities which are found to characterize a corpus of translated texts in relation to either their source texts or a comparable corpus of non-translated texts in the same language are the product of the translation process per se or are the result of mediated communication in general (Chesterman 2007). Indeed, simplification may be a feature not exclusive to translated texts, but common to all texts which imply language contact or intercultural mediation, such as second language writing (Ulrych and Anselmi 2008; Gaspari and Bernardini 2010) or writing about something culturally distant (Becher 2010a). Even assuming that these regularities are specific to translation, it is not clear to what extent regularities in selected corpora of translated texts are due to either cognitively or socially constrained behaviour. In the first case they would classify as universals, with the proviso that they are regarded as tendencies or 'probabilistic regularities' (Toury 2004). In the second case they would classify as historically determined, intersubjective 'norms' (Malmkjaer 2008), which may characterize translation at a specific time, in a specific place, for a specific type of language pair and direction, and for a specific type or genre of texts. Currently, the state of advancement of this type of research does not allow for the drawing of conclusions for a number of reasons, which have been pointed out in the literature and which we will look at summarily below.

First, there is the issue of the paucity of data. The studies produced so far are too limited in number and scope to be conclusive about hypothesized universals and translation norms. The experiments discussed were carried out using corpora or corpus components ranging from the very small (less than 100,000 words) to the still quite small (around 10 million words), as compared to large monolingual corpora which are beginning to be counted in billions of words. The data on which the findings are based are small in size as well as partial: they usually refer only to a specific text type or genre, and each of them only provides information on one or a few linguistic features, which are taken to be indicative of regularities at a higher level of abstraction.

These studies are not always compatible or comparable, as they often differ as regards the design of the corpora (see Chapters 3 and 6) as well as the methodologies and tools used to analyze them (see Chapters 4, 5 and 7). Research has shown that much variation depends on genre, text type and (source) language, and while more studies are being carried out with non-European languages, evidence is still confined to a few languages and genres (mainly literary translation). Most findings tend to confirm the existence of a number of hypothesized universals, but there is also some counter-evidence (e.g. Puurtinen 2003; Saldanha 2004; Corpas Pastor 2008; Wang and Qin 2008). The question remains as to whether different corpus design and methodologies can be claimed to point to compatible findings, and whether different linguistic features can be used as indicators of the same phenomenon.

Furthermore, the phenomena examined are not always clearly defined (House 2008), and the classification of findings in one or the other category is sometimes debatable. In some cases results which were taken to support the explicitation hypothesis can in fact be explained as originating from different proposed universals (Becher 2010a, 2010b), while in others the same studies have been presented in the literature as evidence of different types of translation universals (Mauranen 2008; Laviosa 2008). This proves that there is at least some conceptual overlapping in the definition of these phenomena, and that the relationship between the linguistic features examined and the explicative categories they are supposed to map onto is not always clear.

Finally, some scholars suggest that corpus-based research in descriptive translation studies should find a more robust grounding in Natural Language Processing techniques. According to Silvia Hansen-Schirra *et al.* (2006) there is a gap between high-level phenomena such as simplification and explicitation and the low-level linguistic features which are used as indicators of such phenomena. They argue that while some assumed properties of these phenomena can be tested using measures such as type/token ratio or lexical density that operate at the level of words, others require the analysis of more abstract linguistic features. In order to allow searches based on grammatical relations rather than on simple textual strings there is a need to add explicit linguistic information to corpora through annotation. For example, the German-English parallel corpus set up within the *CroCo* project (Neumann and Hansen-Schirra 2005; Hansen-Schirra *et al.* 2007; Čulo *et al.* forthcoming) aims at filling that gap by allowing for the creation of a catalogue of queries able to retrieve from corpora syntactic features such as raising constructions or cleft sentences based on annotation at the word, phrase and clause level (Vela *et al.* 2007). Gloria Corpas Pastor (2008) also argues that annotation and rigorous statistical techniques may provide more robust ground for corpus-based analysis (see also Corpas Pastor *et al.* 2008). She suggests that word count statistics such as type/token ratio and lexical density are more accurate if based on lemma counts, which allow for different forms of the same lemma to be grouped together (see Chapter 4 on lemmatized corpora). This seems to be especially the case for languages which have a rich morphology, like Spanish, Italian and German.

The search for regularities in corpora of translations has been mostly carried out with the aim of investigating universals, but some studies have concerned themselves with other, more limited objectives. Hannu Kemppanen's (2004) research is a case in point. It examines in depth a specific 'sociologically important' word (*ystävyys*, meaning 'friendship') in a monolingual comparable corpus on Finnish political history including original Finnish texts and translations from Russian, in order to discover ideology-specific features of translated texts (on corpora and ideology see also Olohan 2004:148-149). Ian Williams (2009a, 2009b) investigates theme-rheme progression and verbs that translate 'report' in a monolingual comparable corpus of translated and non-translated Spanish medical research articles in order to devise translation strategies which can help translators approximate the norm established by non-translated texts.

Corpora offer the opportunity to carry out research based on quantitative evidence in a way that would not be possible otherwise. However, evidence of universals, laws or norms of translation can only be derived from the interpretation of replicable and cumulative findings. Regularities of translation, like those of translators and of languages (see below) can only be unearthed through the repeated observation of empirical data and increasingly refined descriptions.

2.2.2 *Regularities of translators*

Translation-driven corpora can be useful not only for research on typical linguistic behaviour of translated texts, but also in the study of individual translations and translators. As opposed to Gellerstam's 'fingerprints' metaphor, which comes from corpus-assisted authorship studies, here we have that of the 'thumbprint' (Olohan 2004:147), of translators leaving their linguistic 'signature' (Baker 2000) in the texts they produce. Different corpus types and combinations can be used to this end, both starting from a source and a target perspective.

Baker (2000) set out to investigate what might be distinctive about the language produced by different translators, starting from the hypothesis that, independently of the source language and of the source text, translators' different profiles of linguistic habits would be manifested through consistently different (unconscious) patterns of choices. To this end, she used a selection of texts from the *TEC*, comparing works by different translators working each from different source texts and languages. The features compared were type/token ratio, average sentence length, and the use of the optional reporting *that* following the verb *say*. In another study and using texts produced by different translators, Baker (2004) also investigated the recurrence of word clusters, repeated strings in expressions such as *on the other hand* and *at the same time*. In both studies, Baker found that translators differ in their use of such features, in most cases also differing from the average data in a reference corpus of non-translated texts (a subsection of fictional texts from the *BNC*). As Olohan (2004) suggests, such studies not only raise the question of investigating the sociocultural environment in which the translation activities take place, but also the issue of distinguishing between idiosyncratic, stylistic and linguistic habits of the translators and "aspects of their works that have been motivated by the source material, the translator's perception of the target readers' needs, expectations, etc." (Olohan 2004:150). Such issues could be partly investigated with another type of monolingual comparable corpus, i.e. one comprising both translated and 'original' texts by the same translator/author.

Research on translator's style also includes quite a few studies carried out with parallel corpora. For instance, Charlotte Bosseaux (2001, 2004, 2006, 2007) investigates how translators manifest their 'voice', their discursive presence in two French translations of Virginia Woolf's *The Wave*. Bosseaux analyzed features such as personal pronouns, time and space adverbials and verb tense in order to determine "whether and how the translator's choices affect the transfer of narratological structures" (Bosseaux 2004:108). Marion Winters (2004, 2007, 2009) studied modal particles and speech-act reporting verbs in two different German translations of the same source text, F. Scott Fitzgerald's *The Beautiful and Damned*. Gabriela Saldanha (2005, 2011) looked at the strategies used by two different translators to translate into English source language words, using a parallel corpus containing both the translations and their source texts of Spanish and Portuguese parallel fiction. She found that one translator (Margaret Jull Costa) makes comparatively greater use of italics, thus emphasizing readability in her translations, while the other (Peter Bush) makes a comparatively greater use of source language words. Similarly, Zanettin (2001b) looked at the different strategies used to translate foreign words by the two Italian translators in the parallel corpus of Rushdie's novels. Jan Rybicki (2006) analyzed two translations from Polish into English of three novels by Henryk Sienkiewicz. By using statistical techniques such as multivariate analysis Rybicki was able to discriminate the characters' idiolect, i.e. words and patterns typically used in dialogues by different characters. He then compared the two translations, in order to observe whether similar patterns were obtained, and found that that was not the case.

Stig Johansson (2004) used a corpus containing a short story and a scientific article translated from English into Norwegian by ten professional translators, to investigate whether any systematic variation could be detected and the extent to which such variation could be attributed to individual stylistic choices or to source language interference. The analysis focused on syntactic changes, more specifically on the subject of the first clause of declarative sentences. The overall tendency was to preserve the subject. In those instances where some change took place (10% of the sample) many shifts were caused by differences between languages, even though there seemed to be "no clear borderline between structural and stylistic differences" (Johansson 2004:49). Also, there was much variation in individual preferences depending on the type of text and the individual translator. However, there seemed to be some correlation between patterns of syntactic changes, and Johansson suggests that a systematic analysis of linguistic features in alternative translations of the same source texts could help identify distinct profiles for individual translators or groups of translators. He also suggests that individual choices can be explained in terms of Toury's (1995) dichotomy of adequacy and acceptability. Translators seem to either tend to conform to the rules and conventions of the target language (acceptability), or to preserve source linguistic features (adequacy).

Corpus-based studies of the translator's style and voice can also usefully incorporate the investigation of paratextual data such as translator's notes, prefaces, etc. (Hermans 1996, 2010; Schiavi 1996).

2.2.3 Regularities of languages

Corpus linguistics has not only spawned a host of studies on regular patterns of behaviour of translations and individual translators, but has also decisively contributed to a revival of contrastive linguistics. In turn, contrastive descriptions are important to translation studies in that they provide the touchstone for assessing the extent to which typical features of translated texts and behavioural patterns of translators are determined by the source language.

Before we provide examples of some research topics and methodologies in corpus-based contrastive studies, it is perhaps useful to distinguish among different types of parallel corpora and say a few words about how the analysis of parallel corpora differs from that of comparable corpora, both monolingual and bilingual. Most parallel corpora used in descriptive translation studies are corpora of literary works, or of fiction, at any rate. Parallel corpora can be monodirectional, as for example the corpus of German source texts and English translations in Kenny (2000) and the corpus of English source texts and Italian translations in Zanettin (2001b). They may contain only one text pair (Váradi 2008) or more works by the same author (Zanettin 2001b) or by different authors (Kenny 2000), and by the same or by different translators. A parallel corpus may also contain more than one translation of the same text(s) into different languages, what Johansson (2003) terms the 'star model'.

Contrastive studies are often based on findings from two sets of parallel corpora, one into each direction of translation. Examples of such bidirectional parallel corpora are the *ENPC* for English Norwegian and *COMPARA* for English and Portuguese. The *ENPC* was created in the mid-1990s in Oslo under the direction of Stig Johansson. It has since generated a large number of studies and has served as a model for corpus projects in other languages. The corpus size is about 2.6 million words, about 650,000 words for each of the four subcorpora, and contains 10 to 15 thousand word samples from 100 text pairs, 50 in each direction of translation. Of these, 30 are from fictional texts and 20 from non-fictional texts. *COMPARA* is an English-Portuguese bidirectional parallel corpus which has been developed from the late 1990s to 2008. Its size is approximately 3 million words in total and it contains 75 different pairs of original and translated extracts from fictional texts published since 1837, written by 35 different authors and translated by 45 different translators. *COMPARA* is freely accessible through an online interface, and will be used for a practical exercise in the Tasks section.

Multilingual corpora can include one or more translations of the same texts into different languages, in multiple directions of translation. This corpus configuration, termed by Johansson (2003) 'diamond model' (see § 2.1 above) is best exemplified by the Oslo corpus network, which was built using the *ENPC* as a first building block and enlarging the languages and translation directions to include German, Dutch, French and Portuguese. An increasing complexity in the design of a corpus involves increasing problems of representativeness, comparability, and balance, which will be discussed in Chapter 3.

The analysis of parallel corpora may take advantage of the same methodologies used in the analysis of comparable corpora, for each subcorpus (translated and non-translated texts). Statistical measures of lexical variety, lexical density and collocational patterns can be derived from automated analysis, and lexical creativity can be explored starting from word frequencies and monolingual concordances independently of whether the texts in a corpus are translated or not. However, one of the main advantages of parallel corpora consists in being able to explore parallel concordances, i.e. to view extracts of the source texts paired on the screen with corresponding target text extracts, or vice versa. Parallel concordances can be read sequentially, according to their order in the texts, as in Øverås (1998) and Johansson (2004), or they can be manipulated and grouped on the basis of linguistic patterns. Figure 2.3 shows a parallel concordance of the word 'Zulu' in a short novel by Salman Rushdie and its renderings in two different Italian translations. Examples are in the order in which they appear in the text.

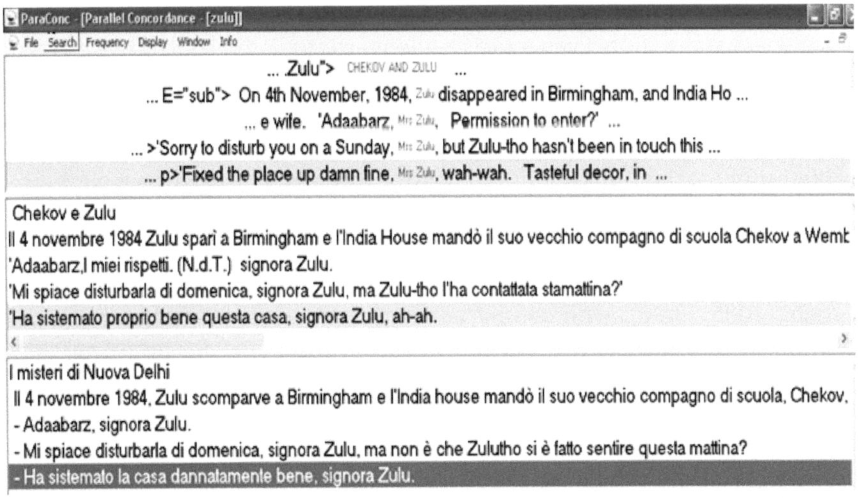

Figure 2.3. Comparing two different translations of the same source text

Bidirectional parallel corpora allow for reciprocity. Aspects and features of two (or more) languages are first brought together through translation, then the analysis is extended to take into consideration the range and frequency of correspondences, and in a cyclical fashion to include other source features which generate the same correspondences, and other translations of these corresponding features in original texts.

Johansson (1998) exemplifies this methodology presenting an investigation of two words, one in Norwegian and the other in English. Looking at how the Norwegian modal particle *nok* is translated into English, he found that the highest frequency is '0 correspondence', meaning that very frequently the modal particle is not directly translated. The second highest correspondence for *nok* is the word *probably*. He then looked at how *probably* is translated into Norwegian, when not as *nok*. An analysis of the correspondences showed the most likely translations of *probably* are in fact the words *sannsynligvis* and *antageligvis*. Similarly, Johansson illustrates how the English noun *mind* has no straightforward equivalent and is translated into Norwegian in many different ways.

Research using the Oslo corpus network and involving various language pairs (English/Norwegian, English/Swedish, English/German, Norwegian/German, etc.) examined, from a contrastive perspective, features such as sentence openings, thematic structure, when-clauses, cognates, connectives, coordination and discourse-structural salience, time and space adverbials, discourse particles, and the *that's what* construction type (see Johansson and Oksefjell eds. 1998).

Some contrastive studies focus on lexical features, while others on syntax, semantics or pragmatics. A corpus-based study in contrastive pragmatics is Aijmer's (2008) investigation of the different realizations of discourse particles in English and Swedish, both in original texts and in translations from the other language. Contrastive semantics is the focus of Diana Santos' (2008) study on the meaning of *result* associated with the English present perfect and its realization in Portuguese translation. Even more frequent are studies in contrastive grammar, for instance Noëlle Serpollet's (2008) study of the English translations of French mandative expressions, Liu's (2004) study of reporting verbs in original and translated English and Chinese fiction, Jiří Rambousek and Jana Chamonikolosová's (2008) study of the translations of English existential *there* in Czech, and Tomás Váradi's (2008) study of noun phrase modification structures as realized in a Hungarian translation of an English novel (George Orwell's *1984*).

A different methodology is adopted in a contrastive study by Ana Frankenberg-Garcia (2005, 2006), who compared the frequency of use of loan words in non-translated, original writings as well as in translations, for both English and Portuguese. She found that, on the one hand, contemporary native-English writers use loan words much more frequently than their native-Portuguese counterparts, from a wider range of languages. On the other, she also found that readers of English are more likely to encounter loan words in original than in translated texts, while the opposite is true for readers of Portuguese. This suggests that, while a 'minor' language like Portuguese may have a higher tolerance for translation interference than a 'major' language like English (Toury 1995:278), the latter may be less conservartive than the former as concerns original writing.

To conclude this first part of the overview with the kind of cautionary remarks which are often found in translation-driven corpus-based studies, it is often the case that the analysis of corpus data, be they monolingual, bilingual or multilingual, comparable or parallel, can profit from being carried out in conjunction with the use of other corpus resources in both source and target languages, including monolingual reference corpora not specifically created for translation purposes. Furthermore, corpus findings should not only be triangulated against other corpus data, but also be assessed against knowledge external to the corpus such as the specific editorial and publishing circumstances under which the texts in a corpus were produced.

2.2.4 Learner translation corpora

The learner translation corpus contains learners' translations, which can be compared with: a) the source text(s); b) the translations of the same source texts by professional translators; c) comparable, non-translated texts in the target language. There can be different directions of translation and more than two languages, so that a corpus including learners' translations can take any of the configurations described for other types of translation-driven corpora, including the 'star' and 'diamond' models.

Learner corpora have been collected since the 1990s for use in second language acquisition studies (Granger 1998). Learner corpora such as the *International Corpus of Learner English (ICLE)*, consisting of essays written by advanced learners of English as a Foreign Language (EFL) from different native language backgrounds, have provided evidence of some major differences in the frequency of use of key grammatical, lexical and discourse features of the target language by second language learners vis-à-vis native speakers/writers of that language. Sylviane Granger (1999) compared error tagged corpora of English texts produced by French EFL students with a comparable corpus of texts produced by English native speakers. The aim was to identify learners' difficulties in order to devise more effective pedagogical tools. Ute Römer (2007) compared the use of *if*-clauses in a corpus of German learner English with that of two other corpora, one containing textbooks of English as a Foreign Language and the other a subcorpus of the *BNC*. She found that the use of this feature by German advanced learners differs both from the usage norm of British native speakers of English (as represented by a subset of the *BNC*) and from the norm put forward in EFL teaching materials.

One of the first studies using a learner translation corpus is that described in Bowker and Bennison (2003). The authors explain how they created an archive of translations by students. The database includes, besides the translations themselves, information about source text, author, date, native language, etc. After this information has been recorded by the students using an input template, different corpora can be extracted from the archive using the prototype Student Translation Tracking System developed by the authors. Such corpora can contain, for example, all translations of a given text, all those from a given language, all those by students having the same native language, all those produced at the same or at a different stage of instruction, or a combination of these criteria. The corpora thus created can then be analyzed using external software such as *WordSmith Tools* and *ParaConc* in order to identify areas of difficulty for learners and study both the process and the product of translation.

A larger database of texts by translation learners is the *Learner Translation Corpus* (*LTC*) created under the *MeLLANGE* project by an international academic and industrial consortium. The *LTC* is a multilingual annotated corpus whose core is composed of translations produced by trainee translators (http://corpus.leeds.ac.uk/mellange/ltc.html). It contains source texts of 4 different text types (legal, technical, administrative, and journalistic) in 11 European languages (Danish, German, Greek, English, Spanish, Catalan, Finnish, French, Italian, Dutch, Portuguese) and their translations into and from these different languages. The *LTC* contains 429 translations by students (350 words each on average), 232 of which are annotated for translation errors, and 55 translations by professional translators, together with the source texts for all translations (Castagnoli *et al.* forthcoming). The translations are lemmatized and annotated for part-of-speech (see Chapter 4 on annotation) as well as for errors according to a hierarchical scheme of error typology which provides for a range of either content-related or language-related errors. The *MeLLANGE LTC* is an open-ended project, and the corpus is freely available on the Web. The last task in this chapter provides the reader with some guidelines for browsing the *LTC* and observing the results of searches.

One of the main problems in corpus studies of translations carried out by learners seems to be the overall design of the corpus, which includes many variables, and makes it difficult to interpret the results. learner Translation corpora rely heavily on annotation not only because each text in the database must contain detailed information which is then used in order to extract a corpus from it, but also because, in order to study systematic variation in the language of translator trainees, a consistent tag set for errors must be devised and applied to the translated texts. Furthermore, since descriptive categories can overlap, the annotation of a corpus for errors is far from straightforward: for instance, it may not be easy to draw a dividing line between lexical and syntactical errors, nor to account for severity of errors. While the annotation process can perhaps to be automated to some extent, error detection ultimately rests on the researcher applying the annotation to stretches of words, and this increases the risk of intersubjective disagreement.

Corpora of learner translations can provide synchronic and diachronic studies with evidence of the development of translation skills over time and of the variability of learner output depending on the source language, the direction of translation (from/into a first/second/foreign language) and the level of language proficiency of the learner. They can also be used to identify specific areas of difficulties in specific translation situations, for instance when translating learners typically produce different profiles of translations depending on the target language. According to the *MeLLANGE LTC* website, translations from French into German display a high percentage of errors in the areas of terminology, verb aspect and use of prepositions, whereas translations from French into Italian are mostly characterized by awkward style and punctuation and misinterpretations of source text meaning.

Corpora which include texts translated or independently produced in a second or foreign language by learners or professionals can also provide useful theoretical insights. For instance, Corpas Pastor (2008) carried out her case studies of universals using various combinations and types of corpora of translated Spanish, including corpora of texts translated (from English) by trainee translators. Gaspari and Bernardini (2010) suggest that by comparing a corpus of translations with a corpus of EFL writing in the same language it may be possible to distinguish between what is specific to translation and what is more generally a feature of 'intercultural writing'. Should systematic similarities be detected between translation and interlanguage, it is hypothesized that these could be accounted for by the notion of mediation rather than translation universals.

2.2.5 *Interpreting and multimodal corpora*

The vast majority of corpus-based translation research has been based on corpora of written texts, created from printed and electronic sources. However, some studies have also presented a rationale and suggestions for research based on interpreting corpora (Shlesinger 1998, Wallmach 2000, Setton 2002), and some preliminary studies have also been conducted on film dubbing and on conference interpreting. The *Forlixt multimedia corpus* of screen translations (Valentini 2006, Heiss and Soffritti 2008), for instance, comprises original and dubbed films together with the transcriptions of dialogues and has been used for translator training activities. The *European Parliamentary Interpreting Corpus (EPIC)* (Russo *et al.* 2006, Monti *et al.* 2005), which contains transcripts of source speeches and corresponding interpreted versions in English, Italian and Spanish has been used to test lexical simplification using the indexes of lexical density and variety proposed by Laviosa (1998b, 1998c). Contrary to written translation, interpreted texts seem to display a tendency towards more complexity as compared to source texts in the same language. On the basis of these findings, and of her own analysis of two comparable corpora, one of interpreted texts and one of written translations, Shlesinger (2009) hypothesizes that, much like written translation, interpreting may be a language variety, distinct both from written translation and original oral production in the same language.

Spoken corpora are also a component of multimodal corpora, in which the transcriptions are linked to the audiovisual recordings of the communicative event. The creation of multimodal corpora is not devoid of technical problems, and the feasibility of working with large collections of audiovisual data in addition to written transcriptions is a fairly recent technical achievement. Furthermore, quantitative methodologies may have a lesser impact on corpus-based dialogue/service interpreting studies not only because of the inherent difficulties of creating multimodal corpora, but also because studies in oral communication, especially when a high degree of interaction among different actors is involved, necessitate a qualitative approach to the data such as those developed in discourse and conversation analysis (see Zanettin 2009b for a survey of issues concerning the creation and use of multimodal corpora).

A special type of multimodal corpus is one containing the transcriptions of translation process data, together with the data themselves (Göpferich 2010, see § 4.2.3). Some scholars (Alves *et al.* 2010) also propose to combine product- and and process-based approaches and to analyze keystroke logging, eye tracking, and retrospective verbalizations together with the translations produced by the subjects in order to identify translation units associated with cognitive effort during a translation task.

2.3 Corpus-based translation teaching and learning

Corpora have been used not only in descriptive research but also in other areas of translation studies, such as translator and interpreter training and computer-assisted translation. In educational settings, corpora have been used mainly in three distinct but related areas, i.e. language teaching, translator training and terminology. The variety of corpora used ranges from monolingual to bilingual and from comparable to parallel, from small and specialized to large and general. Activities involving the use of corpora have been devised both for translation (e.g. Bowker 1998) and language learners (e.g. Zanettin 2009a). Corpus use may take place prior to, during and after the translation activity proper, and involves the use of different corpus types (Aston 2000). Activities for translation trainees described in the literature have been carried out using small and large monolingual target corpora, as well as bilingual comparable and parallel corpora. The use of corpus resources by the language and translation learner may involve not only the exploitation of existing corpora, but also the creation of small, *ad hoc* ones. Less documented is the use of corpora and creation of corpora among professional translators. As Aston (2009:x) points out, this is probably because, "[r]egardlessly of its potential to improve translation quality ... corpus consultation remains time consuming, and corpus construction enormously more so", and thus "[n]ot all translators appreciate that corpus use may have a medium or long-term payoff which can override what they often perceive as short-term disadvantages" (*ibid.*).

While this volume is not specifically concerned with the use of corpus resources by translation trainees and professionals, the information on corpus construction and analysis should be of interest for them as well. In particular, issues concerning the design of Do-It-Yourself corpora for pedagogical applications will be taken up in Chapter 3, while issues concerning the analysis of corpus data will be addressed in Chapters 5 and 7 for monolingual and parallel corpora, respectively. The reader is referred to the publications listed in the further reading section of this chapter for a survey of the uses of corpora in translator education.

2.4 Computer-assisted translation and computational linguistics

A third area of interface between corpus linguistics and translation studies concerns the application of computational linguistics, and corpus linguistics in particular, to the creation of tools for machine assisted translation. Computational linguistics (also referred to as NLP, Natural Language Processing) is concerned with "the scientific study of language from a computational perspective"[2] and can be considered a branch of computer science as well as a branch of linguistics. Corpus linguistics represents, in this respect, a data-driven approach to NLP which is based on statistical and empirical methods. In contrast, an approach which relies on transformational rules is known as 'knowledge-based' or 'hand-crafted'. Since the beginning of the 1990s, corpus linguistics has rapidly become a major research approach in NLP, and corpus-based methodologies have increasingly been used in areas such as automated word-class tagging, sentence parsing, word-class disambiguation and anaphora resolution, which were previously dealt with through rule-based models. Areas of application include automated information retrieval, content and document analysis, abstracting and lexicography, and speech recognition (Kennedy 1998:276-278). Computational linguists have taken great advantage of the availability of large quantities of text in electronic format, and have also been instrumental for the creation of corpus tools and resources to be used in translation studies, among other disciplinary fields.

The influence of corpus linguistics has been particularly felt in the area of

[2] *The Association for Computational Linguistics* (2005) <http://www.aclweb.org/archive/misc/what.html>. Accessed on 30 March 2011.

machine (assisted) translation. One of the major achievements in this area is the creation of systems for assisting technical translators by managing and re-using past translations. Software applications range from word processing macros to fully-fledged translator workstation suites, which include a translation memory (TM) management system, a machine translation (MT) system proper, a terminology management database, a concordancing utility and importing and exporting modules (for the distinction between TMs and parallel corpora, see § 6.4). Example-based and statistical machine translation has increasingly replaced rule-based machine translation as an approach, and millions of users avail themselves of online machine translation systems such as Google Translate, which are largely based on parallel corpora.

Another application of multilingual corpora to the development of tools for translators is the *Turicor* project at the University of Malaga, Spain (http://www.turicor.com/indexeng.htm), which aims at developing a prototype corpus-based system for the automatic text generation of legal documents (tourism contracts) in four languages, on the basis of both parallel and comparable corpora.

The problem with parallel corpora is that their construction is rather laborious. A call for papers for the workshop on *Building and Using Comparable Corpora*, held at the 2008 *Language Resources and Evaluation Conference* (*LREC*), states that research in comparable (bilingual) corpora is motivated by the scarcity of parallel corpora, since "beyond a few language pairs such as English-French or English-Chinese and a few contexts such as parliamentary debates or legal texts, [parallel corpora] remain a scarce resource, despite the creation of automated methods to collect parallel corpora from the Web".[3] A few parallel corpora are available either as sets of aligned text pairs (on alignment see Chapter 7) or through online interfaces. Possibly the most famous parallel corpus is the Canadian Hansard containing the French and English transcriptions of the debates of the Canadian House of Commons and Senate, updated daily and accessible through the TransSearch interface (http://www.tsrali.com/). Several years of proceedings of the European Parliament in 11 languages are also available, as is the *Acquis Communautaire*, i.e. the total body of European Union (EU) law applicable to the EU Member States, comprising 22 languages, 231 possible language pair combinations and 462 language pair directions in 463,792 texts totalling over one billion words. The Acquis Communautaire is freely available both as a multilingual parallel corpus and as a multilingual translation memory. The *Europarl* corpus is also freely available as a multilingual parallel corpus, and is accessible through the free *Open Source Parallel Corpus* (*OPUS*) query interface developed by Jörg Tiedemann at Uppsala University. The *OPUS* project, which also contains parallel corpora in the field of software documentation and subtitles, among others, will be examined in Chapter 7.

---

[3] http://www.limsi.fr/~pz/lrec2008-comparable-corpora/cfp-lrec2008-comparable-corpora.html. Accessed on 20 March 2011.

2.5 Tasks

2.5.1 Experimenting with the TEC

This task replicates Olohan's and Baker's (2000) analysis of the optional *that* using the monolingual comparable corpus *TEC*. To carry out this experiment you first need to launch the custom-built concordancer which is used to access the *TEC* corpus.

1. Go to: http://ronaldo.cs.tcd.ie/tec2/jnlp/ and click on the icon in the top and centre of the page to launch the *TEC* application. The program will download and install itself.[4] You can also save the application file and launch it directly from your computer in the future (a copy of the program can also be found in the DVD accompanying this volume). Say 'yes' to all dialog boxes until the MODNLP/tec concordance browser opens.

2. In order to obtain data about the optional reporting *that* you need to extract concordances for all forms of the reporting verbs SAY and TELL. For instance, to search for all instances of the form *said* followed by *that*, you need to type *said that* in the *Keyword Search* box. To retrieve instances of *told* followed by an object pronoun type *told me*, then *told her*, etc. you should repeat the search for all forms of the two verbs. For help formulating your searches read the notes on query language syntax in the help file. Click on *Help* in the main menu bar, then select *Contents*. As you can see, there are almost 20,000 occurrences of the form *said* alone. In order to make this task more manageable, let us compare the use of the optional *that* in translations from Italian with the use of the optional *that* in translations from German (or any other language).

3. From the menu select *Options* → *Select Sub-Corpus*, then select *Italian* as a source language. Click on *Apply*, then *OK* to confirm your selection.

4. Search for the word *told*, then sort the results according to the first word to the right of the search word. This should allow you to browse results grouped according to the pronoun that follows the verb form. You need to examine the concordance lines to distinguish between forms that do or do not involve the use or omission of the optional *that*. In relevant concordance lines identify and count those where the optional *that* is used and those where it is omitted. To count the occurrences of *told* followed by the optional *that*, sort your concordances according to the second word to the right. Fill in the first line of the form below with

[4] Having been written in the Java programming language, the *TEC* application does not require a specific operating system and installation procedure.

the number of lines in which *told* is followed by the optional reporting *that* and those in which the optional *that* has been omitted. Then repeat for each of the other verb forms and compute the respective percentage values.

Form	*Number of that*	*Number of zero*
Tell		
Tells		
Told		
Telling		
Say		
Says		
Said		
Saying		
Total numbers		
Total %		

5. Repeat steps 3 and 4, selecting German (or any other language) as a source language and compare your results with those for Italian (or any other language). Is the optional *that* omitted more often in texts translated from Italian or in those translated from German? What other searches can you perform to test your hypotheses? Can you think of alternative ways to conduct your searches? Be aware that your raw data at this point do not tell the whole story. In order to compare the figures for the two languages you need to know the size of the two subcorpora and to establish a correlation between the number or occurrences and the size of each subcorpus.

6. Explore the options provided by the *TEC* application. What options are available as concerns the selection of subcorpora, search options, corpus documentation? Which options as available for the display of results? Can you think of any other feature you would like to see implemented?

2.5.2 *Experimenting with COMPARA*

In this task you will use the Portuguese-English parallel and reciprocal corpus *COMPARA* to have a look at parallel concordances and replicate the exercise in task 1. Like the *TEC*, *COMPARA* is freely available online. It can be accessed through the online query interface at the *COMPARA* website.

1. Go to: http://www.linguateca.pt/COMPARA/
In the English version of the front page, click on the *Simple Search* link.

2. Click on the *From English to Portuguese* tab, then type the word *tell* in the search box and click on *Search*. How is *tell* usually translated into Portuguese?

3. Go back to the *Simple Search* and look for translations of the phrase *told me*. In order to replicate the experiment conducted with the *TEC*, you can compare the use of the optional reporting *that* in translations from Portuguese and in original English texts. You are thus interested only in the English "monolingual comparable" components of *COMPARA*. For this, select the *Advanced Search* from the menu.

4. In *Tab 1* select *From English to Portuguese* as a search direction. Then click on *Tab 2* and type *"told" "me"* in the search query box. Note that you must surround each word with double quotation marks. Click on *Tab 3*, then on *Tab 3.3.* and select *Search only from source texts to translations*. Submit your query. Your search results will thus be restricted to English source texts (aligned with their Portuguese translations).

5. In order to obtain fewer and thus more manageable results for this task, restrict the comparison only to the occurrences of *told* followed by an object personal pronoun. As opposed to the *TEC*, the *COMPARA* corpus is linguistically annotated. This means, for instance, that you can formulate the query so as to search for all personal pronouns. To do so, in *COMPARA*, you need to type the following search expression *"told" [pos="PP.*"]*. In case you want to narrow down your results, you can restrict your search to, for instance, forms of the present perfect or past perfect of *tell* followed by an objective personal pronoun (e.g. have told me/had told her). Search for *[lema="have"]"told"[pos="PP.*"]*.

6. Repeat your search in the subcorpus of English translations. This time click on *Tab 3.3.* and select *Search only from translations back to source texts*. Your search results will thus be restricted to English translations (aligned with their Portuguese source texts). Examine your results for both searches and distinguish between forms that do or do not involve the use or omission of the optional *that*. In relevant concordance lines identify and count those where the optional *that* is used and those where it is omitted. To count the occurrences of *told* followed by the optional *that*, search for *"told" [pos="PP.*"] "that"*. Fill in the form below with the number of lines in which *told* is followed by the optional reporting *that* and those in which the optional *that* has been omitted.

Told + PP	*Number of that*	*Number of zero*	*% of that*	*% of zero*
Non-translated texts (English)				
Translated texts (English)				

Should your findings be confirmed by similar results for all forms of the verbs TELL and SAY, could you hypothesize that (literary) translations from Portuguese into English are more 'explicit' than original English texts?

7. Explore the options provided by the *COMPARA* interface. What functions are available as concerns the selection of subcorpora, search options, corpus documentation? Which options are available for the display of results? Can you think of any other feature you would like to see implemented?

2.5.3 Experimenting with the LTC

In this task you will take a look at the *Learner Translation Corpus* (*LTC*), using the online query interface of the *MeLLANGE* project.

1. Go to: http://corpus.leeds.ac.uk/mellange/ltc.html and click on *MeLLANGE* query interface in the menu on the left hand side.

2. Select *MeLLANGE LTC* from the *Select corpus* drop-down menu, and then *linguistic information* as "type of information needed".

3. On the left hand side, select *legal* as text type, *French* as source language, *English* as target language and *Inappropriate Collocation* as error type (LA-TL-IC, see Figure 2.4 for *Error typology* and acronyms). Then click on *Get concordances*. In the results page you should see different types of sentences, distinguished by a different background. A yellow background (Original Context) identifies the French source context for an English translation which contains the inappropriate collocation. A red background (Target Sentence) identifies the sentence which contains the error. The orange background (Reference Context) is for a translation by a professional translator, a white background (Alternative student contexts) is for alternative translations of the same sentence by different learners. Hovering the mouse over the error label

in the Target Sentence shows a proposed correction. You should have found two instances of translations of legal texts from French into English which contain an error marked as "inappropriate collocation".

4. Go back to the search page. This time select *both* as "type of information needed", and experiment with different selection criteria. Be aware that you might need to reload the search page for it to function properly, and that some "cells" may well be empty (e.g., no translations of journalistic texts from German to Spanish by students having Japanese as their second language).

Figure 2.4. MeLLANGE *Translation error typology*

2.6 *Further reading*

Various standard textbooks on corpus linguistics are available, including McEnery and Wilson 2001 (second edition), Kennedy 1998, Meyer 2002.

Good book-length introductions to corpus-based descriptive translation studies, with an emphasis on monolingual comparable corpora, are Laviosa (2002) and Olohan (2004). Various edited collected volumes combine a translation studies and a contrastive linguistics perspective, for instance Granger *et al.* (2003), Anderman and Rogers (2008), and Xiao (2010). Various collections or monographs on corpus-based contrastive studies have been published, for instance Johansson and Oksefiell (1998), Santos (2004), and Johansson (2007).

The use of corpora in translator and interpreter training contexts is discussed in many articles published in miscellaneous volumes. A series of conferences especially devoted to Corpus Use and Learning to Translate (CULT) has generated focused collected volumes (Bernardini and Zanettin 2000, Zanettin *et al.* 2003, Beeby *et al.* 2009).

An introduction to corpora in translator education is provided by Tengku Mahadi *et al.* (2010). Some space is devoted to educational issues in Bowker and Pearson (2002), and in Meyer (2002) and Hunston (2002).

An introduction to the use of corpora in computer-assisted translation is provided by Somers (2003a).

3. Corpus design and acquisition

To construct a corpus may mean quite different things and involve a range of different activities and costs. It may consist of the apparently straightforward procedure of downloading Web pages from the Internet, or be a rather complex project with different stages and significant costs. Martin Wynne (2008), head of the Oxford University Computing Services, in response to a query in the Corpora List asking about corpus construction costs and requirements, posted the following list of steps and factors which may be involved:

- planning the project
- allocating or hiring staff, getting rooms, buying computers, arranging all the infrastructure; or paying for the costs of these things to your institution, or arranging permission to use them
- setting up a computing infrastructure for your project data and communications (text storage, version control system, intranet, wiki, etc.)
- obtaining the texts (selection, obtaining permissions, downloading/ digitising, collecting and marking up metadata, quality control)
- transforming the texts to a common format appropriate for further processing and annotation
- devising an annotation model
- training annotators
- manually annotating the corpus
- checking the corpus: size, sampling, text integrity, mark-up errors, annotation accuracy and consistency
- documenting the corpus and annotation
- making the corpus available, and continuing support for its storage, use and licensing
- long-term archiving and preservation

Wynne suggests that in order to estimate the costs of a corpus project one should calculate person-hours costs for each aspect involved. Costs will of course differ according to the project focus and the resources available so that "for some projects, the biggest cost will be the digitisation of the materials. For others, it will be paying for permission to use them. For some, it will be to construct a schema for annotation. For many it will be to do the annotation, etc." (Wynne 2008 online).

This chapter discusses corpus design issues pertaining to the creation of translation-driven corpora, including monolingual, bi- and multilingual. First, it summarizes the main corpus design criteria which differentiate a corpus from a random collection of texts, and discusses these criteria in relation to translation-driven corpora. Then it discusses issues of corpus acquisition, which may present a project team with problems related to research time and costs, such as those needed to locate text copies and obtain copyright permissions. Once they have been physically and legally acquired, the texts are converted into corpus items.

Most of the projects mentioned in Chapter 1 involved the digitization of textual material from printed sources, either by typing in or scanning texts available in print. More recently, the surge of the Internet as the most comprehensive and accessible repository of textual material has raised issues of corpus design and construction regarding the feasibility and desirability of using the Web as a corpus or as a source of corpus material. On the one hand the availability of large quantities of texts in 'native' electronic format has created new opportunities for corpus-aided investigations, and on the other it poses new challenges with respect to the design and creation of corpora. These issues are discussed first by looking at the Web as a corpus 'surrogate' (Bernardini *et al.* 2006:10), then by considering how the Web can be used as a source of corpora, both general and specialized, and which can range from quick-and-dirty disposable Do-It-Yourself corpora to more carefully constructed ones.

Following corpus design and acquisition, corpus texts are proofread, if scanned from printed sources, or imported and converted, if already existing in electronic format, then they are manually or (semi-)automatically annotated (see Chapter 4) before being further processed (see Chapter 5 and Chapter 6).

3.1 Corpus design

Standard definitions of corpus stress that the size must be substantial – quantitative considerations are at the core of corpus-based studies – and that it must contain texts collected with a specific purpose in mind. Biber *et al.* (1998:12), for instance, define a corpus as a "large and principled collection of natural texts", and Bowker and Pearson (2002:230) as a "large collection of authentic texts that have been gathered in electronic form according to a specific set of criteria". The texts in a corpus should also be 'authentic', i.e. written for purposes other than linguistic research, and they should be available for research purposes in electronic form.

The size of a corpus (§ 3.1.1), as well as other design criteria, will vary according to the purpose for which it is designed, and the total number of words may be a parameter not set once and for all. Many corpus projects, for example those behind *TEC* and *COMPARA*, are of an open-ended nature and the corpora have grown in size accordingly since their inception.

Corpora designed to function as general reference and thus "to provide comprehensive information about a language" (Sinclair 1996:online) need of course to be much larger than specialized corpora, whose scope is limited to one specific aspect or variety of one (or more) language(s). A specialized corpus may be restricted to include only a specific text type (e.g. journal articles) or texts belonging to a specific subject domain (e.g. medicine), or texts by a specific group of text producers, for example language learners or translators. Translation-driven corpora can thus be considered special-purpose corpora, since translation acts as a constraint when mapping the universe of texts to be represented by the corpus.

A second major issue in corpus design is that of corpus composition (§ 3.1.2).

Given that a corpus will include only a sample of a language or of a specific variety of it, the question arises as to which criteria are applied to define the text population to be sampled and which are used to select textual items to be included in a corpus.

Sampling issues lead to considerations regarding representativeness, balance and comparability, which are first discussed in general terms in relation to the design of both general and specialized corpora (§ 3.1.3). The bilingual, parallel, bidirectional, English-Italian *CEXI* corpus is then used as a case study to illustrate design issues in translation-driven corpora (§ 3.1.4).

3.1.1 Size

The size of existing corpora, as expressed in number of words, varies from the very small to the very large. The idea of what constitutes a 'large' corpus has itself changed over time. The *Brown corpus* contains 1 million words of American English, or 500 text samples from publications listed in the 1961 catalogue of library holdings of Brown University, from 15 different textual categories. The total number of words in the *Brown corpus* is that of ten full novels or Sunday newspapers. A remarkable enterprise at the time, this corpus can be considered rather small by the standards of the so-called 'second-generation' general monolingual corpora of the 1990s. The *British National Corpus* (*BNC*) contains 100 million words of British English, including 10 million words of transcribed spoken language from texts dating from 1975 to 1991.[1] As opposed to the original version of the *Brown corpus*, the *BNC* was annotated for part of speech and included extensive header information encoded in SGML (and later XML, see Chapter 4 on annotation standards). Corpora from the 2000s often contain several hundred million words, and dictionary publishers currently claim that they use very large corpora (330 million words for the *Longman Corpus Network*, 550 million for the *Collins Cobuild Bank of English*); the Brigham Young University (BYU) *Corpus of Contemporary American English* (*COCA*) contains over 400 million words, while the *Sketch Engine* online corpus building and query system is a commercial service which provides access to pre-loaded corpora of 60 million to 2 billion words for several languages. Languages currently represented in the Sketch Engine corpora include Chinese, English, French, German, Italian, Japanese, Portuguese, Spanish and Slovene. The texts contained in these corpora are either Internet documents only or a mix of native electronic texts and printed texts, and the corpora are annotated.

The size of corpora keeps growing at a steady pace, mainly as a result of the increasing availability of texts in electronic format, which has diminished the time and costs of digitization. Size often becomes a decisive factor in assessing the reliability of corpus findings, since statistical considerations play an important role when it comes to drawing generalizations about one state of affairs in a language or language variety, for instance, when defining the meaning and us-

[1] http://www.natcorp.ox.ac.uk/. Accessed on 20 March 2011.

age of a word or making hypotheses about universal properties of translation. Zipf's law (1935) states that, in any given text or corpus, about half of the words will occur only once, a quarter only twice, and so on. Accordingly, the one million *Brown corpus* has 69,002 different word forms, of which 35,065 occur once only. The commonest word, *the*, has a frequency of 69,970 and is almost twice as common as the next most frequent one, *of*, at 36,410. According to Sinclair (2005:online), at least twenty instances are needed "for even an outline description of the behaviour of a word to be compiled by trained lexicographers". Thus, large numbers of words in a corpus are needed to draw generalizations about but a few core lexical items. Furthermore, the investigation of units of language larger than a single word will require increasingly larger corpora, since "the occurrence of two or more words together is inherently far rarer than either on its own" (*ibid.*). Accordingly, the estimate of a suitable size for the corpus will become increasingly more complicated (*ibid.*):

> To estimate roughly the size of a corpus for retrieval of a combination of two objects, first estimate the size you will need for the less common object on its own and then raise that figure by an order of magnitude. If there are 20 instances per million words for each of two words in a phrase, then twenty million words is likely to provide 20 instances of the pair (rather than the 5 billion projected by the arithmetic); if there are three of this frequency than [sic] 200 million words will probably be enough.

Size is also related to the specificity of the corpus: the more specialized a corpus, the more likely it will be that a typical term or phrase from the domain in question will recur in it.

As for other types of corpora, the size of translation-driven corpora may vary considerably. It may go from 1,000 to 100,000 words for specialized corpora such as the bilingual comparable or monolingual corpora of the target language used in translator training (e.g. Zanettin 1998, 2001a, Bowker 1998), up to several hundred million words for very large parallel corpora. The corpora used for the studies described in Chapter 2 mostly consist of a few million words. As of 2003, the last date the site was updated, the *TEC* contained 10 million words, and is only one component of a monolingual comparable corpus which altogether has about 20 million words. The *ENPC*, which was compiled and completed in 1996, contains 2.6 million words in two languages and four components, while *COMPARA* contains 3 million words altogether. On the other hand, the *OPUS* multilingual parallel corpus (Tiedemann 2009) contains about 100 million words in 11 European languages (about 10 million words per language). The *Acquis Communautaire* multilingual parallel corpus (Steinberger *et al.* 2006), which comprises the total body of European Union law, totals around one billion words in 22 languages.

The texts in these corpora belong to only one or a few text types (e.g. written fiction, academic texts, transcriptions of parliamentary proceedings, legislative texts), and can thus be considered special corpora. What they have in common is that at least a component of the corpus consists of translated texts. Some studies make use of even smaller subcorpora, setting a further limit to the claims and generalizations that can be made based on the findings.

3.1.2 Composition

Diversity in a corpus is ensured not only by the number of textual items, but also by the length and completeness of each individual text item. Corpora such as the *Brown corpus*, the *BNC* and the *ENPC* only include text extracts of approximately the same length, i.e. chunks of 2,000, 45,000 and 10-15,000 words, respectively. Corpora such as the *TEC* and *COMPARA*, on the other hand, include only full texts, which may range in length from 100 words (some newspaper articles in the *TEC*) to 100,000 words. In principle, there is no reason why a corpus should not include full texts only. The decision to include text extracts rather than full texts is usually dictated by constraints imposed by size limits. For instance, in order to provide for internal diversity, the 2.6-million-word *ENPC* could only include small text samples, whereas corpora which aim at textual completeness like the *TEC* need to be much larger in size in order to compensate for the lack of diversity. Thus, the *ENPC* contains extracts from 30 novels translated into English, averaging about 12,500 words each for a total of about 700,000 words. The *TEC* contains 81 translated novels but its overall size is about ten times that of the *ENPC* subcorpus of translated English texts.

Bowker and Pearson (2002) list eight criteria which should be taken into account in the design of corpora. These concern mainly the construction of monolingual corpora to be used in language for special purposes (LSP) studies, but are also relevant for translation-driven corpora. Apart from size and number of texts, these criteria are: medium, subject, text type, authorship, publication date and language.

By 'medium' Bowker and Pearson refer to the communicative format of the source texts, i.e. whether they are printed matter, oral communication or electronic texts such as Web pages, email messages or chat logs. This volume mostly deals with corpora of written texts, from both printed and electronic sources. Chapter 4 will briefly examine issues relating to interpreting corpora, in which transcriptions may contain utterances in one language interspersed with their translations into another, and transcriptions may be aligned to an audiovisual recording of the communicative event.

Subject and text type are especially relevant criteria in the design of specialized corpora. Given the multidisciplinary nature of many subject fields, when designing a specialized corpus (or subcorpus) it may be difficult to establish the boundary between two subject matters, as well as the level of generality which may determine the inclusion of a text into a given specialized subject field or its exclusion from it. When creating a specialized corpus care should also be taken in evaluating text type. Texts can be classified according to the level of communication, i.e. whether communication takes place between experts as in research papers, or in the various types of expert to non-expert communication, such as that present in textbooks, informative and promotional literature, instructional texts, newspaper articles, etc. Bowker and Pearson (2002:53) suggest that provisional criteria such as those concerning subject and text type may be established at the outset of a project to be later refined by adding material to the corpus.

Authorship and publication date are important criteria to assess the relevance and reliability of the texts included in a corpus. For instance, while publication in print usually involves a process of quality control, this is not always the case for electronic publication. Thus, care should be taken in assessing the authoritativeness of sources, especially when evaluating Internet texts. A synchronic corpus containing only 'current' texts may be obtained by restricting the publication date to a given period of time and used to investigate, for instance, general features of translated texts. A diachronic corpus may instead be used to compare the evolution of translation strategies and norms over time.

Finally, by 'language', Bowker and Pearson refer not only to the language in which the texts are written but also to the production mode (translations vs. non-translations) and the identity of the authors, that is to say whether they are native speakers of the language or not. Thus, monolingual 'reference' corpora are often designed to exclude translations and texts written by non-native speakers, on the basis that these are non-standard varieties of that language. However, it can be argued that translations should be part of a reference corpus insofar as translation is a common and legitimate instance of textual production in the target culture. Similarly, the native speaker category is not necessarily an overriding one. For instance, academic English is a variety of language which is more akin to an international lingua franca produced mostly by competent non-native speakers, than to a native, regional variety of it (Mauranen and Hynninen 2010).

3.1.3 Representativeness and comparability

A corpus should not only be as large as possible, but also map onto the different textual categories of the language (or language variety) it wishes to represent. Representativeness is ensured by segmenting into an appropriate number of categories the textual universe addressed by the corpus compilers, and the definition of internal categories will depend on the type of corpus. For a corpus of newspaper texts, relevant categories could be genre or geographical provenance; for a corpus of printed books, they could be categories drawn from bibliographic classifications; for a corpus of academic texts, categories relating to disciplinary fields. Parameters determining the inclusion as a member of a category will differ depending on how each category is defined. For instance, to ensure the distribution of a wide enough range of texts within the category "written fiction", relevant parameters might be author, publisher and date of publication. In translation-driven corpora these parameters have to apply to both source texts and translations.

According to Atkins *et al.* (1992:6) in order to offer "a manageably small scale model of the linguistic material the builder wishes to study" a corpus must be balanced, where balancedness basically means proportionality (Leech 2007:136). In other words, the size of a (sub)corpus must be proportional to the relative frequency of occurrence of these texts in the textual categories represented by it. To allow for generalizations to be drawn from these categories, the latter should in turn be subdivided into further subcategories, each of which should be proportionally populated.

However, representativeness is a very elusive concept, often something to strive for rather than something which can reasonably be attained. Given the number of variables to be taken into consideration in the design of a corpus and the practical limitations often posed by funding, copyright restrictions, etc., it is usually unlikely that the ideal corpus can be constructed. Furthermore, representativeness can be seen not only as a descriptive concept, but also as a normative one. It can reasonably be asked 'of what' and 'according to whom' a corpus should be representative.

For instance, the *British National Corpus* (*BNC*) is often taken as reference for general British English, and parts of it have been used as a comparable component in some corpus-based translation studies. While its size (100 million words) has now been surpassed by that of "third- generation" corpora, the *BNC* can still be regarded as a very reliable resource not only because it is still large enough by current standards, but also because it contains a variety of text samples of written and spoken language from a wide range of sources, as it was carefully

> designed to represent a wide cross-section of current British English, both spoken and written. [It contains] extracts from regional and national newspapers, specialist periodicals and journals for all ages and interests, academic books and popular fiction, published and unpublished letters and memoranda, school and university essays [and] unscripted informal conversation, recorded by volunteers selected from different age/region/ social classes in a demographically balanced way, together with spoken language collected in all kinds of different contexts, ranging from formal business or government meetings to radio shows and phone-ins. (*BNC* home page).

However, the "cross section" of British English represented by the *BNC* is obviously skewed in favour of written language. Spoken English is severely under-represented, as the corpus contains 'only' 10 million words of transcribed speech, or one tenth of it. While this imbalance is not surprising given the effort necessary to record and transcribe spoken language and 10 million words of transcribed and annotated speech still represent a very remarkable achievement, the *BNC* certainly cannot claim to 'represent' British English as a whole. In this respect the *BNC* Sampler, a 2-million-word subset of the *BNC* which contains half spoken and half written material, compiled "to mirror the composition of the full *BNC* as far as possible" (*BNC* website) is certainly more balanced than the full *BNC*, though because of its size it contains too few texts for each of its subcategories to justify claims of representativeness beyond a few core lexical and syntactic features.

The internal subdivision of the *BNC* categories has been questioned by Lee (2001, see also Aston 2001), who has reservations about its representativeness when examined using an alternative classification based on genres rather than broad domains. Ahmad (2008) surveys the composition of a number of large corpora used in lexicographical research and finds that they all seem to contain a preponderance of texts used by 'educated native English speakers'. In particular, the written component of the *BNC* appears to be dominated by texts published by a small group of metropolitan publishers from Southern England, and the tabloid format is under-represented in the newspaper category if this category is to be based on publication/circulation figures (Ahmad 2008:88-90). Ultimately, the concept of representativeness in general corpora is based on an ideal linguistic standard on which a group of corpus compilers decide to agree.

The concept of representativeness has been discussed not only as concerns large, monolingual reference corpora, but also in relation to specialized corpora. Linguistic production is of an open nature, and it is impossible for a general corpus to contain a sufficient number of text categories and a sufficient number of texts within each category to fully represent any given language. Specialized corpora, by contrast, can not only be smaller in size than general corpora, but also aim at reaching a higher degree of precision with regard to representativeness. McEnery and Wilson (1996:147-167) hypothesize that certain genres of writing, which represent a constrained subset of a natural language, i.e. sublanguages, are subject to closure at various levels of language description. As new words and new texts are added to the corpus, lexicogrammatical and stylistic variation tend to increase at a lesser pace than they do in a general corpus, since as new texts are added the same words, phrases and textual structures are repeated more often and more frequently, until very few new features are added when a new text is added. According to Seghiri and Corpas Pastor (2009:88) "once a certain number of texts have been included [in a corpus], the number of types does not increase in proportion to the number of words the corpus contains". Corpas Pastor and Seghiri (2007) discuss the software application ReCor, which implements a formula "to determine the minimum size of a corpus and the quantity that must be reached for it to begin to be representative" (*ibid.*:on-line). They show how, in a specialized comparable corpus dealing with general conditions in vacation package contracts in Spanish and English, the threshold at which enlarging the subcorpus does not contribute significantly to represent a wider spectrum of words is reached at a different size for the two subcorpora. Seghiri and Corpas Pastor underline that this method can only be used *post-hoc* to determine whether a corpus has reached the minimum size required, and not to determine the size of the corpus beforehand.

The sampling criteria used for translation-driven corpora should be similar to those used to determine the composition of any corpus, whether large and general or small and specialized. They include size, text extent (i.e. whether the texts in the corpus are full texts or limited samples), date of production/publication, and genre or text type. Thus, a corpus of translations ideally designed to represent the features of translated language should be sufficiently large and balanced, and each of its subcategories should contain a sufficiently large number of texts. Furthermore, corpora of translations are subject to constraints determined by their translation status. The distribution of texts within each subcategory should cover a wide number of source languages, authors and publishers, but also different translators and publishers. For instance, the *TEC* specifies a first-level distinction among four subcorpora, i.e. fiction, biography, newspapers and in-flight magazines. The texts in each subcomponent are then classified according to a taxonomy which specifies information about the source text (language, mode, status, place of publication, date), source text author(s) (name, gender and nationality), translator(s) (name, gender, nationality and employment status), the translation itself (mode, extent, publisher, publication place, date), and the translation process (translation direction, mode and type). Thus the *TEC* will represent translated English to the extent that the sum of its subcomponents is representative of it. Each of its subcomponents (e.g. fiction) will represent its target populations to the extent to which the internal distribution of textual items is sufficiently large and varied. For instance, in order to make uncontroversial claims about features common to 'translated English fiction', it should contain a large number of texts from many different source languages, each with a good distribution of source text authors and publishers, translators, etc.

Since corpus-based translation studies usually implies the comparison of data from two or more subcorpora, one of which is made of translations, the design of the corpus as a whole, be it monolingual or bilingual, will depend on the design of the subcorpus of translations. In other words, "[o]nce design decisions have been taken on a corpus of translations, the non-translation component can then be modelled on the translation component" (Olohan 2004:42). Echoing the title of an article by Laviosa (1997), "how comparable can a comparable corpus be?", the comparability of two subcorpora should be assessed using the same criteria for both of them, translated and non-translated texts. This may be difficult to achieve on all dimensions: for instance, the fiction component of the *TEC* and the subset of the *BNC* used as a comparable subcorpus have the same overall size. However, the *BNC* contains mostly text samples of the same length, whereas the *TEC* contains only full texts of varying length. Thus, the non-translated subcorpus contains a larger spread of texts than the translated one, and the linguistic features compared will be unevenly distributed across the two subcorpora.

Comparability should be assessed not only regarding overall size, textual length and completeness, but also regarding composition. The criteria which can be used to describe the population of translated fiction in one language are not necessarily the same used to describe non-translated fiction in that language, and both may differ from those which describe fiction (translated or not) in another language. So, for instance, even assuming that a corpus of translated fiction may be representative of fiction translated into that language, a parallel corpus containing its source texts for a given language will not be representative of fiction in that language, since source language texts were not in fact selected to be representative of source language fiction. As Kenny (1998:53) explains, "it is in the very nature of translation that new genres are introduced from one literature to another, and there may be nothing 'comparable' in the host literature to a text introduced to it through translation from another textual tradition".

More in general, representativeness and comparability are conflicting goals: "an attempt to achieve greater comparability may actually impede representativity and vice versa", and "as one nears to perfection in comparability, one meets with distortion in terms of representativeness, and vice versa" (Leech 2007:142). Aspects relating to representativeness and comparability, together with other corpus design issues, are exemplified in more detail in §3.1.4 by looking at the design of a bilingual, parallel and bidirectional – or reciprocal – corpus. Further aspects involved in the design of parallel and comparable corpora are discussed in Chapter 6.

3.1.4 Case study: the CEXI corpus

CEXI, which stands for *Translational English Italian Corpus*, is a research project initiated at the School for Translators and Interpreters of the University Bologna (Zanettin 2000, 2002a, Bernardini 2003, 2005, Bernardini and Zanettin 2004). The project envisioned the creation of a well-thought-out 'representative' bilingual, parallel, bidirectional and translation-driven corpus to be used both as a resource for descriptive studies and as an aid for language learning and translator training.

Ideally, the composition of the corpus would have allowed not only for the analysis of parallel subcorpora into the two directions of translation, but also for the analysis of monolingual comparable subcorpora (translated vs. non-translated texts in the same language, for both languages), as well as for the analysis of a bilingual comparable corpus of non-translated texts in the two languages.

Eventually, the *CEXI* project did not result in the creation of a corpus. Project funding was not renewed, and the collection of copyright permissions (see §3.2) proved to be a long and often unsuccessful process. However, while a well-constructed, bilingual and bidirectional parallel corpus of English and Italian is still needed, a discussion of the issues considered when designing the *CEXI* corpus may still offer some useful advice to compilers of translation-driven corpora.

The texts to be included in the corpus were chosen according to selection criteria, which defined the external boundaries of the textual population to be represented, and descriptive criteria, which established the number and extent of the texts to be included in the corpus, and the internal categories into which each subcorpus is subdivided.

Selection criteria are external to the composition of the corpus. These included medium, corpus type, and time of publication: the corpus was to contain only electronic versions of printed books, either source texts or translations, published in the previous 25 years (1976-2000), with some motivated exceptions for a few long-selling English translations. It was decided to include only adult prose writing, to the exclusion of children's literature, schoolbooks and simplified readers, poetry, comic books and texts written for the stage. The countries of publication were restricted to Italy, the UK and the US. Finally, both production and reception criteria were considered as concerns the distribution of authors, translators and publishers in the corpus. Thus, on the one hand candidates for inclusion in the corpus were selected on the basis of random sampling in order to obtain a balanced distribution of authors, translators and publishers, and on the other, best-selling works and authors were privileged among candidate titles in order to account for readership figures. To avoid a possible further variable, works self-translated by their authors were also discarded.

Descriptive criteria referred to the internal composition of the corpus in terms of its overall size, number and extent of the texts, and internal categories. Given that the envisaged overall size had been established at about 4 million words, or one million words for each subcorpus, it was clear that, to ensure variety in the distribution of texts in each subcategory, the most workable option was to include limited extracts rather than full texts. Thus, following the *ENPC* model, it was decided that the corpus would include 320 text samples of about 12,500 words each, i.e. 160 texts pairs or 80 texts for each subcorpus. While not being substitutes for full texts, text samples have the advantage that, being of the same length, they are more amenable to statistical analysis. It was also hoped that copyright clearance would prove easier to obtain for text extracts than for full texts.

In order to define internal categories within each subcorpus, and draw up a list of candidate texts for inclusion, a preliminary investigation was carried out based on book publishing literature and statistics from bibliographic sources. After looking at specialized publications such as *European Bookseller* and *Publishers Weekly*, it was decided to adopt a broad distinction between fiction and non-fiction and to split the corpus evenly between the two. This solution, which has the advantage of obtaining comparable quantities of data for fiction and non-fiction, is also based on publication figures (Berla 1993, Vigini 1999).

The main source of data used to select the texts to be included in the corpus was the *Index Translationum* database, which is the most comprehensive international bibliography of translations.[2] An analysis of the database, together with a survey of book publishing magazines and other sources, suggested that not only the flow of fiction translations from English into Italian is much more substantial than in the opposite direction (both in absolute numbers and as a proportion of total production), but also that different types of fiction get translated into Italian and into English. Translations from English into Italian, which account for about one third of all books sold (Lottman 2000), are mostly from best-selling authors such as Michael Crichton, John Grisham and Stephen King, popular romance and detective stories, and are usually published by a few big Italian publishers. The situation is quite different in the UK and the USA, where translations account for between 2 and 3% of all titles, and translations from Italian are a minor percentage of these (Hale 1996:27, Venuti 1995:12-15). They are rarely best-sellers and mostly belong to what has been called "difficult literary fiction" (Schiller 1993:28), published in translation by small, specialized

---

[2] See the *Index Translationum*'s FAQ Page, available at http://portal.unesco.org/culture/en/ev.php-URL_ID=7810&URL_DO=DO_TOPIC&URL_SECTION=201.html. Accessed on 20 March 2011.

publishers. Similar imbalances also occur in translated non-fiction, where texts are unevenly distributed across the respective subject categories. For instance, books belonging to the religion and entertainment categories are those most translated from Italian into English, representing almost half non-fiction translations, whereas books in the sciences categories are translated in a much higher percentage from English into Italian than vice versa.

While the subcorpora of translated texts, if designed to be representative of translations from Italian into English and vice versa, are not comparable, the non-translational subcorpora are neither representative nor comparable, both in the same language and across languages. The four subcorpora which form a bidirectional parallel corpus cannot be assumed to mirror each other precisely, and such a corpus is "reciprocal" only as far as size is concerned, not as regards the relationship of each subcorpus to the textual population it is supposed to represent.

The non-translational subcorpora are, in fact, modelled on the translational ones, and they thus mirror their composition rather than being designed to represent book production or reception in the respective countries. Thus, the fictional component of the Italian non-translational subcorpus, being mostly composed of "high-quality" literary fiction, is not representative of book production in Italy since it does not contain Italian best-sellers and popular fiction. Conversely, the fictional component of the non-translational English subcorpus only includes best-sellers and popular fiction. This lack or representativeness is even clearer when we look at the composition of the Italian and English non-translational, non-fictional subcorpus components with respect to data for book production for non-fiction works in Italy, the UK and the USA. What gets translated into English from Italian source texts bears little correspondence to what is published in Italy. Conversely, the design of the English subcorpus of source text does not reflect book production in the UK and the USA.

The subcorpora of translations and non-translation, for both languages, are not comparable since their composition is different. For Italian, popular translated fiction would be compared with high-brow non-translated fiction, while the opposite would be true for English. The same lack of comparability also holds for the non-fictional subcorpus components, where non-fictional categories are represented in different proportions. Moreover, the English and Italian subcorpora of non-translated texts are not comparable either, since both their fictional and non-fictional components are not only non-representative of book production or reception in the respective countries, but also contain a different distribution of texts within each subcorpus component. A comparison of the non-translational subcorpora would thus reflect the picture that readers have of foreign languages and cultures through translation, rather than actual 'native' language production and consumption in the respective languages.

The overall design of a bilingual, bidirectional parallel corpus such as *CEXI* clearly derives from its 'target' orientation, meaning that a concern with the representativeness of the subcorpora of translated texts also dictates the composition of the non-translational subcorpora. In order for these to become comparable, both within and across languages, enough text pairs should be added to each subcorpus to even up all categories. However, this would make the non-translational subcorpora less representative than before. On the other hand, if the number of text pairs in each component were adjusted so as to reflect different publication figures and account for text production policies in the different countries, the non-translational subcorpora would become more representative, but at the same time the translational subcorpora would become less representative, and less mutually comparable within and across languages.

A flexible approach would thus be needed to allow for monolingual and bilingual comparative analyses using a bidirectional parallel corpus. But even resorting to a dynamic composition of subcorpora, in which texts were selected on the basis of the specific type of analysis at hand, a reciprocal corpus may still not be sufficient to allow for effective representativeness, since not all text types are translated from one language to the other. It may also be argued (see § 3.1.3) that translations should be included in a (sub)corpus which aims at representing textual production in a given language, as translation is a legitimate form of textual production and contributes to the shaping of a language as much as other textual practices. This is even more the case in countries like Italy, in which translation accounts for a much larger share of published books than it does in the US and the UK. Furthermore, while a representative subcorpus of Italian non-translated fiction should contain texts belonging to Italian popular fiction genres, it would be difficult to include them in a parallel corpus since they are rarely translated into English. Thus, parallel corpora may also need to be supplemented by texts which have not been translated.

3.2 Corpus acquisition and copyright

Once a corpus has been designed, texts must be located and acquired, and corpus compilers must address the problem of copyright permissions. The issue of copyright clearance is a rather thorny one in corpus construction, and while it has been "brought up periodically for discussion by corpus linguists, there is as yet no satisfactory solution to the issue of copyright in corpus building" (McEnery *et al.* 2006:77). Copyright laws and practices may vary considerably in different countries. For instance, in "EU countries, the term of copyright for published works in which the author owns the copyright is the author's life time plus 70 years. Under US law, the term of copyright is the author's lifetime plus 50 years; but for works published before 1978, the copyright term is 75 years if the author renewed the copyright after 28 years" (*ibid.*). If resources are to be made available over the Internet the situation can be even more uncertain as no general agreement has been reached on the status of electronic texts available online.

Accordingly, there is much variation in the approaches adopted by corpus compilers to secure public access to and distribution of corpus resources. Generally, when seeking to approach a copyright holder, a distinction should be made between asking permission to use a text for non-profit making academic research as opposed to commercial purposes. The approach will also be different depending on whether the texts for which copyright permission is requested are to be digitized or are already available in electronic format. Most translation-driven corpora examined so far consist of electronic versions of printed text, often books such as novels or academic works. In such cases there is usually a clear copyright owner, imprinted in the opening pages of each book. The copyright owner, usually the author or the publisher, must be located and asked to send the corpus compilers a written permission to use one or more texts for the purposes of the project. This process, which was also adopted for the construction of the *ENPC* and the *TEC*, is described on the *COMPARA* website:

> Permission requests are sent to the copyright holders of the texts we want to use. They can be authors, translators, publishers or a combination of them. If the copyright holders are deceased, permission requests are sent to their heirs. We begin by asking for permission to use source texts, and only apply for translation permissions after the source texts ones have been granted.[3]

When asking for permission, it may be important to specify that the use of a text as part of an electronic corpus will preclude access to the text in its entirety by the user as part of the specifications of the corpus analysis software. Luz and Baker (2000:online) describe the set of corpus indexing, storage and retrieval tools developed as part of the *TEC* project, and explain that

> [the material in the TEC] is subject to copyright restrictions. In order to be able to make the corpus accessible as a resource for researchers and translators while abiding by copyright laws it was necessary to protect the original texts. This was done by allowing only indirect access to the texts, via the concordance server and browsers. The system architecture described [in the paper] satisfies this constraint, since the clients only receive lists of words drawn from a variety of texts, and their immediate contexts.

A sample letter granting permission for limited use, to be sent together with an accompanying letter explaining the purpose of the project and the use which will be made of the text(s) for which permission is sought, may run as follows:

> This letter will confirm that permission is granted to create an electronic version of the following texts, for use in the research project "[Project Name]" at "[Institution Name]".
> The term of this licence is for the life of the texts, and will not infringe any copyright or other legal rights of any third party, and no additional permission from any third parties will be necessary for use of the texts within the [Project Name].

[3] COMPARA Help Page available at http://adamastor.linguateca.pt/COMPARA/construcao_compara.php. Accessed on 25 August 2010.

> Author, (Translator), Date, *Title*, Place of publication: Publisher.
> --
> --
> Permission is granted on the condition that the electronic corpus will be used for non-profit academic research only. Access to the texts included in the corpus will be restricted to students enrolled and staff currently working at the [Institution Name] or other academic institutions participating in the project. Access to the corpus will in any case be limited to a maximum of 400 words of continuous running text.

Finding copyright holders, sending letters and keeping track of requests may be a taxing matter. Addresses may become obsolete, copyright holders may deny permission, ask for a sum of money not budgeted for in a project, or perhaps simply fail to reply to a request letter, even after acknowledging receipt. In some cases, a negative reply or no reply may result from the copyright holder not properly understanding what a corpus is and the purpose for which the permission should be granted. It is up to the corpus compilers to approach copyright holders effectively and argue their case convincingly. In some instances it may be useful to approach copyright holders in person, or to state in a certified written communication that permission will be taken for granted unless otherwise stated by the copyright holders. In any case, obtaining permission for a large number of texts can be a daunting experience.

A different approach is that taken by Mark Davies, the creator of the 400-million+-word *Corpus Of Contemporary American English* (*COCA*, 1990-2011) and other large monolingual corpora at Brigham Young University. The texts in the *COCA* come mostly from periodical publications (newspapers, magazines and journals) and the corpus is equally subdivided into five genres, four written (fiction, academic article, news report, research article) and one spoken (transcriptions of unscripted TV and radio conversations). The text sources were already available in electronic format, and were downloaded from the Internet manually or through a set of automated routines (Davies 2009a). Rather than seeking permission for each textual item in the corpus, Davies assumed that the format of presentation – that is to say the way texts in the corpus are displayed to the user – make their use in a corpus fall under the practice of fair use. As generally applied to printed texts, the doctrine of 'fair use' (in the US) or 'fair dealing' (under Common Law) allows for the use of short extracts of copyrighted material without the need to obtain explicit permission from copyright holders. The standard length of text extracts generally tolerated under fair use conventions does not exceed 400 words for prose texts, 40 lines or one quarter from a poem, etc.[4] After carefully considering the issue and consulting with lawyers who specialize in Internet copyright law, the author of the *COCA* decided that,

[4] See examples from http://jhepp.library.jhu.edu/drupal/fairuse. Accessed on 10 February 2011.

since access to the corpus contents through the Web interface prohibits access to entire texts and "it would be difficult for end users to re-create even one paragraph from the original text, and it would be virtually impossible to re-create an entire page of text, much less the entire article",[5] availability of the *COCA* to the general public can be considered to fall under fair use. Davies supports this approach "which relies on limited access to the original text via small snippets from the Web interface" (*ibid.*) on the 'snippet defence' used by Google Books. This search function provides access to the contents of thousands of copyrighted books allowing for the visualization of small textual portions, a policy which Google maintains is legal under fair use. Other reasons which favor Fair Use status are, according to Davies, the purpose and character of the use (academic, non-commercial), the fact that the corpus contains mostly non-creative works, and that its use has little or no effect on the copyright holder. Whether or not the *COCA* is an infringement of copyright laws can only be established by a court of law, as in all cases of fair use, but the *COCA* seems to be establishing itself as an unchallenged precedent as concerns publicly available corpora.

The decision to seek formal permission or presume fair use also depends on the source format of the texts included in a corpus (e.g. printed fiction as opposed to non-fictional electronic texts). Moreover, the increasing global availability of texts in electronic format (witness the extensive digitization of libraries and the diffusion of electronic books) points perhaps to a better ease of access to electronic sources for corpora and for a more relaxed attitude towards the contents of corpora in connection with copyright issues. However, any decision ultimately rests with the corpus compilers, who should carefully consider the options at hand.

Still different is the case of small and 'virtual' corpora which are created for private purposes, whether by professional translators, researchers and students (see § 3.3.2.2). These DIY corpora are usually created by individuals with a specific purpose in mind and are not available to the general public. They are often of a disposable nature, and are not meant to be redistributed. Various researchers have discussed the use of such corpora, which often are created by downloading from the Internet texts whose copyright status in not always clear, in translator education (e.g. Maia 1997, Bowker 2002b, Zanettin 2002b, Varantola 2003, Wilkinson 2006). Bowker and Pearson (2002:59) suggest that, since copyright laws for electronic texts are still unclear, "[i]n order to be safe, you should contact the owner of any text that you want to include in your corpus and obtain his or her permission". Often, however, copyright permissions do not seem to be a major concern in the literature on research or teaching applications of DIY corpora.

3.3 Web corpora

The exponential growth of the Internet in the new millennium has led some scholars to adopt a different approach to corpus size and composition. The World

---

[5] 'Copyright issues', by Mark Davies at COCA's website, http://www.americancorpus.org/. Accessed on 10 February 2011.

Wide Web is the largest content distribution system and the most extensive and accessible repository of textual data. Estimates of the size of the Web in total number of words have been attempted at various times, showing an increase from about 7,000 million words of running text in 1996 to about 60,000 million in 1999 (Grefenstette and Nioche 2000), to 2,000 billion in 2003 (Kilgarriff and Grefenstette 2003:337), to about 8,000 billion in 2005 (Gatto 2009:20, 42n). Over the same period the share of texts in English, initially the overwhelming majority language, has diminished to proportionally less than one third of the total, while other languages have increased at an even faster rate of growth. As of the end of 2010, some estimates put its total size at over 100 billion pages.[6]

The Web is an almost exhaustive – rather than representative – corpus of the language used in electronic written communication, itself one of the main modes of linguistic communication in the world. However, while the Web is a gargantuan and growing collection of electronic texts, by mixing together languages, text types, genres, etc., it seems to lack the main criterion which defines a corpus, that of having being designed and assembled for the purpose of linguistic investigation. There is in fact little reason to resort to the Web as a corpus if an alternative can be found in a well-designed corpus. For many general investigations concerning frequent and stable features of English the *BNC* will be of better use than any 'Web corpus'.

The main advantage of the Web over 'proper' corpora lies in its tremendous size, which compensates to some extent for the uneven quality of the texts it contains. In fact, even very large and well-designed monolingual corpora can provide data for a relatively few features of a language, since as Kilgarriff and Grefenstette argue (2003:336)

> although 100 million is a huge number, and the *BNC* contains ample information on the dominant meanings and usage patterns for the 10000 words that make up the core of English, the bulk of the lexical stock occurs less than 50 times in the *BNC*, which is not enough to draw statistically stable conclusions about the word. For rare words, rare meanings of common words, and combination of words, we frequently find no evidence at all.

Since the Web is much larger than any purpose-built corpus in existence, for many languages and language varieties it may be the only 'corpus' available, and ultimately, while "[t]he web is not representative of anything else ... neither are other corpora, in any well-understood sense" (Kilgarriff and Grefenstette 2003:343).

Two options are basically available in order to use the Web as a corpus resource: the first is to use the Web *as* a macro-corpus, and apply a number of parameters to restrict the results of searches to 'slices' of the Web (Bergh 2005),

[6] See e.g. http://edudemic.com/2011/01/how-big-is-the-internet/. Accessed on 31 December 2010.

much as one would use parameters from descriptive criteria in a corpus to select subcorpora from it. This means shifting the focus from the design behind the collection of texts to the strategies which can be used to select appropriate texts from the Web and to the interpretation of search results. The second option is to use the Web as a source of texts, i.e. select texts from the Web and use them as sources of textual material to be included in large and robust corpora such as the *COCA*, as well as in 'quick-and-dirty' DIY disposable corpora. Having no control over the overall design and composition of the Web the researcher or translator can still use its contents for linguistic investigations, provided appropriate subcorpora are extracted from it.

3.3.1 The Web as corpus

Apart from its anarchic lack of design, a major difference between the Web and 'proper' corpora concerns the way linguistic data are accessed, displayed and interpreted. While corpora are analyzed through software specifically created for corpus analysis, the Web is accessed primarily through commercial search engines such as Google, Bing or Yahoo! The issue here is whether and to what extent commercial search engines can be used for purposes of linguistic research, and whether software can be created to provide an alternative, more linguistically focused access to Web data.

When one is using commercial search engines the first problem is formulating a query in order to get only relevant results. For instance, by using specialized terminology as search input, it is possible to restrict the type and content of the documents retrieved. Words and terms pertaining both to text type and content can be used in a search to filter out many unwanted documents. A search for documents containing both the word 'mouse' and the word 'computer' will hopefully weed out most references to the animal. A search for documents containing the word 'mouse' but not any of the words 'computer', 'software' or 'hardware' will instead largely narrow down the documents retrieved to those mentioning the rodent. Even more importantly, searches for extended phrases, which are likely to retrieve only a few if any instances from corpora of even hundreds of millions of words may return relevant documents from the Web. While typically not having the same capabilities of corpus software (e.g. the use of regular expressions, see Chapter 5), search engines such as Google allow for some flexibility, for instance for the use of wildcard characters. A search for *"who is a * member of the"*, where the asterisk represents one or more intervening words in the phrase delimited by quotation marks, will produce a list of modifiers of the word 'member', such as' founding', 'former', 'retired', 'prominent', 'proud', etc.

By carefully playing around with the formulation of queries for searches and refining search parameters researchers, translators and language learners alike can select relevant subcorpora, i.e. 'slices' of the Web (Hubbard 2005, Bergh 2005, Gatto 2008, Zanettin 2009a). For instance, by using the advanced search options of search engines it is usually possible to tailor a search by restricting access to data by language and regional provenance, indicating a country and an Internet domain (for instance ".ac.uk" and ".edu" to select an "educational and academic" variety of English), or a specific Internet address (for instance wikipedia.org or elsevier.com). It is also usually possible to search within categories determined by search engines, such as 'finance', 'travel' or 'sports'. Furthermore, some search engines cover specialized "subwebs" restricting a search, for instance, to news (e.g. Yahoo News and Google News), academic publications (Google Scholar) or books in print (Google Books). Other options available include for instance the possibility to limit a search by file type (for instance to PDF files, which usually have a less volatile content than files in other text formats) and by date range.

However, while a combination of search criteria may help the user to restrict the scope of a search, the data provided by search engines are of a different nature from those provided by a well-designed corpus, both quantitatively and qualitatively. The quantity of data retrieved is often unmanageable and not easily interpretable and does not offer an indication of the external boundaries or of the internal subdivision of the "Web subcorpus" selected. Quantitative results, as expressed in number of hits, only provide a rough if not confusing indication of standard usage. While it may be useful to know that a certain linguistic form does not occur at all on the Web, even thousands of occurrences of one particular form could still only be evidence of a minority or inconsistent usage.

Besides the challenge of formulating appropriate queries and of selecting appropriate 'Web subcorpora' using 'filters' such as language, Internet domain, topic categorization, etc., the use of linguistic data from the Web is problematic in that search engines fail to present results in a format suitable for linguistic analysis.

The display format of the results retrieved by a search consists in a list of links to the indexed documents, each accompanied by a short extract containing the query string. However, the way results are ordered by search engines is not determined by linguistic criteria (Bergh 2005:30-33). Commercial considerations as well as other ranking criteria determine the order of presentation of search results and this order is extremely volatile. It is specific to one search engine or the other, and changes when using the same search engine at different times. In any case, the ordering or results does not reflect criteria of frequency and authoritativeness. Furthermore, while results as displayed by a search engine may seem to resemble those displayed by a concordancer, search engines do not allow for their manipulation. Results can only be arranged in the order and format provided, and occurrences cannot be displayed in KWIC format (see § 5.2.2), sorted or otherwise categorized.

The issue of how to present results from the Web as corpus in a format amenable to linguistic analysis has been addressed, at its simplest, by *WebCONC*[7] (Hüning 2001-2002), a 'linguist's search engine' which allows the user to restrict a Google search by language, to one or more domain(s), and to use regular expressions in searches. *WebCONC* acts as an interface between the end user

[7] http://www.niederlandistik.fu-berlin.de/cgi-bin/web-conc.cgi?sprache=en/. Accessed on 01 October 2011.

and search engines, allowing the display of search results in a concordance-like format as in Figure 3.1.

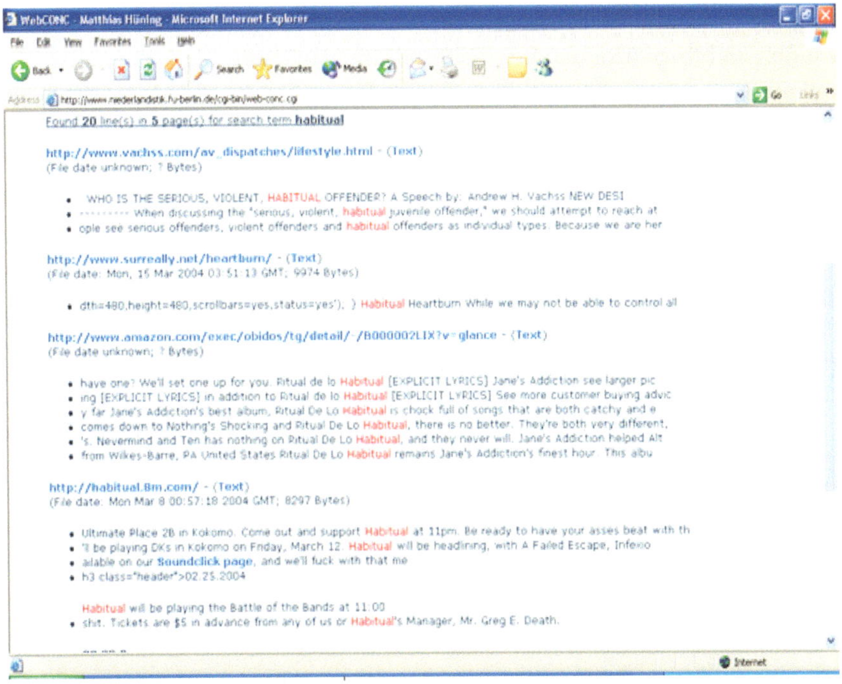

Figure 3.1. Results of a search for 'habitual' using WebCONC

More sophisticated applications, which in fact treat the Web as a source of corpora to be further processed before being made available for linguistic analysis (see § 3.3.2), are *WebCorp Live*[8], *WebAsCorpus*[9] and *KWiCFinder*.[10] *WebCorp Live*, developed at the Research and Development Unit for English Studies at Birmingham City University since 2000, is an interface which allows the user to choose among a number of search engines, and build on their advanced search features to filter results by Internet domain, textual domain (based on the Open Directory categorization), and date range. As opposed to *WebCONC*, *WebCorp Live* makes it also possible to improve precision by adding a 'word filter' which limits the results of a search only to documents which contain (or do not contain) one or more specific words, so as to restrict the number of instances per site to one, and exclude hyperlink text, email addresses and other distracters from searches (Renouf *et al.* 2007).

In order to allow further manipulation of search results, services such as *WebCorp Live* and *WebAsCorpus* operate in a cache mode, storing on the server

[8] http://www.webcorp.org.uk. Accessed on 20 March 2011.
[9] http://webascorpus.org. Accessed on 20 March 2011.
[10] http://miniappolis.com/KWiCFinder/KWiCFinder.html. Accessed on 20 March 2011.

a copy of the results, where they remain available for a short period of time and can be downloaded to a local computer. By doing this, the system basically creates a corpus from the Web from which concordance lines can be sorted, collocations generated and other relations between words can be computed. Figure 3.2 shows the first 25 hits of a search for "habitual" in a subcorpus of British broadsheet and tabloid newspapers, sorted according to the first word to the right.

A similar approach is also taken by *KWiCFinder* (Fletcher 2004), which is not an online service that creates a cache copy of the Web subcorpora retrieved on the server, but a stand-alone program which must be downloaded and run from the desktop, and which stores corpora locally. Figure 3.3 shows the results of a search for the word 'translators' in the stand-alone *KWiCFinder* Online Research Tool.

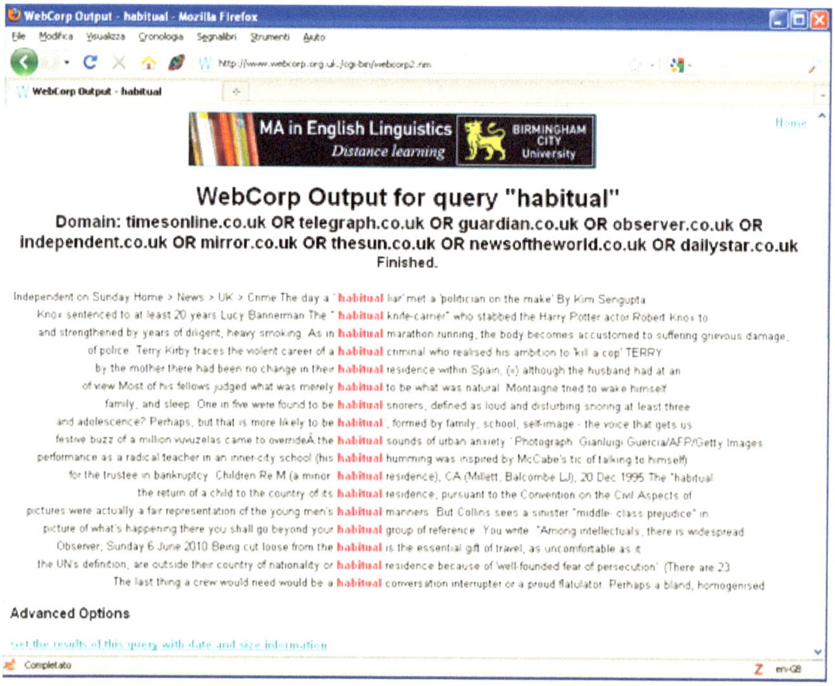

Figure 3.2. WebCorp Live *output for the query 'habitual'*

These enhancements go a long way towards solving the problem of using the Web as a suitable source of text-linguistic information, but the searches are often slow and do not solve the problem of the relevance and reliability of the documents retrieved.

3.3.2 *The Web as a source of corpora*

The Web can be used not only as a corpus 'surrogate' (Bernardini *et al.* 2006:10), but also as a source of texts for corpora. First- and second-generation corpora included mostly digitized versions of printed material, as other types of language

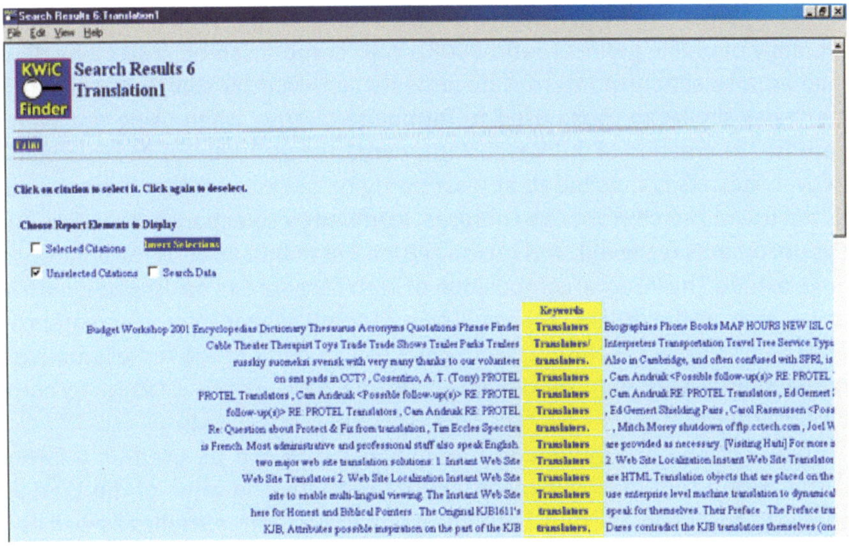

Figure 3.3. KWiCFinder *output of a search for the word 'translators'*

production such as spoken language and handwritten or otherwise 'non-printed' material were indeed harder to include. By the same token, many current corpus projects use the Web as a source of corpora because electronic texts are now more readily available than printed texts and because, since corpora are laborious and expensive to build, using texts already available in electronic format allows to save on corpus construction times and costs. Furthermore, while access to and use of some textual archives available online may come at a price, the status of Web documents as concerns copyright restrictions appears to be regulated by laxer criteria than for printed publications.

A corpus may of course include texts from more traditional media such as print, transcriptions of oral language, etc. together with native electronic, or only contain texts from the Internet. In principle, the selection of texts from the Internet should be guided by the same design criteria used in the creation of more 'traditional' corpora. Thus, depending on the purpose for which a corpus is built and on the textual universe addressed, its reliability will depend on its size, its composition, subject, text type, and balance among its internal components. These are language-external criteria, that is, the selection of texts to be included in a corpus depends on categories defined prior to the analysis of the linguistic contents of the texts. Such a corpus is for instance the *COCA* (Davies 2009a). The corpus "is composed of more than 400 million words in more than 160,000 texts, including 20 million words each year from 1990-2009" (Davies 2009b:online). Davies (*ibid.*) argues that the *COCA* is as balanced a corpus as the *BNC*, while at the same time being 4 times as large and updated at the rate of 20 million words per year. The sources of the *COCA* for written genres are electronic versions of 'traditional' texts from printed genres, and the Web at large is not considered as a source of data.

Given the difficulty in describing the contents of the Web and in creating a typology of online genres (Gatto 2008), Web corpora can be created by downloading a selection of Internet documents retrieved by search engines using strategies similar to those used to formulate queries when using the Web as corpus. The creation of 'mini-webs' (Bernardini *et al.* 2006:10), or scale models of Web subsets is thus based at least partly on language-internal criteria such as the use of search words and phrases, followed by selection and processing of the documents retrieved, and can be carried out manually or be automated to a large extent. The internal composition of Web corpora can be assessed *post-hoc* rather than at the outset (Sharoff 2006a, 2006b), allowing corpus creators and end users to draw conclusions as to what search findings are representative of, rather than assess representativeness on the basis of pre-established corpus design criteria.

Web corpora are by default monolingual, and can be used as reference corpora for a certain language, or language variety. The value of the Web as a source of corpora for corpus-based descriptive translation studies as well as for translator training and practice lies also in the possibility of creating comparable corpora, both general and specialized, by using similar criteria for different languages. Corpora thus created can range from very large general ones to much smaller and very specific ones.

Finally, while translated texts are indeed present on the Web, direct access to Web data does not allow the user to distinguish between translated and non-translated texts, nor does it allow for the display of parallel concordances. The creation of bi- and multilingual parallel corpora using parallel texts available on the Web will be discussed in Chapter 6.

3.3.2.1 General Web corpora

A model for the automated creation of large Web corpora has been devised within the *Wacky!* project (Baroni and Bernardini 2006) and has led to the creation of various corpus products and tools. An offshoot of the *Wacky!* model is, for instance, the implementation by Serge Sharoff (2006a) of a methodology for "creating general-purpose corpora using automated search engine queries". Sharoff has developed a set of open source, large general/reference Web corpora using the same methodology for many languages. Large corpora in 11 languages (English, Chinese, Italian, Japanese, Russian, German, French, Arabic, Spanish, Portuguese and Polish) are available through an online interface known as the 'Leeds collection of Internet corpora'.[11] The first stage of corpus creation follows the steps outlined in Baroni and Bernardini (2004), which led to the creation of the freely available *BootCaT* (Bootstrapping Corpora and Terms from the Web) tools.[12] The procedure is described on the website of the Leeds collection of

---

[11] At http://corpus.leeds.ac.uk/internet.html. Accessed on 12 February 2011.

[12] The *BootCaT* tools can be downloaded from: http://bootcat.sslmit.unibo.it/. Accessed on 12 February 2011.

Internet corpora by Sharoff who recounts how the text collection can begin by selecting as search words "about 500 words from a list of the most frequent word forms". These words "must be sufficiently general", that is they should neither belong to a specific domain nor be function words. For the English corpus the initial wordlist was derived from the *BNC* frequency list, and then used to automatically produce a list of 5000-6000 Google queries. Each query consists of 4 words randomly selected from the list, and the first 10 documents resulting from each query are downloaded to make the corpus. The third step is processing the downloaded documents. Web documents are often hypertexts living in a multimedia environment and before being entered in the corpus they are stripped of images, sound, film, navigation frames, unwanted codes and annotation such as HTML tags and Java scripts. Through a series of automated routines the corpus is then also cleared of duplicates and the texts are converted to a common encoding format. Finally they are annotated (lemmatized and part-of-speech tagged), indexed and then queried using the *IMS Open Corpus Workbench* (*CWB*, see Chapter 5). Figure 3.4 is a screenshot of the output of a search for "set + your + [any token] + [any token] + [any pronoun]"[13] in the Leeds 100 million words English Internet corpus.

Figure 3.4. Output of a search in the Leeds English Internet *corpus*

---

[13] The query is formulated in the search syntax used by the Corpus Query Processor (CQP), which is the search tool associated with the *IMS Corpus Workbench* (*CWB*).

The composition of the English Internet corpus was assessed by taking a sample of texts from the corpus and describing them according to a text typology. A comparison with the equal size *BNC* shows that indeed the two corpora are different on a number of parameters such as authorship (e.g. the *BNC* contains a smaller proportion of 'corporate' texts), mode (e.g. the Web corpus contains fewer transcriptions of spoken language) and domain (e.g. the Web corpus contains a higher percentage of texts in the applied sciences).

Based on similar criteria are the Web 'megacorpora' available on the *Sketch Engine* website[14] which include a 1.5-billion-word corpus of British English (*ukWaC*), a 1.6-billion-word corpus of German (*deWaC*), a 1.9-billion-word corpus of Italian (*itWaC*), and smaller corpora in other languages. These corpora are fully annotated and the online interface allows the user to create and sort concordances and wordlists, plus a series of additional features (see Chapter 5).

General Web corpora can be used as reference in corpus-based translation research when triangulating findings from smaller monolingual and bilingual translation-driven corpora. They can either supplement and extend the information derived from traditional monolingual corpora such as the *BNC*, or act as the sole reference for languages for which other corpora are not available.

3.3.2.2 Specialized Web corpora

The use of the Web as a source of small, specialized corpora goes back to the practice of collecting Do-It-Yourself Web corpora for use in translator training and practice (e.g. Bowker 2002b, Zanettin 2002b, Varantola 2003). According to Varantola (2003:56-57) "the knowledge and skills needed in the compilation and use of corpus information for individual translation assignments" should be part of translators' competence. The advantage of such corpora, which are basically a collection of domain-specific Internet documents, is that they can be created *ad hoc* as a response to a specific text to be translated and can therefore be very precise. DIY Web corpora are also of an open-ended nature, as new material can be added as a translation need arises, and are disposable (Varantola 2003) or virtual (Ahmad *et al.* 1994). Not being meant as permanent resources, they can be disposed of as soon as a translation assignment is completed, thus arguably making the issue of copyright permissions irrelevant.

The procedures used to assemble Web documents for a specialized DIY Web corpus are basically the same used to perform queries and evaluate search engine results when using the Web as a corpus. The advantages over simply using the Web as a corpus are that once a Web corpus is assembled it can be analyzed more easily through corpus linguistic techniques. Small DIY specialized Web corpora can be created by manually saving individual documents in a local folder, and can be analyzed using stand-alone corpus concordancing software such as *WordSmith Tools* and *AntConc* (see Chapter 5). Zanettin (2002b), for instance, illustrates an experiment in translator training in which students were

---

[14] http://www.sketchengine.co.uk/. Accessed on 20 March 2011.

asked to first setup a 'workstation' comprising various tools and resources (a concordancing program, an Internet browser and search engines, word processors, etc.) and then create a corpus to be used during a translation assignment. Operational instructions regarded the formulation of appropriate queries, followed by perusal of results, processing of selected documents into the corpus and analysis of the data with *WordSmith Tools*. The compilation of the corpus was performed on a cyclical basis, in that in the process of translating and analyzing the corpus students were prompted to perform new searches and add material to the corpus. The corpora created were rather small, ranging between 10 and 50 texts and between 5,000 and 40,000 words each. However, they proved to be highly useful for understanding and translating specific terminology, collocations and phraseology when dealing with texts such as scientific articles, catalogues and promotional material. Sánchez-Gijón (2009) suggests protocols to help students formulate queries, evaluate results and process Web documents in order to create DIY Web corpora.

In the experiment described in Zanettin (2002b) the students started by first looking in dictionaries, term banks and online glossaries in specific fields and establishing equivalence between terms in the source texts and in the target language. Queries were then refined while translating and checking hypotheses during revision. The evaluation of the results, which determined the inclusion or not of a text in the corpus, was carried out by scanning documents for content rather than for terms. The relevance of a document was usually decided after considering both verbal and visual clues (titles, layout and images), text type, style and register and overall content. For instance, a student translating a catalogue of luxury textiles discarded texts from the website of a museum dealing with African traditional textiles and clothing; a student translating a bicycle locks catalogue discarded a newspaper article on urban safety. The reliability of the texts was further assessed by looking at their authoritativeness. Bad translations were discarded, and texts produced by recognizable bodies and authorities within the relevant discourse communities (experts, producers, public and private agencies and associations) were privileged.

The compilation of specialized Web corpora can be carried out not only manually but also in a fully or partially automated way using software specifically created for this purpose such as the *BootCaT* front-end application. In any case the construction of a reliable corpus will depend on the successful formulation of queries and on the evaluation of search results. The challenge in the formulation of queries is to come up with a list of words or terms which will strike a balance between precision and recall (see §5.2.2), determining the number of relevant documents retrieved by a search. When Web corpora are collected automatically, the corpus compiler can exert various degrees of control on what is being collected and on the processing of the texts. A very useful tool is the *Sketch Engine* online corpus query system. Besides providing access to a number of pre-loaded general reference corpora (including the *BNC*) and 'Web megacorpora' for different languages, it allows registered users to create their own DIY Web corpora using a version of the *BootCaT* tools integrated in the system. The creation of a corpus from the Web is carried out through a series of steps which use modular components, guiding the user through procedures similar to those used in the construction of the Leeds Internet corpora mentioned in the previous section. First, the user provides a name, an ID and further descriptive information about the corpus, and specifies the annotation templates to be used in the compilation of the corpus. A number of default annotation schemes ('configuration templates and sketch grammars', see Chapter 5) are provided for some languages and new customized ones can be added and selected. Once setup options are specified, the user can start adding text files to the corpus. Programs such as *WebCorp Live* and *KWiCFinder*, provide a corpus linguist's interface to the Web as corpus by making 'raw' Web data more manageable. The *Sketch Engine*, in contrast, assists in creating a corpus by allowing for a cyclical procedure and a number of refined options. Following the steps defined by the *BootCaT* tools the user provides a list of 'seeds' (words or phrases) and specifies a numbers of search parameters, such as the type of files to be retrieved (HTML, PDF, Word, etc.), the Internet domains and subdomains and one or more words and/or phrases that must be contained (whitelist) or not (blacklist) in the documents retrieved. The user can set additional parameters, fine-tuning options such as the number of 'seeds' to be used in each query, the number of results to be downloaded per query and the total number of queries, as well as a lower and an upper limit to the size and the number of words of the files to be retrieved. Results are displayed as a list of links grouped by query (queries are based on random combinations, i.e. 'tuples', of the seeds provided), and it is at this stage that they can be individually scrutinized in order to decide whether to include them in the corpus or not. Then, selected documents are downloaded to the server and further processed, i.e. converted to a common encoding format and stripped of unwanted tags and text, duplicates and near duplicates, etc. Finally the corpus is compiled, i.e. it is annotated and indexed, ready to be analyzed through the online interface.

The results of a *BootCaT* run create an initial 'corpus collection' which can be used as a basis to add material and refine the corpus. The 'seeds' to be used in a second run can be automatically extracted from the initial corpus collection by comparing a frequency wordlist for that collection with that of a larger corpus available in the *Sketch Engine* website. Wordlists will be dealt with in more detail in Chapter 5, but in short this list of keywords for a given corpus is obtained by comparing the relative frequency of each item in both lists. Thus, the list will include only words that are not only frequent in the smaller corpus, but which are comparatively less frequent in the larger corpus. The system provides a list of keywords for the corpus, which can be selected (or not) as seeds for a new *BootCaT* run. The results are stored as a new collection on the side of the initial one, and the newly accrued corpus can in turn be used as input for a new list of keywords. Each text in each collection in a corpus is still available for inspection, both through a link to the original Web document and as a raw, unannotated text file, and can be deleted from the corpus at a later stage.

As an example, a small specialized corpus on 'human geography' was created by using as the initial input from which to extract seed words the frequency list from the entry 'human geography' in Wikipedia. A list of keywords was obtained by using the *BNC* frequency wordlist as a reference (see § 5.2.1 for a description of this procedure). The resulting wordlist contained 20 words with a minimum frequency of 5, and from these 10 content words (geography, physical, human, social, geographies, include, work, geographer, cultural, economic, space, spatial) were selected and used as a set of 'seeds' for a *BootCaT* run. The search was restricted to PDF files coming from servers in the British academic domain (.ac.uk), and to the first ten hits for each of ten Yahoo! queries, each query containing a random quadruplet, i.e. a tuple of 4 seed words. In order to filter out texts which are either too short or too long, further settings included the specification of the minimum and maximum file size (between 5 and 2000 Kb) and of the minimum and maximum number of words which a file must contain (between 300 and 10,000 words) in order for it to be added to the corpus. The search returned about 80 pages, of which about half were finally selected and downloaded. This resulted in a corpus of about 200,000 words, and it took about 20 minutes before the corpus was ready for analysis with the *Sketch Engine* (see Figure 3.5).

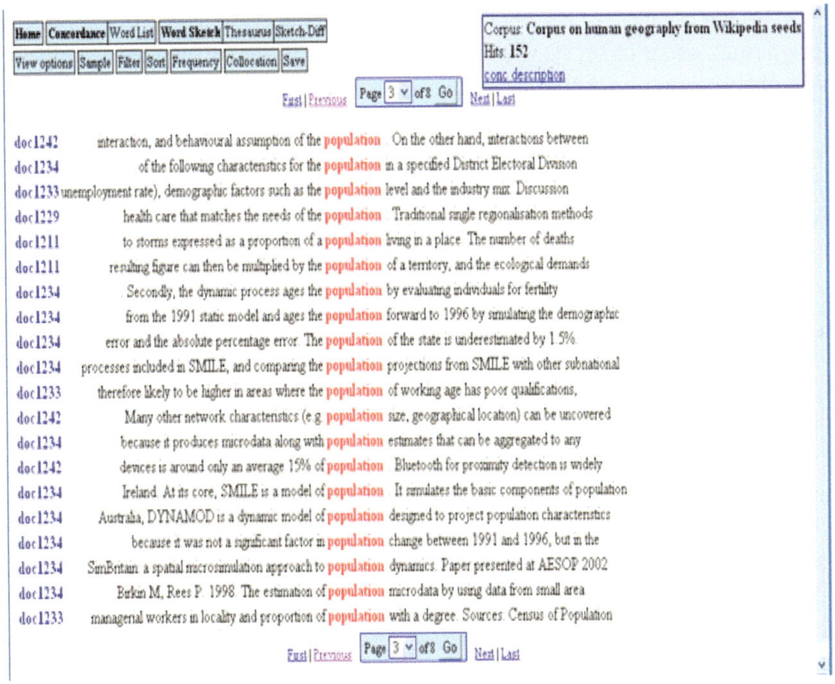

Figure 3.5. A screenshot from the Sketch Engine

By using default options even an inexperienced user may create a rough-and-ready disposable DIY corpus which may prove quite useful to assist in a specific translation task or project (Ferraresi 2009). A careful use of tools such as the *Sketch Engine*, however, may also result in the making of well-constructed, specialized, bilingual comparable Web corpora for use in descriptive studies.

3.4 Conclusions

Like for any corpus project, the design of a translation-driven corpus may change from that of an *ideal* corpus to one where expectations have to be adjusted to general constraints such as project funding, copyright restrictions or lack of appropriate corpus material or tools. Such constraints may be even more taxing in the making of parallel corpora where texts come in pairs and both source and target texts must therefore be available. For instance, copyright restrictions may apply to both the source text and the translation, and thus further complicate the process of copyright clearance.

Some difficulties may also be encountered during the following stages of corpus acquisition. As we shall see in Chapter 4, processing the texts for inclusion in the corpus and then for annotation can also be laborious and error-prone. This is the case not only when digitizing printed texts through scanning and proofreading, but also when creating corpora from native electronic texts, a process which may imply various problems related, for instance, to format conversion and clean-up. In conclusion, in any corpus project a balance has to be sought between the creation of an ideal versus an opportunistic corpus. The ideal corpus design must come to terms with practical problems concerning the quantity and type of the source material available, and this will be reflected in the make-up of a corpus. While some form of reconciliation between the two poles seems to be rather standard practice for available corpora, researchers should be aware of the possible shortcomings of the corpus they are using when interpreting the data, since these may in turn result in a distorted representation and skew the results of studies.

3.5 Tasks

3.5.1 Corpus building project outline

The aim of this task is to help you focus on the main aspects involved in corpus design and construction. Some of these have already been discussed, and others will be considered in the following chapters. At the end of Chapter 6 you will be asked to revise your project outline using a checklist. Go through the different points and if possible discuss them with a fellow student or researcher. Write down notes concerning each aspect, on the basis of what you already know and of your expectations. At this stage you should outline a project for an ideal corpus, which you will be able to reconsider later in view of its implementation.

1. Project objectives and general description
Describe the aim of a research project involving the creation of a corpus to assist in translation research or teaching, and how you would use the corpus once it is available.

2. Corpus description
Sketch out a description of the corpus/corpora involved in your project. What type(s) of texts would you include in the corpus/corpora? In which languages/translation directions?

3. Corpus annotation
Is there a need to annotate your corpus? What would need to be annotated and how? What type of extralinguistic information about the texts in the corpus should be documented? What kind of information about the language in the texts would you like to add to the plain text, if any?

4. Corpus analysis and accessibility
What uses would you envisage for the corpus once it is created? For example, personal research, work with students, a resource to be made available to the wider research community, etc.

3.5.2 Manual creation of a DIY monolingual corpus

In this task you will manually create a sample specialized corpus by searching for, selecting and downloading electronic documents from the Web. This task is preparatory to the following one, in which you will be asked to replicate the procedure with the help of the *BootCaT* front-end application to create a bilingual comparable corpus.

1. Decide on a subject field/topic for your specialized corpus. Here are some suggestions:
   - A monolingual comparable corpus of "Contact" and "Legal" textual blocks in corporate websites (e.g. original Spanish Web pages and Web pages localized into Spanish, Jiménez-Crespo 2010).
   - A monolingual corpus on a specialized subject such as cosmology, retinopathy, or the European Monetary Union. In the table below some keywords are listed which can be used as search words for these subjects/topics. Use several words at a time for your searches.

Subject/Topic	Keywords
Cosmology	universe, galaxies, bang, cosmic, astronomers, Hubble, theory, space, matter, clusters
Retinopathy	retinopathy, diabetic, diabetes, retinal, patients, microaneurysms, fundus, duration, baseline, screening
European Monetary Union	euro, currency, states, currencies, participating, economic, stability, exchange, convergence, treaty

2. Fill in the table below with project details. Estimate the number of texts and the number of words which can be collected in about one hour of work.

Topic/Subject	
Text type(s)	
Publication dates	
Authorship	
File type(s)	
Number of texts	
Number of words	

3. Use a general search engine (e.g. Google, Altavista, Yahoo!, Bing) or the search facilities of specific online databases (e.g. electronic journals your university subscribes to) to find suitable texts for your corpus.

4. Save your corpus files in a personal folder. Within this folder you can create subfolders as needed, e.g. one for each language.

5. Examine search results in detail, if necessary by skimming the actual documents from the list of candidate texts in order to assess the relevance of each document for your corpus, and decide whether or not you want to include it. Use the *Save as...* function of your browser or PDF document reader (for PDF documents) to save the texts in the folder you created in text-only format (.TXT). Create a table using as a model the table below, and fill it in with as many details as possible – minimally file name and URL – to keep track of the documents in the corpus.

File name	URL	Title	Author	Date	N. of words	Notes

6. On the basis of the time you have spent searching, assessing, saving and documenting the texts in your corpus folder, and of the current corpus size, estimate the time it would take to create a corpus of about 50,000 words.

3.5.3 Automatic creation of a DIY bilingual comparable corpus

In this task you will create your own bilingual comparable corpus using the *BootCaT* front-end graphical interface. If you have done the previous task you should have become acquainted with details which should help you assess the authoritativeness and reliability of the texts before including them in the corpus. These include details about the URL, file format, visual presentation, etc. While the system will help you to process your corpus, you will still have to gauge its composition.

1. Go to: http://bootcat.sslmit.unibo.it/
Download and install the *BootCaT* front-end graphical interface most suited to your software configuration. A copy of the program (Windows version) is also available on the DVD.

2. Choose one of the following subjects/topics: Cosmology, Retinopathy, the European Monetary Union, and start creating your comparable corpora. First create a corpus in English.

3. Launch the *BootCaT* front-end. From the *Edit* menu select *Options*, and specify a working directory in your computer where you will store the corpora which you will be using for the activities in the Tasks section. Then click on *Next.*

4. Provide a name for the corpus and select a language, then click on *Next.*

5. Type in all the keywords for the chosen subject/topic from the table below, one per line.

Cosmology	Retinopathy	European Monetary Union
universe galaxies bang cosmic astronomers Hubble theory space matter clusters	retinopathy diabetic diabetes retinal patients microaneurysms fundus duration baseline screening	euro currency states currencies participating economic stability exchange convergence treaty

6. In the next steps, you can set a number of parameters which will increase the accuracy of your corpus. For the purpose of this exercise, set the value for *Tuple length* at 5, and that for *Number of tuples* at 10. This means that the search will retrieve only documents which contain at least 5 of your keywords (randomly selected), and that the system will generate 10 such queries based on the list of 'seeds' you provided. Then click on *Next.*

7. Set the number of pages per query to 10, then click on *Collect URLs*. When this is done, click on *Next*. In the list of results, untick irrelevant links if present. Base your decision on the URL or, if necessary, click on the links and inspect the pages. When you have decided on the texts to include in the corpus, click on *Next*, then on *Build the corpus* and wait until all the pages are downloaded. Then click on *Open corpus folder* to see your corpus.

8. Repeat steps 2 to 7, this time for a different language. As *seeds*, you can use the Italian keywords in the table below, or provide a translation of the English keywords in your language of choice. Remember to select the appropriate language from the drop-down menu.

Cosmologia	Retinopatia	Unione monetaria europea
universo galassie teoria Hubble bang radiazione materia big densità ammassi	retinopatia pazienti diabetica diabete proliferante diabetici soggetti prevalenza retinica insulino	euro moneta monetaria stabilità unione monete fase tassi convergenza scambio

You will use the corpora in Chapter 5 when experimenting with corpus analysis software.

3.6 Further reading

A good introduction to corpus design issues is John Sinclair's 'Corpus and Text: Basic Principles' (2005), the first chapter of the online volume *Developing Linguistic Corpora: a Guide to Good Practice*, edited by Martin Wynne. The book is available at http://www.ahds.ac.uk/creating/guides/linguistic-corpora/index.htm and contains other useful introductory chapters. Chapters 1, 3 and 4 of Lynne Bowker and Jennifer Pearson's *Working with Specialized Language. A Practical Guide to Using Corpora* (2002) also provide useful guidelines, with a special emphasis on specialized corpora. A discussion of the issue of representativeness, in light of the shifting focus from the printed to the digital world as a data source is provided by Geoffrey Leech's 'New resources, or just better old ones? The Holy Grail of representativeness' (2007), in volume 59 of the series Language & Computers on *Corpus Linguistics and the Web* edited by Hundt *et al.*

On the design of bilingual bidirectional parallel corpora, see the *English-Norwegian Parallel Corpus Manual* by Johansson *et al.* (1999-2002) available online at http://www.hf.uio.no/ilos/forskning/forskningsprosjekter/enpc/

ENPCmanual.html. Further discussion on the issues of comparability and reciprocity is provided by Federico Zanettin in 'Parallel Corpora in Translation Studies. Issues in Corpus Design and Analysis' (2000) in *Intercultural Faultlines*, edited by Maeve Olohan (reprinted in vol. IV of the series Critical Concepts in Linguistics on *Corpus Linguistics* edited by Wolfgang Teubert and Ramesh Krishnamurthy).

Not much has been written about copyright issues in relation to corpus construction, apart from a few remarks in corpus linguistics textbooks. A short but informative chapter on copyright can be found in McEnery *et al.* (2006).

For general information about the corpus linguistics approach to Web data see the special volume of the journal *Computational Linguistics* (vol. 29:3) on the Web as corpus, edited by Adam Kilgarriff and Gregory Grefenstette (2003). The collection *Wacky! Working papers on the Web as Corpus* (2006) edited by Marco Baroni and Silvia Bernardini, available at http://wackybook.sslmit.unibo.it/ includes a description of the approach and the tools used for the automation of Web harvesting procedures used to create both general and specialized corpora from the Web. Maristella Gatto's *From Body to Web* (2009) discusses practical applications of approaches to the Web as corpus and the Web as a source of corpora for contrastive linguistics and translation studies.

4. Corpus encoding and annotation

The Electronic Text Center of the University of Nebraska-Lincoln Libraries defines text encoding as "a process whereby documents are transferred to an electronically searchable format for scholarly research".[1] According to this definition, then, all electronic text corpora are encoded since texts are basically strings of characters which are codified by computers as sequences of binary digits. The digital format is in fact what makes textual documents searchable by using strings of characters as search words.

The first schema for encoding characters in computer-generated text was the American Standard Code for Information Interchange (ASCII), which could handle 128 different characters, more than enough to cover those of the American keyboard. The original ASCII code set, which became an international standard in 1972 (ISO 646), was based on a combination of seven bits and was superseded by various complementary and competing 8-bit extensions in order to increase the number of characters sufficiently to handle most European and Asian languages. The ASCII code set has now become obsolete, and has been replaced by Unicode, a truly multilingual character set which can handle tens of thousands of characters. Unicode not only allows for data interchange across systems and platforms but also for the display of multilingual documents. Different versions of Unicode, or Unicode Transformation Formats (UTFs) have been developed since the 1990s. After reviewing various technical aspects involved in the use of different character encoding formats, McEnery and Xiao (2005) recommend UTF-8 as a suitable format for corpus construction.

While character encoding was a paramount issue in first- and second-generation corpus projects, it may be less so when creating corpora in the 2000s. However, since a corpus project may make use of existing corpora and software created according to past standards, and may in turn be used in the future in conjunction with corpora created according to new standards, the need to pay attention to character encoding should not be overlooked, and the character encoding used should be clearly documented in a corpus project.

The term 'encoding' has also been used in conjunction with or as a synonym for words such as annotation, markup and tagging. In corpus linguistics, annotation means more properly the enrichment of plain text with information regarding linguistic as well as other aspects. The process of adding annotation to a text is called markup, and is usually carried out by tagging the text, i.e. inserting tags next to text segments.

We can distinguish between two main types of annotation or markup, i.e. procedural or presentational markup and descriptive or structural markup. Procedural markup concerns information about the visual formatting of a text, for instance regarding the font type and size of titles or the way in which 'foreign

---

[1] Available at http://cdrh.unl.edu/articles/guide_site/intro.php, accessed on 10 September 2009.

words' are displayed in the text. Descriptive markup concerns instead the content of a document both as regards linguistic and extralinguistic information, such as bibliographic information about a text, information about its logical structure, and information about smaller textual units, down to the orthographic word and even to word parts (morphemes). Each word can be annotated at various levels of linguistic analysis: most commonly, annotated corpora are tagged for part-of-speech (*POS* tagging), and lemmatized. *POS* tagging consists of labelling each word according to its word class as noun, verb, adjective, etc. Lemmatization consists instead in labelling each word with its base form, so that, for instance, 'is' and 'was' can be labelled as forms of the lemma 'be'. Syntactic annotation is often referred to as parsing. In a 'parsed' corpus each syntactic constituent is assigned a label in accordance with the linguistic theory which informs the analysis. Furthermore, semantic and discourse annotation can also be added. A word like 'run' can be labelled as 'verb' for part of speech, as a 'form of the lemma RUN', as (part of) a verb phrase, etc. In a multilingual corpus, annotation can include references to other texts and languages, related to either documentary information (e.g., information about the source text of a translation), structural information (e.g. information about a relationship of correspondence between a constituent in the Source Text and another in the Target Text), semantic annotation (e.g. information about word sense or standard translation equivalents for a word), and so on.

As stated in Chapter 3, written corpora can be created either by digitizing printed texts such as books and newspapers, or from native electronic texts such as HTML, Word or PDF files. Some corpora may also contain a mix of texts from these different sources, depending on the type and purpose for which they were created.

When printed texts are used as data sources, the encoding process begins with typing in or scanning the texts and, by using an Optical Character Recognition (OCR) program, transforming the signs on the paper into computer processable data. Setting up and assisting the OCR program to scan a printed document, obtain a suitable plain text electronic version of it, and save it as a file in the computer can be a time-consuming and often laborious task. While scanners and OCR programs may have reached a high degree of accuracy, digitized texts still need to go through some sort of human 'proofreading', in order to remove errors and convert them into a standard electronic format. The following checklist, adapted from the *COMPARA* website (Frankenberg-Garcia *et al.* 2008:online), illustrates the type of manual interventions required after automated OCR has been carried out:

- Remove extra-linguistic elements (e.g. page numbers and images)
- Mark up chapter titles as such
- Correct misprints
- Normalize orthography (in older texts)
- Normalize hyphens, dashes and bullets across languages
- Normalize quotation marks and apostrophes across languages

- Mark up author's notes and move them to immediately after the sentence to which they refer
- Mark up translator's notes and position them beside the text to which they refer
- Mark up text highlighted in italics or bold as either 'title', 'foreign', 'proper name', 'citation' or 'emphasis'
- Convert and save the text into appropriate character encoding format

When digitization has been accomplished, documentary information must be recorded for each text, either minimally in the file name or as structured information associated with each text. Electronic texts can then be post-processed and enriched with text-linguistic annotation if so envisaged by the project.

Native electronic texts must also be processed before they become part of a corpus. For instance, a PDF file which is first downloaded from the Internet must be cleaned, converted and standardized into plain text format, before documentary information is associated with it and the text file is possibly annotated. The same also applies to other types of electronic documents to be included in the corpus. For instance, in HTML Web pages the text 'proper' is often surrounded by extratextual information such as navigational links and menus, which corpus builders may want to remove before further processing the documents (see Chapter 3).

4.1 Corpus-based translation studies and corpus annotation

The extent to which annotation should be among the main concerns of corpus compilers depends, of course, on the purpose of a project. Whether a corpus is created for use in descriptive translation studies, machine translation, computer-assisted translation or translator training will greatly influence the choices about annotation which are made when a project is being designed. This chapter is primarily concerned with annotation for descriptive translation studies, thus covering the 'middle' ground of the continuum between the two extremes of not being concerned with annotation at all and of granting annotation a central place in a project.

Computer-Assisted and Corpus-based Machine Translation, as subfields at the crossroads of Computational linguistics and Natural Language Processing, tend to focus more on using available resources than on corpus design. Research is primarily concerned with processing existing parallel corpora so that they can be used as a database to retrieve past translations and use them as material for new ones. 'Pure' corpus-based machine translation (statistical and example-based MT), as well as translation memory (TM) systems all rely on aligned parallel corpora, in which source text units are paired with their translations. The applications of NLP/CAT/MT to corpora include the development of methodologies for statistical alignment and of annotation schemes to be used in parallel and multilingual corpus processing. Encoding standards such as the XML Corpus Encoding Standard (XCES) for use in the encoding of language corpora, including multilingual and parallel aligned ones, and the Translation Memory Exchange (TMX) format, an industrial standard for the exchange of translation memories between different TM systems, have been developed for use by research and professional communities.

This chapter is mainly concerned with how translation-driven corpora, either mono- or multilingual, can be enriched with documentary, structural and linguistic annotation. Procedures and annotation standards such as XCES and TMX, which can be used to align and annotate parallel corpora for descriptive translation studies and translator education, will be dealt with in more detail in Chapter 6.

Annotation details will of course be a main concern in corpus creation for researchers in descriptive translation studies who wish to create robust corpus resources and tools. Different annotation options are available to corpus compilers, and the choice between one or the other is often dictated by the knowledge required to use specific corpus compilation as well as corpus analysis tools.

At the other extreme are translator trainees and professional language service providers who, of course, are interested in using corpus resources rather than in developing them. Even translators, however, may want to be involved in corpus construction when, for example, no other corpora are available for certain languages or language varieties. They will however need to minimize time and effort taken by text collection and post-processing. In this case translation practitioners may either use plain text corpora or resort to a commercial system like the *Sketch Engine*, which automates the procedures for collecting documents from the Web using existing search engines (see Chapter 3) and the procedures for streamlining post-processing (character conversion, cleaning of documents, annotation, indexing, etc.). It also provides an interface for querying the annotated corpus (see Chapter 5). The *Sketch Engine* allows users to add linguistic annotation to a corpus of texts downloaded from the Web using the *BootCaT* procedure described in Chapter 3, or to mark up a pre-existing plain text corpus uploaded by the user. The corpus is supplied with summary documentary information provided by the user, then linguistically annotated using a pre-loaded annotation scheme (or one provided by the user). A translation practitioner can thus quickly assemble a DIY Web corpus, and have it annotated and ready for consultation in a matter of minutes.

In descriptive translation studies researchers are perhaps more interested in using freely available resources and tools to annotate documentary and translation-specific information than in devising schemes for linguistic annotation. These are discussed in Chapter 5, together with other corpus processing and analysis software.

The Web can be a legitimate source of texts for creating specialized monolingual or bilingual corpora to be used in descriptive translation research, especially if no other corpus resources exist. Regardless of the provenance of the texts included, corpus resources created for research in descriptive translation studies should be more robust than the 'virtual' and 'disposable' DIY Web corpora used in translation practice, meaning that a corpus should have the attributes of stability, flexibility and accessibility. Since creating an electronic corpus for research purposes is usually a medium- or long-term project, and many difficulties can be encountered along the way, the resources created may well be a permanent asset and should be constructed according to sound criteria and principles.

In order to make these resources available to the wider research community, it is essential to provide adequate documentation for the corpus and its contents. Stability also means that corpora should not depend on specific people or software. Since the final users may be different from the people who created it, a corpus should provide for the possibility of further elaborations and unexpected types of investigations. New users may also want to supply additional annotated information or, given the comparative nature of most corpus-based studies, they may want to use only selected parts of a corpus to create a subcorpus for use in conjunction with other subcorpora.

Finally, translation-driven corpus resources should be designed and implemented with the provision of being distributed across different software platforms, and the data should be as far as possible accessible to the wider research community. While electronic corpora - as opposed to paper corpora - allow for larger-scale investigations, results may vary depending on the nature of the data and the tools used to investigate them. So, ideally, the data and the tools themselves should be openly available and accessible to researchers for cross-validation of results. To this end, the adoption as far as possible of common encoding standards seems an advisable choice to ensure access, reuse and exchange of corpus resources by the research community.

4.2 Annotation for descriptive translation studies

The annotation of information in a corpus may be related to three different aspects: documentary information about the texts in a corpus as a whole, documentary information about each text in the corpus, and structural information about the texts themselves, including linguistic information about each word in each text.

General information about a corpus concerns the character encoding format adopted throughout, the annotation scheme adopted in the corpus project, and taxonomical information which defines the categories according to which each text in the corpus is classified. Information about each text in the corpus may be crucial for the selection of corpus data and for the interpretation of results. To make sense of the words, it is necessary to know where the words come from. Structural information about linguistic units shorter than the full text may be essential to selectively retrieve single words or stretches of language according to their position in the text and to lexicogrammatical or other categories previously annotated.

In its simplest incarnation a corpus may include plain text files, each containing a series of 'words' separated by white spaces. Documentary information about the texts can be minimally encoded in more or less explicit file names, to which

```
<?xml version="1.0"?>
  <doc>
    <title> This is the title</title>
    <p>This is the text</p>
  </doc>
```

Metatextual information is enclosed between angle brackets and is thus separated from textual content, which is here highlighted for better display. Each textual element is enclosed between a start and an end tag. The latter has the same name as the start tag, but is preceded by a slash sign. The elements are arranged into a hierarchical structure nested inside a root element. The tag in the first line <?xml version="1.0"?> is called an "xml declaration" and identifies the XML document as such. There follow two textual elements (title <title> and paragraph <p>). These are nested inside the main document <doc> element.

Each element can be expanded to contain further parameters, called attributes, which specify properties of the element. Each attribute has a name and a value, written within the start tag of an element after the element's name. The word 'went' may be enclosed between tags in XML format as follows:

```
<w id="23" lemma="go" pos="VVD">went</w>
```

This is encoded as a <w> element (meaning 'word'). The start tag has three attributes, *id*, *lemma* and *POS*, each separated by a space from the preceding element name or attribute. Each attribute has a value joined to the attribute by an equals sign ("=") and enclosed between quotation marks. The attribute *id* is a unique identifier, expressing the progressive position of the word in the text; in this case 'went' is the 23rd word. The attribute *lemma* has the value 'go', that is the base form of the lemma which includes 'went'. The attribute *POS* specifies the word class (part-of-speech) the word 'went' belongs to, expressed by the value 'VVD', a synthetic notation for 'past tense form of lexical verb'.

There are two possible types of XML documents: so-called 'well-formed' XML documents are those which are conformant to XML syntax, as in the examples above. XML per se, however, does not specify the content of the tags and the relationships among them. A 'valid' XML document is instead defined as a well-formed XML document which conforms to an XML Schema, that is, "a description of a type of XML document, typically expressed in terms of constraints on the structure and content of documents of that type".[3] XML Schemas are expressed in programming languages such as the Document Type Definition (DTD) language, which is a set of instructions about which attributes, elements and values are admissible and how XML documents which belong to the same class (like texts in a corpus) should be interpreted by an XML application such as a Web browser or a concordancer. A Document Type Definition is common to a set of XML documents and makes them portable from one application to another. Often stored

[3] http://en.wikipedia.org/wiki/XML_schema. Accessed on 08 October 2009.

in a file external to the main XML document, the DTD states how a specific type of XML document is to be dealt with by text processing software. XML applications can be quite complex, and a large number of XML Schemas and DTDs have been written for such diverse applications as "business-to-business" and financial transactions, publishing and mathematics. Specific DTDs have also been developed for electronic texts and corpora, among which are the DTDs for documents annotated according to the Text Encoding Initiative (TEI) encoding scheme, and for corpora annotated according to the XML Corpus Encoding Standard (XCES) guidelines (see Luz 2011 for further details on XML).

The guidelines for text encoding suggested by the Text Encoding Initiative, an international consortium which has produced a de facto standard for scholarly work with electronic texts, are suitable for a minimalist approach to annotation as well as for supporting deeper encoding. TEI documents are 'valid' XML documents, and the TEI guidelines are designed to allow for encoding of a wide range of texts (TEI Consortium 2009). The TEI website lists over 120 projects which have adopted the TEI guidelines. For example, within the corpus linguistics community, the TEI guidelines have been implemented in the *British National Corpus* and in the XML Corpus Encoding Standard. The TEI scheme offers the corpus encoder a set of predefined tags for document elements and structural relations between them, providing a framework for the annotation of structured information in a header and in the text itself. A simple TEI document could be represented as follows:

- XML declaration
- TEI DTD declaration
  - Header
  - Text

After the XML declaration there follows a DTD declaration, which associates the XML document with a given DTD. A minimum of two elements are then required, a header (the electronic title page) and a text, each of which can contain further nested elements. An actual version of such a document looks like this:

```
<?xml version="1.0" encoding="UTF-8"?>
<!DOCTYPE TEI PUBLIC "-//TEI//DTD TEI Lite XML" "http://www.tei-c.org/
release/xml/tei/custom/schema/dtd/teilite.dtd">
<TEI>
   <teiHeader>The header goes here</teiHeader>
   <text>The text goes here</text>
</TEI>
```

In this case the DTD is TEI Lite, a basic DTD which follows TEI guidelines giving specifications for most commonly used tags. The TEI Lite DTD is in a file named 'teilite.dtd', in this case the one available online at the TEI website (but the file could be placed elsewhere, including on a local computer). There follows a main

<TEI> element which contains a TEI header <teiHeader> and the text element itself <text>.

TEI has been criticized for being too complicated and cumbersome for people interested in studying language or translation rather than in the workings of computers. In other words, translation studies researchers as well as translation learners and practitioners may want to make sure that the advantages to be gained from annotating a text are not outweighed by the expenditure of time and effort. However, a basic understanding of XML TEI may be a price worth paying for the better processing and hence analysis of electronic texts, a price affordable if one wishes to create robust resources for corpus-based translation studies. While creating a corpus may require time and effort, to which annotation may add a considerable amount, only by making corpus resources public and by agreeing on standards for their encoding will it be possible for research to be replicated, findings to be cross-checked, and evidence accumulated. Furthermore, XML TEI standards allow for the adoption of a variable range of layers of annotation, including minimal annotation consisting of a simple header and the plain text. While corpora designed for different purposes may require different degrees of encoding, all the texts within any given corpus are likely to share a common layer of structural and metatextual information. Adopting XML TEI does not mean that all corpora have to be encoded to the same level of detail or use the same theoretical approach. TEI seems to be flexible enough to ensure that minimal encoding can be accomplished without too much effort during corpus creation.

The annotation of a corpus using XML, TEI and XCES standards certainly requires an understanding of how annotation schemes work. However, simple annotation procedures may be streamlined with the help of annotation protocols. Simple instructions may be followed during text preparation, for example in order to add structural annotation to a text while proofreading scanned material, as described for instance in the guidelines for text preparation for the *COMPARA* parallel corpus (Frankenberg-Garcia and Santos 2003). A number of XML authoring tools exist which can suit a variety of budgets and annotation requirements, and simple software applications may be developed to mediate between the corpus compiler and the encoding system through a number of automated routines. For instance, basic documentary annotation may be inserted by devising a template with obligatory and optional fields to put structured information into a text header.[4] Those interested in the annotation of linguistic information may then add further annotation layers using available corpus tools and services.

---

[4] While in principle an XML document can be created with any text processor, software specifically designed to create TEI documents is scarce and indeed it has been argued that the shortage of TEI conformant tools may be a major hindrance to its becoming a more widely adopted standard. XML is a relatively recent development, so it is hoped that more XML/TEI text processing software will be developed in the future.

4.2.1 Documentary information

XML provides the syntax for annotating information about texts in such a way that it can be automatically interpreted by corpus management software. The TEI guidelines define the grammar and the semantics for encoding information about each text in a corpus as well as about the corpus itself. The guidelines provide a set of labels (tags) which can be used for inserting information elements in a structured way, indicating which elements are obligatory and which are optional, and the attributes and values which each element must or may take. The TEI consortium endeavoured to account for a large number of textual annotation projects, including bibliographical listings, dictionaries, manuscripts and, of course, corpora. The TEI guidelines were designed to be customized, and are therefore both flexible and complex. In order to help users deal with such flexibility and complexity the TEI consortium offers a number of tools "for creating, editing, transforming, and publishing TEI documents and schemas"[5], as well as a set of freely available pre-defined customizations. These include *TEI Corpus*, a simple template which provides minimal specifications for encoding TEI conformant linguistic corpora (Ratz n.d.), and TEI Lite, a subset of the full TEI encoding scheme which, according to its authors, should be able to accommodate "90% of the needs of 90% of the TEI user community... particularly by beginners and by big institutional projects that rely on large teams of encoders to markup their documents" (Burnard and Sperberg-McQueen 2006:online).

As seen in the previous section, a TEI conformant document must contain at least two elements, Header and Text (nested within the root TEI element). The following examples are based on the specifications for simple TEI Lite headers, as described in the TEI Lite manual.

A TEI header element <teiHeader> may contain four main elements: "file description" <fileDesc>, "encoding description" <encodingDesc>, "profile description" <profileDesc> and "revision description" <revisionDesc>. The file description element contains a bibliographic description of the electronic file, and this is the only obligatory element of the header. In its turn the <fileDesc> element must include three mandatory elements (title statement <titleStmt>, edition statement <editionStmt> and source description <sourceDesc>). The <titleStmt> element must include a title element <title>, the <editionStmt> element must contain elements providing information concerning the publication/distribution of the electronic document, either in simple prose within a paragraph <p> element or inside structured elements such as <publisher>, <date>, etc. Finally, the <sourceDesc> element, which records details of the source or sources from which the computer file is derived, must contain either a simple prose description or more rigidly structured bibliographic information. Thus, a well-formed and valid TEI header for a text published on the Web, the Wikipedia entry for *Art*, may look as follows:

[5] http://www.tei-c.org/Tools/#body.1_div.3. Accessed on 20 March 2011.

```
<teiHeader>
    <fileDesc>
        <titleStmt>
            <title>Art: from Wikipedia, the free encyclopedia. A TEI
            compliant version</title>
        </titleStmt>
        <publicationStmt>
            <p>This document is in the public domain. It contains a text-only
            version of a Wikipedia article freely available under Creative
            Commons licence</p>
        </publicationStmt>
        <sourceDesc>
            <bibl>
                <title>Art</title>
                <idno type="URL">http://en.wikipedia.org/wiki/Art</idno>
                <date>15 October 2009</date>
            </bibl>
        </sourceDesc>
    </fileDesc>
</teiHeader>
```

It is easy to see how this simple template could be used to create TEI headers for a corpus of texts from Wikipedia, by simply providing each text with a title and, within the bibliographic element <bibl> of the source description, the Web address and the day in which the document was downloaded from the Wikipedia website.[6]

A TEI header for a corpus such as those described in Chapter 2 and Chapter 3 (e.g. *CEXI*, *TEC*, CTF, *COMPARA*, etc.) may well be more articulated, and include not only a more detailed bibliographic description in the <fileDesc> element, but also one or more of the other three optional main elements (encoding description, profile description and revision description). Each of these may in turn include more or less structured and detailed information. As an example, the header of a TEI version of *The Name of the Rose* by Umberto Eco, might look as follows:

```
<teiHeader>
    <fileDesc>
        <titleStmt>
            <title>The Name of the Rose: in machine-readable form</title>
            <author>Umberto Eco</author>
            <respStmt>
                <resp>compiled by</resp>
                    <name xml:id="FZ">Federico Zanettin</name>
```

[6] The <idno> element "supplies any number or other identifier used to identify a bibliographic item in a standardized way" (http://www.tei-c.org/release/doc/tei-p5-doc/en/html/ref-idno.html, Accessed on 20 March 2011). The element has the attribute 'type' and the value 'URL', which identifies the source text as an online document.

```
        </respStmt>
    </titleStmt>
    <publicationStmt>
        <availability status="restricted">
            <p>Not available for commercial purposes.</p>
        </availability>
    </publicationStmt>
    <sourceDesc>
        <bibl>
            <author>Eco, Umberto</author>
            <editor role="translator">Weaver, William</editor>
            <title>The Name of the Rose</title>
            <pubPlace>New York</pubPlace>
            <publisher>Harcourt Brace</publisher>
            <date>1983</date>
            <relatedItem type="sourceText">
                <bibl>
                    <author>Eco, Umberto</author>
                    <title>Il nome della rosa</title>
                    <pubPlace>Milano</pubPlace>
                    <publisher>Bompiani</publisher>
                    <date>1980</date>
                </bibl>
            </relatedItem>
        </bibl>
    </sourceDesc>
  </fileDesc>
  <encodingDesc> ... </encodingDesc>
  <profileDesc> ... </profileDesc>
  <revisionDesc> ... </revisionDesc>
</teiHeader>
```

The <fileDesc> element provides information about the electronic text (in the title statement and publication statement) and about the printed source from which the electronic version was derived. The <sourceDesc> element contains not only information about the translated novel but also bibliographic information about the original Italian text. This is contained in the <relatedItem> element nested within the main bibliographic <bibl> element.

The optional encoding description element <encodingDesc> may be used to document the relationship between the electronic file and its source. Information which is common to all texts in a corpus may be recorded in the <encodingDesc> element of a corpus header rather than in each text in the corpus. Such information may concern the corpus project itself, i.e. the purpose for which the corpus was created and the criteria which were used to assemble the texts in the corpus, text sampling methods, editorial principles and practices, taxonomies defining classificatory codes and so on.[7] For instance, the <encodingDesc> element in the header of translation-driven corpora could contain a project description element followed by a classification declaration <classDecl> element referring to and assigning descriptive labels to the classificatory categories used for the texts in the corpus. Thus the <classDecl> element may contain any number of taxonomical descriptions and labels. Categories by which a text can be identified may include domain (e.g. imaginative or informative) and subdomain (e.g. quality fiction, detective fiction, applied science, religion, etc.), translation status (original or translation), the language in which the source text was written, age and gender of the translator, as in the following fragment.

```
<encodingDesc>
    <projectDesc>
    <p>Project description:...</p>
    </projectDesc>
    <classDecl>
        <taxonomy>
            <category xml:id="domain">
            <catDesc>Domains</catDesc>
            <category xml:id="main_domain1">
            <catDesc>imaginative</catDesc></category>
            <category xml:id="main_domain2">
            <catDesc>informative</catDesc></category>
            <category xml:id="sub_domain1.1">
            <catDesc>imaginative: quality fiction</catDesc></category>
            <category xml:id="sub_domain1.2">
            <catDesc>imaginative: detective fiction</catDesc></category>
            <!—other imaginative subcategories here-->
            <category xml:id="sub_domain2.1">
            <catDesc>informative: applied sciences</catDesc></category>
            <category xml:id="sub_domain2.2">
            <catDesc>informative: religion</catDesc></category>
            <!—other informative subcategories here-->
            </category>
        </taxonomy>
        <taxonomy>
            <category xml:id="textStatus">
            <catDesc>Text status</catDesc>
            <category xml:id="original">
```

[7] This information, which should be included in the corpus header rather than in the text header, is here integrated into the text header for illustration purposes only.

```
        <catDesc>original</catDesc></category>
        <category xml:id="translation">
        <catDesc>translation</catDesc></category>
        </category>
    </taxonomy>
    <taxonomy>
        <category xml:id="sourceLanguage">
        <catDesc>Source Language</catDesc>
        <category xml:id="lang_eng">
        <catDesc>English</catDesc></category>
        <category xml:id="lang_ita">
        <catDesc>Italian</catDesc></category>
        <!—other source language categories here-->
        </category>
    </taxonomy>
    <taxonomy>
        <category xml:id="translator_gender">
        <catDesc>Gender of translator</catDesc>
        <category xml:id="male"><catDesc>male</catDesc>
        </category>
        <category xml:id="female">
        <catDesc>female</catDesc></category>
        <category xml:id="unknown">
        <catDesc>unknown</catDesc></category>
        </category>
    </taxonomy>
  </classDecl>
</encodingDesc>
```

The compilers of the *TEC* suggest other categories which may be relevant for the analysis of translated texts, such as for example the nationality and employment status of the translator, the direction of translation (into or out of the mother tongue) and the nationality of the source text author (Baker 2004). The <encodingDesc> element may also include other elements, documenting copyright status, tag usage, and character encoding.

The third part, “Profile description”, contains information about the languages used in the text and a <text class> element which groups information about the nature of the text in relation to the taxonomies adopted. The fragment below, for instance, which again refers to the English translation of the novel by Umberto Eco, identifies the language in which the text is written (English), the domain (imaginative), the subdomain (quality fiction), its status (translation), the source language (Italian) and the gender of the translator (male).

```
<profileDesc>
    <langUsage>
    <language ident="EN-GB" usage="20">British English</language>
    </langUsage>
```

```
    <textClass>
    <catRef target="main_domain1 sub_domain1.1 translation lang_ita male"/>
    </textClass>
</profileDesc>
```

Taxonomical information is contained within a <catRef> “empty” element, that is an element which does not include any content to be displayed. An empty element tag resembles a start tag but contains a slash before the closing angle bracket.

Finally, the fourth main element of the TEI header, “Revision description” is used to document any editorial changes made to the electronic document at different times by different people, in other words it is the history of the electronic text. The fragment below specifies the date the text was converted into UTF-8 format, and the author of the change, identified by the acronym which refers back to the ‘id’ specified in the initial <titleStmt> element.

```
<revisionDesc>
    <change who="FZ"when="2009-10-11">Converted to UTF-8
    </change>
</revisionDesc>
```

A full version of the simple well-formed, valid XML TEI compliant version of the English translation of Eco’s text (without the text itself) is provided below.

```
<?xmlversion="1.0"encoding="UTF-8"?>
<!DOCTYPETEIPUBLIC"-//TEI//DTDTEILiteXML""http://www.tei-
c.org/release/xml/tei/custom/schema/dtd/teilite.dtd">
<TEI>
<teiHeader>
    <fileDesc>
        <titleStmt>
            <title>The Name of the Rose: in machine-readable form</title>
            <author>Umberto Eco</author>
            <respStmt>
                <resp>compiled by</resp>
                <name xml:id="FZ">Federico Zanettin</name>
            </respStmt>
        </titleStmt>
        <publicationStmt>
            <availability status="restricted">
            <p>Not available for commercial purposes.</p>
            </availability>
        </publicationStmt>
        <sourceDesc>
            <bibl>
                <author>Eco, Umberto</author>
                <editor role="translator">Weaver, William</editor>
```

```
                <title>The Name of the Rose</title>
                <pubPlace>New York</pubPlace>
                <publisher>Harcourt Brace</publisher>
                <date>1983</date>
                <relatedItem type="SourceText">
                    <bibl>
                        <author>Eco, Umberto</author>
                        <title>Il nome della rosa</title>
                        <pubPlace>Milano</pubPlace>
                        <publisher>Bompiani</publisher>
                        <date>1980</date>
                    </bibl>
                </relatedItem>
            </bibl>
        </sourceDesc>
</fileDesc>
<encodingDesc>
        <projectDesc>
        <p>Project description:...</p>
        </projectDesc>
        <classDecl>
            <taxonomy>
                <category xml:id="domain">
                <catDesc>Domains</catDesc>
                <category xml:id="main_domain1">
                <catDesc>imaginative</catDesc></category>
                <category xml:id="main_domain2">
                <catDesc>informative</catDesc></category>
                <category xml:id="sub_domain1.1">
                <catDesc>imaginative: quality fiction</catDesc></category>
                <category xml:id="sub_domain1.2">
                <catDesc>imaginative: detective fiction</catDesc></category>
                <!—other imaginative subcategories here-->
                <category xml:id="sub_domain2.1">
                <catDesc>informative: applied sciences</catDesc></category>
                <category xml:id="sub_domain2.2">
                <catDesc>informative: religion</catDesc></category>
                <!—other informative subcategories here-->
                </category>
            </taxonomy>
            <taxonomy>
                <category xml:id="textStatus">
                <catDesc>Text status</catDesc>
                <category xml:id="original">
                <catDesc>original</catDesc></category>
                <category xml:id="translation">
                <catDesc>translation</catDesc></category>
                </category>
            </taxonomy>
```

```
            <taxonomy>
                <category xml:id="sourceLanguage">
                <catDesc>Source Language</catDesc>
                <category xml:id="lang_eng">
                <catDesc>English</catDesc></category>
                <category xml:id="lang_ita">
                <catDesc>Italian</catDesc></category>
                <!—other source language categories here-->
                </category>
            </taxonomy>
            <taxonomy>
                <category xml:id="translator_gender">
                <catDesc>Gender of translator</catDesc>
                <category xml:id="male"><catDesc>male</catDesc>
                </category>
                <category xml:id="female">
                <catDesc>female</catDesc></category>
                <category xml:id="unknown">
                <catDesc>unknown</catDesc></category>
                </category>
            </taxonomy>
        </classDecl>
    </encodingDesc>
    <profileDesc>
        <langUsage>
        <language ident="EN-GB" usage="20">British English</language>
        </langUsage>
        <textClass>
        <catRef target="main_domain1 sub_domain1.1 translation lang_ita male"/>
        </textClass>
    </profileDesc>
    <revisionDesc>
        <change who="FZ" when="2009-10-11">Converted to UTF-8
        </change>
    </revisionDesc>
</teiHeader>
    <text>
        <body><p>Content of the novel</p></body>
    </text>
</TEI>
```

This header provides essential information which identifies a text as part of a corpus. In the following sections the annotation of the text itself will be tackled.

4.2.2 *Structural information*

A text in a TEI-compliant corpus may minimally be presented enclosed within a single paragraph <p> element, nested within the <body> element of a <text> element, as in the fragment below.

```
<text><body><p>The text goes here</p></body></text>
```

Any text annotated following the TEI Lite DTD to the extent illustrated can be processed by annotation-blind text retrieval and concordancing software. Annotation would only have the advantage of associating the documentary information in the header with the text, and making the text available for use in conjunction with similarly encoded ones. This level of annotation is thus a first layer to which further ones may be added, either as envisaged by the original corpus design or by further developments and new versions of the corpus data.

A second layer of annotation is structural annotation. First, a text may contain additional material such as an introduction, a translator's note at the beginning of a translated novel, or a glossary at the end. Such materials would go within the optional <frontMatter> and <endMatter> elements before and after the <body> element, respectively.

The body of a text can be further subdivided into one or more hierarchically lower-level divisions, like the parts and chapters of a novel, or the different blocks of text of a Wikipedia entry. The following TEI-style structural annotation could probably accommodate most written texts:

```
<text>
<body>
<div n="1">
<head>Title of first chapter or text block</head>
<p n="1">First paragraph.</p>
<p n="2">Second paragraph.</p>
<!--more paragraphs-->
</div >
<div n="2">
<head>Title of second chapter or text block</head>
<p n="3">First paragraph.</p>
<p n="4">Second paragraph.</p>
<!--more paragraphs-->
</div>
<div>
<!--more chapters or text blocks-->
</div>
</body>
</text>
```

The <text> element contains just one <body> element, within which each major subdivision is marked by a division <div> element. Each <div> element contains an optional header <head> element and one or more paragraphs. The sequential order of divisions and paragraphs can be explicitly tagged by using the n (number) attribute. Since the sequence of text blocks is a graphical feature of texts, annotation up to the level of the paragraph can be carried out in a semi-automatic fashion, replacing with </p> and <p> tags the hard returns in a plain text file containing the body of a document, and thus converting it into a sequence of explicitly marked paragraph elements. Native electronic texts – as opposed to printed texts – may also contain some kind of structural markup (often in HTML format) which can be retained and automatically converted into TEI XML format. Other structural subdivisions such as subdivisions within main <div> elements, verses, lists, notes, etc., may need to be visually inspected, individually assessed, and manually annotated following the TEI specifications.

The TEI guidelines explain how structural features of written prose as well as other written (and spoken) textual varieties can be accommodated. Encoding issues become of paramount importance in projects involving the creation of interpreting corpora. The design and implementation of an annotation scheme suitable for interpreting corpora may require a sizable effort (Cencini 2002, Cencini and Aston 2002, Sandrelli and Bendazzoli 2006). The internal segmentation of text units in spoken corpora, especially of a dialogic nature, may be difficult to accommodate to the TEI data structure in order to capture the relative timing of different speakers' contributions. The non-hierarchical organization of possibly relevant features of spoken discourse, such as interruptions, pauses, overlapping turns, false starts, etc., conflicts with the constraint of having to nest textual elements within each other. Difficulties increase if TEI annotated spoken corpora of interpreting are to be used in conjunction with the audio or audiovisual recordings of the speech events transcribed (Zanettin 2009b). However, research is under way and new software applications are being devised in order to deal with these issues, some of which will be discussed in §4.3.

4.2.3 *Text-linguistic information*

The annotation of textual units below the paragraph level can be considered a third level of annotation. A first issue, which applies also to the analysis of non-annotated text, is tokenization and sentence splitting. Words can generally be thought of as sequences of characters separated by white spaces, but some 'word forms' may have an uncertain status. When annotating a text or analyzing a non-annotated corpus of English, for instance, it has to be decided whether contracted forms such as "it's" should count as one or two words, and whether the possessive marker "'s" is to be considered as an individual word or as an inflectional morpheme. Sentence splitting, which, in TEI format, is the segmentation of paragraphs into <s> elements that identify sentence-like units, is based on punctuation. However, single and double quotes, commas, and colons may serve different functions, both in narrative and instructional texts, and full stops may be used not only to mark sentence boundaries but also in abbreviations and acronyms. Other segments which perform a specific textual function and need to be treated separately from paragraph and sentence elements include headings, lists, captions, etc. As will become apparent when discussing the alignment of parallel corpora (see Chapter 6), segmentation below the paragraph level is not always a straightforward matter and may require the implementation of complex automatic and semi-automatic routines.

The TEI guidelines also provide for the annotation of other stretches of text which can be of interest as units of analysis in descriptive translation studies. For instance, features such as (translator's) notes and glosses, quotations, foreign words or phrases and proper names may be marked up using appropriate tags, respectively <note>, <q>, <gloss>, <foreign> and <name>. This type of annotation can be carried out manually or semi-automatically exploiting punctuation and typographical features of source texts, for instance quotation marks for direct speech and highlighting devices such as italics for foreign words.

Linguistic annotation at the level of individual words is carried out in TEI by specifying attributes and values for <w> elements. *POS* tagging, lemmatization and syntactic annotation (parsing) can be carried out automatically for many languages using existing tools and resources (see Chapter 5). In simple terms, *POS* tagging can be described as follows: after the corpus has been tokenized, i.e. each 'word' has been defined as a unique entity, each <w> element is expanded to contain a *POS* attribute. *POS* values are taken from a predefined tagset derived from a taxonomy of the different parts of speech, and a program (tagger) associates each word with a *POS* value. First, all words are matched against a predefined glossary and each known word is assigned its most frequent tag. In the next step the program proceeds to disambiguate words which may belong to more than one part of speech, and to assign *POS* tags values to unknown words by exploiting lexical and syntactic regularities. The word 'run', for instance, is more likely to be a verb than a noun if preceded by a noun or a personal pronoun, whereas if preceded by a determiner it is more likely to be a noun. The same logic applies to unknown words. Morphological information may also be made to play a role since, for example, a word ending in *-ly* is more likely to be an adverb, whereas a word ending in *-dom* is more likely to be a noun. *POS* tagging can be carried out at different levels of delicacy, and taggers can be 'trained' to perform consecutive and increasingly refined runs achieving very high levels of precision. *POS* taggers for English have been estimated to achieve precision scores up to 97% (McEnery *et al.* 2006:34), which may be brought even closer to 100% by limited manual intervention.

The following fragment shows how the sentence "Every deaf child, whatever the level of his/her hearing loss, should have the right to grow up bilingual" was annotated using the tagger *CLAWS* (Constituent Likelihood Automatic Word-tagging System).

```
<s>
<w id="5.1" pos="AT1">Every</w> <w id="5.2" pos="JJ">deaf</w> <w
id="5.3" pos="NN1">child</w> <w id="5.4" pos=",">,</w> <w id="5.5"
pos="DDQV">whatever</w> <w id="5.6" pos="AT">the</w> <w id="5.7"
pos="NN1">level</w> <w id="5.8" pos="IO">of</w> <w id="5.9"
pos="APPGE">his/her</w> <w id="5.10" pos="NN1">hearing</w> <w
id="5.11" pos="NN1">loss</w> <w id="5.12" pos=",">,</w> <w id="5.13"
pos="VM">should</w> <w id="5.14" pos="VHI">have</w> <w id="5.15"
pos="AT">the</w> <w id="5.16" pos="NN1">right</w> <w id="5.17"
pos="TO">to</w> <w id="5.18" pos="VVI">grow</w> <w id="5.19"
```

```
pos="RP">up</w> <w id="5.20" pos="JJ">bilingual</w> <w id="5.21"
pos=".">.</w>
</s>
```

CLAWS is only one of a number of annotation services and applications, and the values assigned to *POS* tags will depend on the annotation scheme implemented.

Lemmatization is similarly conducted on the basis of a predefined list of lemma forms, available for many languages. Word forms belonging to more that one lemma can be disambiguated on the basis of *POS* tags, which may also help to assign a base form to an unknown word. The word 'clobs' is more likely to be a form of the noun lemma 'clob' rather than a form of the verb 'clob' if its part-of-speech value has been defined as NN2. Many *POS* taggers and lemmatizers have been developed for English and continue to be developed also for other languages. *CLAWS*, which has been developed at the University of Lancaster since the 1980s (Garside 1987, Leech *et al.* 1994, Garside 1996, Garside and Smith 1997), and a version of which was used to *POS* tag the *BNC*, is available both as a software package and as an annotation service. The free trial version of *CLAWS* will be used to carry out one of the tasks in the practical section of this chapter.

The <w> tag may thus include both *POS* (part-of-speech) and *lemma* (base forms) attributes. The annotation of the word form "ran" may thus look as follows:

```
<w id="23" pos="VVD" lemma="run">ran</w>
```

POS tagging is a precondition for syntactic annotation, or parsing. A parsed corpus contains information regarding syntactic structure, so that the text is broken up into chunks, and function labels are attributed to these in accordance with a formal grammar. Syntactic annotation below the sentence level <s> is provided for in the TEI tagset by clause <cl> elements, each of which can be split into one or more phrase <phr> elements, each containing one or more <w> elements.

A more detailed discussion of tagging and parsing methodologies is beyond the scope of this volume. In the section at the end of this chapter the reader is directed to standard corpus linguistic textbooks, which can be used for further reference.

Further layers of annotation may concern such levels of analysis as co-reference, semantics, pragmatics and stylistics. For instance, a parallel corpus of translations by translation trainees may be manually annotated with comments on translation errors.

The implementation of user designed annotation schemes may however require the adoption of a DTD o XML schema other than the TEI Lite, as well as the use of specialized annotation software. For instance, Göpferich (2010) proposes that the TEI guidelines can be used to provide a standard annotation system for the analysis of translation process data such as think-aloud protocols, which have been used in translation research to provide access to the psychological and linguistic mechanisms involved in the activity of translation (see e.g. Jääskeläinen 2010). She suggests that information about a data session, including information on the project in which the data was collected, the methods of data collection used, and the subjects involved, can be appropriately documented in the header of a TEI document containing an annotated transcription of the verbalizations of the translator's mental processes (think-aloud protocols) together with a description of other actions which may be relevant to the analysis. Göpferich provides a model TEI template file for the transcription of translation process protocols together with the associated XML schema file which is being used in the *TransComp* project to investigate the development of translation competence in students of translation. The *TransComp* corpus of translation process data is being archived and will be made accessible online at the end of data collection.

In the <body> element the transcription of the translator's verbalization is broken up in utterance <u> elements, which are linked to the audio/video recording of the event through start and end attributes, whose values are time stamps. Other elements include <pause> for pauses, <vocal> for vocalized non-lexical phenomena (gulping, laughing, etc.), <shift> for changes in vocal quality and <incident> for other verbalizations such as reading aloud and actions such as consulting a dictionary. Furthermore, The TEI guidelines have been adapted to allow for the annotation of interpretation categories such as translation problems. These are manually coded by enclosing a *type* attribute with the value "problem" in <incident> elements. The cause of the translation problem is then expressed as a value of a *subtype* attribute. The fragment below illustrates the annotation of a translation problem caused by the word 'conditioning' in the source text. The <incident> element also includes a sequential ID and timeline attributes.

```
<incident xml:id="1.2" type="problem" subtype="conditioning"
start="00:06:47" end="00:06:54">ähm: ja das weiß ich immer noch
nicht so recht wie ich das übersetzen soll</incident>
```

As stated above, TEI is not the only available annotation format, and in fact a good many corpus projects make use of other annotation formats compatible with different software platforms. The TEI format is however amenable to being transformed into a database structure, and a TEI compliant corpus is therefore in principle compatible with different corpus management tools. It is easy to convert into and out of other annotation formats, such as for example the one-word-per-line tabular format required by a query system such as the *IMS Open Corpus Workbench* (*CWB*), currently used in a number of corpus projects.

The degree and type of annotation will also depend on the tools which will be used for corpus analysis (see Chapter 5).

4.3 Stand-off annotation

Some scholars, following Sinclair (1987, 1991), define their approach to corpus data as 'corpus-driven', in opposition to the 'corpus-based' approach adopted in other studies. According to proponents of the first type of approach, linguistic annotation (tagging and parsing) imposes a predetermined theoretical outlook at, and a consequent interpretation of, the data. In a corpus-driven approach it is the 'unprejudiced' observation, classification and description of the data which leads to the formulation of new theories or to the revision of existing ones, whereas a corpus-based approach only looks at a corpus as a "repository of examples to back pre-existing theories or a probabilistic extension to an already defined system" (Tognini-Bonelli 2001:84). In order to preserve the integrity of data and be able to analyze them with a fresh eye, these scholars suggest that a 'clean text policy' should be adopted. Other scholars instead see linguistic annotation as an enrichment of raw data which gives them an 'added value' (McEnery *et al.* 2006).

This debate may seem rather pointless, as far as corpus construction is concerned. A corpus is a resource which it is up to the user to analyze choosing an appropriate modality. Thus, it makes sense for a descriptive linguist or a lexicographer to start from 'raw' data and distil the meaning of words from their associated contexts. At the same time, it makes sense for the translation student or language learner to learn from data which are already filtered and analyzed. Annotation, and TEI in particular, is a way to associate metadata with texts. Linguistic annotation is just one possible layer of annotation of a corpus, and TEI simply provides guidelines which make linguistic annotation compatible with the overall annotation framework. The XML data structure allows the user to separate primary data from annotation, so that it is always possible to ignore the latter.

In the fragments presented so far, annotation appears in the form of tags intermingled within the text. The text to be displayed on the computer screen and interpreted by translators, researchers and students is clearly separated from the text enclosed within angle brackets, to be interpreted by the corpus analysis software. This is known as 'internal' or 'inline' annotation.

A different model, which involves a higher level of abstraction, is stand-off annotation. According to the TEI Stand-Off Markup Workgroup (2003:online), "[m]arkup is said to be standoff, or external, when the markup data is placed outside of the text it is meant to tag: before, after, or even outside it altogether. The markup therefore points to, rather than wraps, the relevant data content". Stand-off annotation thus makes it possible to abide by Sinclair's principle that "any information about a text other than the alphanumeric string of its words and punctuation should be stored separately from the plain text and merged when required in applications" (Sinclair 2005:online).

A stand-off annotation model was adopted by the Corpus Encoding Standard (CES) project developed as a part of the EAGLES (Expert Advisory Group on Language Engineering Standards) Guidelines. The CES is compliant with TEI specifications and "is designed to be optimally suited for use in language engineering research and applications, in order to serve as a widely accepted set of encoding standards for corpus-based work in natural language processing applications" (Ide and Priest-Dorman 2000:online). XCES, the XML version of the CES (developed at the Department of Computer Science at Vassar College, Poughkeepsie, New York and at Equipe Langue et Dialogue at LORIA/CNRS, Vandoeuvre-lès-Nancy, France), consists of a set of files containing XCES schemas, DTDs and XSL scripts (these latter transforming XML into HTML files). Annotation following the XCES architecture is rather more complex than simply using a TEI Lite DTD, and the compilation of a corpus which implements XCES guidelines requires the customization and development of software tools.

XML stand-off markup based on the XCES guidelines was, for example, used for the annotation of the *CroCo* German-English bidirectional parallel corpus (Hansen-Schirra *et al.* 2006, Neumann and Hansen-Schirra 2005, Vela *et al.* 2007). The *CroCo* corpus is "tokenized and annotated for part-of-speech, morphology, phrasal categories and grammatical functions" (Hansen-Schirra *et al.* 2006:36) as well as aligned at the level of "words, grammatical functions, clauses and sentences" (*ibid.*). Different layers of linguistic annotation are kept in separate XML files, and annotated elements are linked through a unique ID to a base file consisting of the indexed units in the text.

The following examples, taken from sample XML files from the *MeLLANGE Learner Translation Corpus*[8] *(LTC)*, see Chapter 2, illustrate how stand-off annotation works. Each text (each student translation) consists effectively of six XML files, in which information related to different levels of annotation is stored separately. A base file containing the tokenized translation is linked to a header file containing documentary information. *POS* and lemma information referencing token IDs in the base file are stored in a third file, and a fourth file is used to store information about structural subdivisions. Finally, two further files contain annotation referring to the error annotation scheme devised within the project, with information about Content Transfer errors and about Language errors.

A sample fragment adapted from the original base file is shown below. The <words> element of the XML file contains a list of <word> elements, each of which is identified by a unique sequential id.

```
<?xml version='1.0' encoding='UTF-8'?>
<!DOCTYPE words SYSTEM "words.dtd">
<words>
<word id="word_1">RÉSUMÉ</word>
<word id="word_2">.</word>
<word id="word_3">Emploi</word>
<word id="word_4">et</word>
<word id="word_5">famille</word>
<word id="word_6">des</word>
<word id="word_7">travailleurs</word>
```

[8] http://corpus.leeds.ac.uk/mellange/ltc.html#LTC_annotation. Accessed on 20/03/11.

```
<word id="word_8">.</word>
<word id="word_9">I.</word>
<word id="word_10">Accès</word>
<word id="word_11">à</word>
<word id="word_12">l'</word>
<word id="word_13">emploi</word>
<!—other words here-->
</words>
```

The related header file contains metadata about the trainee translator and the circumstances in which the translation was carried out, including affiliation, level of studies, first and second languages, experience as a translator, and so on. The structure of the header is similar to that discussed in the previous section, and is thus not shown here.

The XML file in which linguistic annotation is recorded contains a <ling_annot> element which itself contains a list of <tokposlem> elements, each identified by a unique *id* and pointing to a specific word in the base file, identified by the value of the *span* attribute. The values of the *POS* and *lemma* attributes specify part of speech and base lemma form for that token.

```
<?xml version='1.0' encoding='UTF-8'?>
<ling_annot>
<tokposlem id="1" span="word_1" pos="NomC" lem="résumé" />
<tokposlem id="2" span="word_2" pos="PONCT-S" lem="." />
<tokposlem id="3" span="word_3" pos="NomC" lem="emploi" />
<tokposlem id="4" span="word_4" pos="C-C" lem="et" />
<tokposlem id="5" span="word_5" pos="NomC" lem="famille" />
<tokposlem id="6" span="word_6" pos="P+D" lem="du" />
<tokposlem id="7" span="word_7" pos="NomC" lem="travailleur" />
<tokposlem id="8" span="word_8" pos="PONCT-S" lem="." />
<tokposlem id="9" span="word_9" pos="CARD" lem="I." />
<tokposlem id="10" span="word_10" pos="NomC" lem="accès" />
<tokposlem id="11" span="word_11" pos="P" lem="à" />
<tokposlem id="12" span="word_12" pos="DetDef" lem="le" />
<tokposlem id="13" span="word_13" pos="NomC" lem="emploi" />
<!—other tokposlem here-->
</ling_annot>
```

Similarly, s-units are listed in a separate file as <markable> elements. They are identified by the "eol" value of the *type* attribute and a *span* value pointing to the first and last word of each s-unit, as shown in the following fragment:

```
<?xml version="1.0"?>
<!DOCTYPE markables SYSTEM "markables.dtd">
<markables xmlns="www.eml.org/NameSpaces/sentence">
<markable id="markable_1" span="word_1..word_2" type="eol" />
```

```
<markable id="markable_2" span="word_3..word_8" type="eol" />
<markable id="markable_3" span="word_9..word_9" type="eol" />
<markable id="markable_4" span="word_10..word_14" type="eol" />
<markable id="markable_5" span="word_15..word_50" type="eol" />
<markable id="markable_6" span="word_51..word_97" type="eol" />
<!—other markables here-->
</markables>
```

While linguistic and structural annotation were carried out automatically, the *Learner Translation Corpus* was also annotated manually by a team who classified and marked up errors in translation learners' output according to the typology devised within the project (see Chapter 2).

The following fragment is taken from the file containing annotation related to one of the two typologies of errors, namely 'transfer of content'. Each <markable> element points to a specific word span which contains the error, in this case the omission, in a text translated from English into French, of a translation for the expressions 'in particular' and 'other'. A note by the annotator explaining what the error consists of is included as a value of the attribute *commentaire_tr-om*.

```
<?xml version="1.0" encoding="UTF-8"?>
<!DOCTYPE markables SYSTEM "markables.dtd">
<markables xmlns="www.eml.org/NameSpaces/content_transfer">
<markable id="markable_43" span="word_168..word_173" commentaire_
tr-om="le traducteur n'a pas traduit 'in particular'" omission="tr-om" />
<markable id="markable_68" span="word_370" commentaire_tr-om="le
traducteur a omis de traduire 'other'" omission="tr-om" />
<!—other markables here -- >
</markables>
```

By separating logical layers of annotation as well as text from annotation, stand-off markup allows for "the annotation of overlapping segments where no dominance relation is involved" (Neumann and Hansen-Schirra 2005). The advantages of stand-off over inline annotation can be especially appreciated with respect to parallel corpora and corpora of spoken interaction such as consecutive or dialogue interpreting corpora. In parallel corpora stand-off annotation can be used to record and store separately alignment information regarding correspondences between pairs of textual units of different length, including paragraph, sentence, phrase and word. Such bi-textual maps can be used as reference for user created annotation systems, regarding for instance translation shifts (Cyrus 2006) or the addition of glosses in translations. Approaches and tools to the retrieval of alignment information from parallel corpora are discussed in Chapter 6.

In corpora containing transcriptions of multi-party spoken interactions, stand-off markup allows for the annotation of overlapping segments of speech, an important feature in the analysis of mediated communication. In multimodal corpora, written transcriptions are linked to the timeline of the video or sound record, and further layers of annotation may be added for describing features of non-verbal communication.

4.4 Conclusions

Annotation is but one part of corpus construction, which can contribute to the creation of stable, flexible and accessible corpus resources for translation studies. In the provision of making these resources available to the wider research community, it makes sense to adopt common standards for their annotation. This chapter has illustrated how the TEI XML annotation standard, which provides guidelines for the annotation of large language corpora, may offer a suitable annotation scheme for translation-driven corpora. The examples discussed have shown how a minimalist structure for corpus texts can be devised following TEI guidelines, allowing the inclusion of a simple header and plain text. The same annotation framework, however, allows for the addition of further layers of annotation, which can often be carried out using existing resources. Annotation can be partly automated and follow a modular approach, in that it is possible to add annotation layers at different stages and according to different research needs.

The activities presented in the Tasks section below are designed to guide the reader through the steps of corpus compilation, and to perform a sample search on an annotated corpus containing documentary, structural and linguistic information in XML TEI format. The corpus, consisting of just one annotated document, will be indexed and queried using *XAIRA*, a software application which is able to operate on any corpus of XML TEI documents. The different steps involved in corpus compilation and analysis, and the software tools which can be used for this purpose, are discussed in Chapter 5.

The implementation of stand-off annotation, in which different layers of annotation are recorded and stored independently of the text itself, can be quite complex and require the intervention of computational linguists and programmers working together with translation scholars. However, stand-off XML annotation seems to be a promising way forward with a view to the interoperability and sharing of corpus resources.

4.5 Tasks

4.5.1 Creating an XML TEI document

In the first task you will create an XML TEI conformant document, starting from a document in PDF format. The text chosen for this activity is the English version of a short text by François Grosjean, *The right of the deaf child to grow up bilingual*, available in PDF format on the author's website. You can also decide to use a different text, for instance one of the versions in a different language of the same text available on the website.[9]

[9] http://www.francoisgrosjean.ch/the_right_en.html. Accessed on 20 March 2011.

1. Create a new empty document, using either a plain text editor such as Microsoft WordPad or an XML editor. Software tools which can be used for the annotation of XML documents are discussed in Chapter 5, where pointers are given to some free XML editors, copies of which are also available on the DVD. Type or copy and paste the following xml declaration on top of the document:

```
-------------------------------------------
<?xml version="1.0"?>
-------------------------------------------
```

followed by the DTD declaration below, pointing to a modified version of the XML version 1 of TEI Lite DTD.

```
-------------------------------------------
<!DOCTYPE TEI.2 PUBLIC "-//TEI//DTD TEI Lite XML ver. 1//EN"
"http://www.intralinea.it/tmp/teixlite_FZ2008.dtd">
---------------------------------------------------
```

Note that the path for the DTD declaration points to a public file available online. You can change the path by replacing the URLs with a local address. The path should point to the place where you have saved a copy of the DTD file (teixlite_FZ2008.dtd), which can be found on the DVD.

2. Insert a <TEI.2> element in your document, and within it an empty <teiHeader> element followed by an empty <text> element.
Your document should now look like this:

```
-----------------------------------------
<?xml version="1.0"?>
<!DOCTYPE TEI.2 PUBLIC "-//TEI//DTD TEI Lite XML ver. 1//EN"
"http://www.intralinea.it/tmp/teixlite_FZ2008.dtd">
<TEI.2>
        <teiHeader>
        <!—the header goes here-->
        </teiHeader>
        <text>
        <!—the text goes here-->
        </text>
<TEI.2>
---------------------------------------------------
```

3. You have created a well-formed xml document. Save it as a file with the name **DeafChild_en.xml** in a working folder in your computer.

4.5.2 Adding a simple header

1. To create a simple TEI header in your document, type or copy and paste inside the <teiHeader> element the XML fragment below, replacing the <!—the header goes here-> placeholder. The fragment contains the <fileDesc> element, which is the only obligatory element in a TEI Lite header. Obligatory elements for this element are nested inside it.

```
--------------------------------------------------
<fileDesc>
      <titleStmt>
            <title><!-- supply a title --></title>
            <!-- can include (author, sponsor, etc.) -->
      </titleStmt>
      <publicationStmt>
            <!-- supply publication information -->
            <!-- can include (publisher distributor authority pubPlace
            address idno availability date p) -->
      </publicationStmt>
      <sourceDesc>
            <p><!-- supply information about the source --></p>
            <!-- can include (p bibl biblFull listBibl) -->
      </sourceDesc>
</fileDesc>
--------------------------------------------------
```

2. Replace placeholders (the text in bold) with the following documentary details, putting each piece of textual information inside the appropriate elements:[10]

- Title of the source electronic text: **The right of the deaf child to grow up bilingual**
- Author: **François Grosjean**
- Publisher: **[you/your institution]**
- Publication place: **[your place of publication]**
- Other information about the source text: **online PDF document available at http://www.francoisgrosjean.ch/English_Anglais.pdf**

3. Compare your document header with the fragment below, and make changes as needed. Then save the file again, but keep it open for use in the next task.

[10] For more details on header annotation see Burnard and Sperberg-McQueen (2006).

```
------------------------------------------
<?xml version="1.0"?>
<!DOCTYPE TEI.2 PUBLIC "-//TEI//DTD TEI Lite XML ver. 1//EN"
"http://www.intralinea.it/tmp/teixlite_FZ2008.dtd">
<TEI.2>
<teiHeader>
<fileDesc>
    <titleStmt>
        <title>The right of the deaf child to grow up bilingual. An
        electronic version</title>
        <author>François Grosjean </author>
        <sponsor>University of Neuchâtel, Switzerland </sponsor>
    </titleStmt>
    <publicationStmt>
        <publisher>[you/your institution]</publisher>
    </publicationStmt>
    <sourceDesc>
        <bibl>
            <title>The right of the deaf child to grow up bilingual</title>
            <author>François Grosjean </author>
            <note>online PDF document available at http://www.
            francoisgrosjean.ch/English_Anglais.pdf</note>
        </bibl>
    </sourceDesc>
</fileDesc>
</teiHeader>
<text>
<!--here goes the text-->
</text>
<TEI.2>
------------------------------------------
```

4.5.3 Marking-up text structure

First of all you need to create a file containing the content of the short article in text only format. The source text is a PDF file, which must be converted to plain text format before markup can be added to it.

1. Download the source PDF file from: http://www.francoisgrosjean.ch/English_Anglais.pdf.
A copy of the PDF file is also available on the DVD.

2. Open the file with Acrobat Reader (if the program is not already installed on your computer you can download a copy from http://www.adobe.com). Save a text only version of the text using Acrobat Reader's *Save as…* function, or copy and paste the text into an empty text file. Edit the text to delete unnecessary hard returns. For example, you may want to move the text of the note to the end of the file.
A clean and edited copy of the txt file is also available on the DVD.

3. After cleaning up the texts, you may insert structural markup by enclosing chunks of text in tag pairs. First, type in start and end tags for the <body> element, then mark up major textual subdivisions using <div> tags. Within each <div> element mark up titles using <head> tags, and paragraphs using <p> tags. You can use the search and replace function to find hard returns and replace them with tags. Additional elements which can be marked up are sentences (use the <s> element), lists (use the <list> element), items in the list (use the <item> element), and the note (use the <note> element).[11]

4. Compare your text with the fragment below, and make changes if needed. Make sure you used both start and end tags for each element, and that tags do not overlap.

<body>
<div><head>What kind of bilingualism? </head>
<p><s>The bilingualism of the deaf child will involve the sign language used by the Deaf community and the oral language used by the hearing majority.</s><s> The latter language will be acquired in its written, and if possible, in its spoken modality.</s><s> Depending on the child, the two languages will play different roles: some children will be dominant in sign language, others will be dominant in the oral language, and some will be balanced in their two languages.</s><s> In addition, various types of bilingualism are possible since there are several levels of deafness and the language contact situation is itself complex (four language modalities, two production and two perception systems, etc.).</s><s> This said, most deaf children will become bilingual and bicultural to varying degrees.</s><s> In this sense, they will be no different than about half the world's population that lives with two or more languages.</s><s> (It has been estimated that there are as many, if not more, bilinguals in the world today as monolinguals).</s><s> Just like other bilingual children, they will use their languages in their everyday lives and they will belong, to varying degrees, to their two worlds -in this case, the hearing world and the Deaf world.</s></p>

---

[11] For a list of basic structural annotation see 'Elements Available in All TEI Documents', *TEI Consortium*, 2010, available online at http://www.tei-c.org/release/doc/tei-p5-doc/en/html/CO.html. Accessed on 12 September 2010.

```
</div>
<!--other div here-->
</body>
------------------------------------------
```

5. Select and copy all the text and paste it into the XML file you created (**DeafChild_en.xml**, which should still be open in your text or XML editor from the previous task). The text should replace the placeholder

<!—the text goes here-->

You should now have a well-formed and valid XML TEI document containing a header and a text with basic markup. You can, if you wish, proceed to validate the document against its DTD (task 4.5.5), or add a layer of linguistic annotation to it before doing so (task 4.5.4). A well-formed and valid version of the XML you should have created up to this point is available on the DVD.

4.5.4 Adding linguistic annotation

To add information about word classes to a TEI document you need to mark up all word forms using the <w> element containing a *POS* attribute and a value for part of speech. In this task, you will add linguistic annotation to your text using the free *CLAWS* online trial service, available at the UCREL (University of Lancaster) website.

1. Go to: http://ucrel.lancs.ac.uk/claws/trial.html
Enter your email address and select the tagset on which to base the annotation (select *tagset C7*), and the annotation format for the output which will be sent to you (select *Pseudo-XML* as output style).

2. In the XML file you created (**DeafChild_en.xml**) select the <body> element and copy and paste it into the text box in the form, then click on *Tag text now.*

3. Copy and paste the XML output into your corpus file **(deafChild_en.xml**), replacing the element you had selected as input. Make sure start and end tags are preserved and save your file.

Before you can add your XML file to a corpus, you need to validate it. You can either use the validating function of an XML editor (see Chapter 5) or *XAIRA*, the indexing and retrieval software which you will be using to query your single-text corpus. If your XML file is not valid, correct any mistakes such as missing start or end <TEXT>, <BODY>, <DIV> or <P> tags, until the document is both well-formed and valid. A well-formed and valid version of the full, tagged XML document is available on the DVD.

4.5.5 *Indexing the corpus*

In this task you will create a corpus containing in fact only one document, in the XML file you have created. Using *XAIRA* you will set up a database structure and index the documentary and linguistic information previously annotated, so that you will be able to use this information when analyzing the corpus. *XAIRA* validates input XML files before adding them to the corpus. (See Chapter 5 on corpus management and indexing procedures).

1. Download a copy of *XAIRA* from http://xaira.sourceforge.net/ and install the program on your local computer. A copy of the program is also available on the DVD.

2. Open *XAIRA* tools, then select *Index wizard* under the file menu. The following list of actions will guide you through input forms and corpus indexing steps:

- In the *Corpus name* form, provide a name for the corpus (e.g. "Literature on bilingualism") and a title statement (e.g. "Corpus created by ..."), then click on *Next*.
- In the *Corpus root* form, provide the name and path for a directory in which to store your corpus. Click on *Next* or provide an alternative path for a new directory.
- In the *Texts* form, use the browse button to select the directory in which your file **deafChild_en.xml** is located, and click on *Next*.
- In the *Mark up* form, select *XML* as corpus format and tick the *Corpus is TEI compliant* box, then click on *Next*.
- In the *File structure* form, leave default choices and simply click on *Next*.
- In the *File list* form, select only the file **deafChild_en.xml**, which will be the only document contained in your corpus.
- In the *Reading files* form, click on *Go!*, wait till the corpus has been indexed and then click on *Next*.
- In the *Language* form, select *English* and then click on *Next*.
- In the *Text delineation* form, tick the *Just use file names* box and click on *Next*.
- In the *Unit delineation* form, select *s* as element and *Auto-number* as attribute, then click on *Next*.

- In the *Word delineation* form, select *w* then click on *Next*.
- In the *Additional keys* form, leave default values and click on *Next*.
- In the *Bibliography* form, select *SourceDesc* and click on *Build now*, then click on *Next*.
- In the *Indexing* form, select *Index*, then tick the *View corpus in XAIRA client* box. Click on *End*.

In the next task, you will be able to perform some queries with the *XAIRA* client on your corpus.

4.5.6 Searching the corpus

This task is a very limited demonstration of the type of searches which can be carried out on a corpus annotated according the XML TEI scheme. Help files and tutorials on *XAIRA* search functions can be found in "Using the *BNC* Baby with XAIRA", available at http://www.natcorp.ox.ac.uk/tools/xaira_search.xml. (See Chapter 5 for a discussion of corpus analysis tools).

1. If not already open, launch the *XAIRA* client and open the corpus you created. To do so, open the file with the extension *.xcorpus in the directory created during the previous task.

2. Carry out a simple search for the word *that* by typing it in the search box at the top left of the program window, then press *Enter*. Under the menu *Query*, select *Concordance*, and you will see a KWIC concordance of the word *that* in your single document corpus.

3. To distinguish between *that* as pronoun introducing a relative clause, and *that* as a conjunction introducing a that- clause, construct a query for the word *that* followed by any verb, i.e. any <word> element with the attribute *POS* set on a verb form value. The following list of actions will guide you through all the steps:

- From the *File* menu select *New Query* under *Query Builder*.
- In the popup window, click on the black box on the left, and select *XML*. In the next popup window select text from the list of options, then click on *OK*.
- Click on the red box on the right and select *Edit*, then *Word*.
- In the popup window type the word *that* in the search box, that click on *Lookup*. You should see that there are 25 occurrences of the word *that* in your document. Select the word *that* in the list of results and click on *Query*.
- Click on the short line below the box to the right, and a new red box

will appear. Click on the red box and select *Edit*, then *Addkey*.
- In the popup window tick the *Any* box and select *POS* from the list of *Keys*, then click on *Refresh*. A list of *POS* values will appear in the results box.
- Select all values beginning with a V, that is all the verb forms, then click on *OK*.
- Click on the short line linking the two boxes and select *Link type*, then *Next*.
- Click on *OK* in the *Query Builder* window. Your query will select only those occurrences of the word that that are immediately followed by a verb form.
- Right-click on one concordance line, and select *Source*. The bibliographic description provided about the source is shown in a pop-up window.

4.6. Further reading

An overview of encoding and annotation issues is provided by three chapters in Wynn's *Developing Linguistic Corpora* (2005, available online at http://ahds.ac.uk/linguistic-corpora/), namely McEnery and Xiao's 'Character Encoding in Corpus Construction', Leech's 'Adding Linguistic Annotation' and Burnard's 'Metadata for Corpus Work'.

Bowker and Pearson's *Working with Specialized Language* (2002) devotes one chapter to an introduction to corpus annotation. A more detailed treatment of technical aspects of linguistic annotation, with pointers for further reading, can be found in the volume *Corpus-Based Language Studies* by McEnery *et al.* (2006).

The *TEI Lite Manual* (Burnard and Sperberg-McQueen 2006), which contains detailed instructions for the annotation of XML TEI conformant documents and corpora, is available in various formats (HTML, PDF, DDT, etc.) at the Text Encoding Initiative website at http://www.tei-c.org/Guidelines/Customization/Lite/. The XCES Corpus Encoding Standard is fully documented and available at http://www.xces.org.

For information on *XAIRA* see *All About Xaira*, available at http://www.oucs.ox.ac.uk/rts/xaira/. The *BNC Handbook* by Aston and Burnard (1998) is a textbook providing worked examples of how text retrieval software such as (a previous version of) *XAIRA* can be used to explore a large corpus, in this case the *BNC*.

5. Corpus tools and corpus analysis

This chapter first provides an overview of the tools available for the creation of corpus resources and for the retrieval and analysis of data from corpora, and then examines the main types of computer-assisted analyses which can be carried out using corpus tools. While the discussion focuses primarily on monolingual corpora, the tools and techniques introduced in this chapter are also relevant for the creation and analysis of multilingual corpora, both parallel and comparable. Tools and resources more specifically conceived of for the creation and use of bilingual and multilingual corpora will be the subject of Chapter 6 and Chapter 7.

The construction, distribution and analysis of corpus resources all rely on both hardware and software tools. Hardware requirements may range from single user workstations to a local network and a dedicated server, and include different devices and equipment, for instance one or more scanners if the project involves the digitization of printed documents. Therefore, at the stage of project design careful consideration should be given to technical and technological aspects. Equally, it should be taken into account that the acquisition of hardware and software resources usually implies the assistance of human personnel to support them, including trouble-shooting computational problems and providing technical backup.

The configuration of the computer infrastructure should provide sufficient means for the storage and backup of tools and data, as well as for accessing them over a distributed environment. If a project aims at making the tools available and providing continuous access to corpus data over the Internet over a period of time, provision should be made for the acquisition and maintenance of a middle or up-range server.

The choice of hardware will also depend on the operating system(s) required by the software used. While most general purpose applications are found under all operating systems, not all applications specifically created for corpus annotation, management and analysis will work in all software environments. Most stand-alone end-user applications will be supported by a Windows operating system, but some of these may not run under Mac OS. On the other hand, some server-side applications such as corpus indexing and management software may only work in a Unix environment. As with hardware, a degree of computational knowledge concerning software is also required. The extent to which this competence can be 'externalized' to net administrators and computer officers or programmers, or required in members of a project team will depend on the scope and focus of a project. Some computational knowledge will of course be indispensable, and it seems advisable that, even if a project does not envision the use of complex software applications or the need to resort to programming expertise, someone on the team should be 'technologically oriented' and able to act as an interface between technical aspects of corpus work and other members of the team.

5.1 Corpus creation and analysis tools

The software applications used in a corpus creation project will vary according to whether the objective of the project is the creation of a 'quick-and-dirty' disposable corpus or of robust and stable corpus resources. The creation of stable corpus resources, whether for local use within a research group or pedagogical institution or for free distribution over the Internet, is likely to involve a team working on various aspects of corpus construction. Standard office applications needed to manage the administrative part of a project (e.g. preparing lists of texts and documenting stages of advancement) may include a word processor, a spreadsheet, a database, and an Internet browser. A collaborative working environment will comprise shared facilities and resources as well as an information and communication infrastructure. This may be set up using freely available Internet communication platforms and services such as a mailing list, a forum, a blog or a wiki, or adopting a personalized content management system (CMS).[1]

Such general purpose applications are then to be joined by more specific corpus creation and management tools, with various pieces of software taking care of different aspects and stages of corpus processing, in a modular configuration. Different applications will be needed to process the texts into a suitable format, to annotate, index and store the corpus, to retrieve the data and display the results of a query. The focus of a project, whether it is on the exploitation of existing corpora, on the collection of new textual materials, on the development of an annotation scheme, or on the creation of corpus processing tools will determine which applications and resources are most appropriate.

The overview which follows includes both commercial and freely available software. The programs mentioned are listed in the last section of this chapter, together with availability details. Copies of freely distributable applications are also available on the DVD.

5.1.1 Text acquisition

The first stage in corpus compilation consists in obtaining clean, text-only versions of the documents to be included in a corpus, or already annotated versions of existing documents. This is done either by digitizing (or typing in) printed text or by converting existing electronic documents from a different format (PDF, HTML, etc.). To digitize printed texts, a good scanner, together with a good OCR program, is needed. Simple editing and find-and-replace functions, which are found in any text editor, can be used to tidy up a text while proofreading. Converting already existing electronic documents into text-only format may involve the use of different software applications, depending on the format of the source texts. PDF files, for example, will first have to be saved to text-only or XML format by a PDF reader or editor. A PDF document saved in text-only format will have to be

[1] CMSs are available both as commercial and free software, but setting up such a working environment will usually require significant computational expertise.

edited, for instance, in order to remove hard returns and edit 'strange' characters (Calzada Pérez and Luz 2006). Again, simple editing and search-and-replace functions may be used to complete text preparation, possibly preserving text structural and formatting information, for example by marking up headers and major textual subdivisions (see Chapter 4).

When using online documents such as HTML Web pages as sources for a corpus, it may be advisable to separate the main body of the text from the accompanying paratextual material. This is what Bernardini *et al.* (2006:20) call the 'boilerplate' "i.e. the linguistically uninteresting material repeated across the pages of a site and typically machine-generated, such as navigation information, copyright notices, advertisement, etc.". The boilerplate may be stripped out of HTML documents by devising a series of routines which take into consideration recurrent structural features. For instance, Bernardini *et al.* (*ibid.*) suggest that since boilerplate sections are rich in formatting information, number of links, newlines, etc., "HTML tag density [is] a fast heuristic method to filter out boilerplate".

When a text file is converted from proprietary formats such as Microsoft Word or public formats such as HTML or XML, it may be useful to retain recoverable formatting information rather than simply stripping the text of all annotation and inserting new annotation from scratch. A variety of software applications are available, often at no or little cost, to assist in converting, for instance, from or into Microsoft Word and HTML or XML format, to convert from XML to tabular format and to convert from one XML format to another (see the software scripts and programs listed at the end of this chapter). Consistent character encoding may also require using different text editing programs and utilities.

5.1.2 *Annotation*

Once clean or partially annotated text files are obtained, they can be tokenized and annotated using appropriate applications. As seen in Chapter 4, annotation in XML TEI format allows corpus compilers to add structured information at various levels, and different annotation layers can be implemented through different tools.

Contextual and metatextual information about each document can be entered through an input template and stored in a standard header, associated with a text which can then be marked up through a mix of manual and automatic means. Given that an XML file only includes plain text, manual annotation can in principle be carried out by any text editor compliant with the Unicode character encoding standard. However, a number of specialized text editors are also available. These offer advanced search-and-replace functions and tagging facilities such as syntax highlighting, which may greatly facilitate the annotation of an XML text. XML text editors are software applications specifically designed to create XML files by supplementing the functions of a plain text editor with a number of features to assist users in inserting elements, attributes and values in accordance with a specific XML DTD or Schema. Various XML editors are available either as freeware, shareware or as commercial products. Freely available XML editors can be found by searching sites such as SourceForge (http://sourceforge.net/) and CNET.com (http://download.cnet.com/). These include, for instance *XML copy editor*, *Rinzo XML editor*, *XML Marker*, and *XML Pad*. Professional software providing advanced functionalities which assist in editing and validating XML documents include *<Oxygen/> XML editor* and *Altova XMLSpy®*, to mention only a couple.

While standard text headers can be created by means of model templates and input forms, linguistic annotation relies on applications which can perform the required operation automatically. Various tokenizers, chunkers, taggers, parsers, lemmatizers, and so on are available for a number of languages. These applications come either for free or at a cost, either as stand-alone packages to be downloaded and installed on a local machine, or as online services to be accessed and run on a remote server. Free annotation software generally has a cost in terms of the knowledge required to adapt the application used to the requirements of a specific corpus project. It may involve some programming skills and often the use of a Unix/Linux working environment in addition to the software on users' workstations. On the other hand, online services come at a price and may be less flexible and adaptable. The *CLAWS* tagger for English developed at the University Centre for Computer Corpus Research on Language (UCREL) of the University of Lancaster is offered both as licensed software (running on a Unix system) and as an in-house tagging service, whereas text is sent to UCREL in electronic form and is returned *POS* tagged within an agreed time schedule. UCREL also offers the online trial service used for task 4.6.4, and a Web-based interface (*WMatrix*, Rayson 2009) for the annotation of corpora using the *CLAWS* and *USAS* (*UCREL Semantic Analysis System*) annotation tools as well as standard corpus analysis tools.

A popular free application is the *Tree Tagger* developed at the Institute for Computational Linguistics of the University of Stuttgart. The *Tree Tagger* is both a *POS* tagger and a lemmatizer, adaptable to different languages on the basis of a lexicon and a manually tagged training corpus, and it has been used to tag German, English, French, Italian, Dutch, Spanish, Bulgarian, Russian, Greek, Portuguese and Chinese texts. The *Tree Tagger*, together with parameter files for many languages, is freely available for research, education and evaluation as executable code for Unix, Windows and Mac operating systems. Another popular non-commercial application is *TnT* (short for *Trigrams'n'Tags*), a statistical part-of-speech tagger provided with parameters for German and English and trainable on different languages and tagsets. Other annotation tools, sometimes taggers bundled together with tokenizers, lemmatizers, parsers and so on, sometimes as separate applications, are available for still more languages.

Other layers of annotation may be added using custom-built or adapted annotation software. For instance, a version of *MMAX* was used to manually implement XML stand-off annotation of clause alignment of the *CroCo* corpus (Hansen-Schirra *et al.* 2006), and for marking up errors in learner translations within the *MeLLANGE* project (see Chapters 2, 3 and 4).

5.1.3 Corpus management and query systems

Once a corpus has been compiled, it needs to be managed in order to be submitted to various types of analyses. Software tools for corpus management and text retrieval range from stand-alone corpus analysis software programs of the type generally known as 'concordancers' to applications designed to make corpus resources available to the larger research community, and provide access to annotated and indexed data residing on a remote server.

Whereas the different operations related to text retrieval and display are integrated into the user interface of concordancers, in tools based on a server-client architecture different pieces of software are responsible for indexing, storing, querying and retrieving results.

In order to grant access over the Internet to large quantities of annotated text, a corpus must first be indexed, i.e. transformed into a database managed through a server-side application which retrieves the results of a query formulated by the user. The results of the query are then displayed on a user interface in a format amenable to analysis, for instance as a KWIC concordance or as a list of keywords ordered by saliency.

Applications for the management of annotated corpus resources which are freely available for research purposes include *XAIRA*, the *MODNLP-tec* suite and the *CWB*. *XAIRA*, which was used in Chapter 4 to compile and search a sample micro-corpus, is an open source software toolkit which includes an indexer and server/client applications, i.e. a program residing with the corpus in a local or remote corpus server which is used to retrieve the data, and a user interface installed on client computers. *XAIRA* is a platform-independent tool, distributed as a Windows release and available as source code for other operating systems. It can be used with any XML annotated corpus, especially with TEI-conformant documents, and it has been adopted by a number of corpus projects, including the *American National Corpus* (*ANC*, Ide and Suderman 2006), the Italian newspaper *La Repubblica* corpus (Baroni *et al.* 2004), and the *Lancaster Corpus of Mandarin Chinese* (*LCMC*, McEnery and Xiao 2004). *XAIRA* is Unicode compliant; it can thus work with any language, and exploit XML-style annotation at its fullest using the XML Query Language (XQL).

In Chapter 2, the *TEC* client was used to explore the *Translational English Corpus*. The program, which was originally developed for accessing the *TEC*, has grown into a less corpus-specific tool, and is now also used with the *European Comparable and Parallel Corpora (ECPC*, Calzada Pérez and Luz 2006, see Chapter 7). The software is available not only as a client, but also as an open source platform which comprises a set of independent applications: an indexer, a server-side application and a user interface (the client). *MODNLP-tec* works with XML texts, putting together a corpus-specific non-TEI header and a lightly tagged text. Corpora are queried through the XQuery query language.

A different approach, not based on XML, is offered by the *Corpus Workbench* (*CBW*) developed at the *Institut für Maschinelle Sprachverarbeitung* (*IMS*) at the University of Stuttgart. The *CWB* uses a specific input format, i.e. text files in which each token in the corpus, including punctuation marks, is placed at the start of a new line, and is followed by annotation in tabular format. The *CWB* is an open source "collection of tools for managing and querying large text corpora (100 M words and more) with linguistic annotations"[2], which is being used by many different corpus projects, including the Portuguese *Corpógrafo* (see Chapter 8) and *COMPARA*, the *Czech National Corpus* and the *OPUS* multilingual parallel corpus[3]. Both the *Sketch Engine* and *BNCWeb* provide access to a version of the *BNC* in which XML annotation has been converted into the 'vertical' format used by the *CWB* and *Manetee* systems. The *CWB* and *Manetee* are Unix based and use a specific query language, CQP (Evert 2005). However, a Windows version of the *CWB* is also currently being developed.

A further option for indexing and searching large corpora is that of using a relational database. This is the approach chosen by Mark Davies for the Brigham Young corpus collection, which includes the *COCA* and the *BNC* as well as other large corpora of English, Spanish and Portuguese (Davies 2009a). All the corpora hosted at Brigham Young University use the same system. In the case of the *BNC*, XML markup was converted into a set of tables which can be queried through SQL, the query language for relational tables. The BYU corpus collection relies on proprietary architecture built using commercially available general-purpose database management software (Davies 2009a).

Each of these approaches and tools has its pros and cons and specificities. For instance, while both *XAIRA* and *MODNLP-tec* are based on XML annotation, currently they cannot handle parallel texts. The *CWB* can deal with XML information only to a certain extent, but provides support for parallel corpora. On the other hand, *XAIRA* is distributed as a Windows application (with source code available for other operating systems), the *CWB* is still preferably used under Unix/Linux, while *MODNLP-tec* is written in the Java programming language and is therefore platform independent.

5.1.4 Data retrieval and display

While some software packages such as *XAIRA* and *MODNLP-tec* include client applications which are installed on local workstations and used for corpus interrogation and data display, other applications do not provide a graphical user interface. For example, since the *CWB* only provides a command line user interface, corpus projects which adopted the *CWB* as a backend platform to perform corpus management and query operations developed their own custom graphical interface for online access to and display of corpus data. For instance, task 2.6.2 was carried out using the graphical interface created for the *COMPARA* corpus. The Leeds Internet corpora referred to in Chapter 3 also rely on the *CWB*, as does the *OPUS* multilingual parallel corpus (see Chapter 6 and Chapter 7), and each of these projects has developed a custom graphical end-user interface. Task 5.6 in this chapter involves the use of the *Sketch Engine*, which provides a service

---

[2] http://sourceforge.net/projects/cwb/. Accessed on 02 February 2011.

[3] Alternative platforms are Manatee/Bonito (Rychlý n.d.), which uses an input format and query language similar to the *CWB*, and *Poliqarp* (Janus and Przepiórkowski 2007), developed and used for a Polish corpus project, the *IPI PAN* Polish corpus.

for the whole corpus construction and analysis continuum, from the creation of DIY Web corpora (see Chapter 3), to the addition of linguistic annotation (see Chapter 4) to corpus management and query using a version of the *Manatee* corpus manager tool, and corpus analysis using the purpose-built user interface. Other approaches to corpus management also need to integrate already existing resources with newly created ones. For example, a custom Web-based user interface had to be created to query the BYU corpus collection.

A corpus available in text-based format can also be queried using stand-alone corpus analysis applications such as concordancing packages. Concordancers are usually general-purpose corpus software, i.e. not created for use with a specific set of data. They offer an all-in-one solution to text retrieval and display. Users select their corpus by choosing files and directories, and queries are performed on the fly. Concordancers are readily available, both as commercial software and as freeware running on a Windows or multiplatform environment, and do not require much technical know-how. Once the program has been installed on a computer, the user simply needs to select the files and search them. However, when not working with indexed data, concordancers tend to be slow, hence they perform better with small corpora. Furthermore, while some concordancers can make some use of in-line annotation, they cannot exploit it to its full potential like corpus management systems, and are therefore best suited for analyses based on plain text corpora.

A list of concordancing programs is of course bound to be outdated, in that new software applications appear regularly, new and improved versions of existing software are developed, while some are discontinued. A tentative list as of 2011 includes commercial packages such as Michael Barlow's *MonoConc Pro*, Mike Scott's *WordSmith Tools*, Chris Greaves' *ConcGram* 1.0 and R. J. C. Watt's *Concordance*, and free applications such as Scott Piao's *Multi Language Corpus Tool* (*MLCT*), Lawrence Anthony's *AntConc*, Alan Reed's *Simple Concordance Program*, and Matthias Hüning's *TextSTAT*.

Both text-based and index-based tools offer basic access to corpora through wordlists and user-defined searches, and differ in how they allow the user to formulate queries and display results. Software packages such as these have different merits in terms of functionality, performance and usability, and differ in how they treat the input (i.e. the kind of searches they allow) and the output (in terms of how search results are displayed). Some programs have limited search functions and can only handle very limited amounts of data, while others offer fast and flexible searches and more advanced tools and utilities.

Each software product has its own specific features, and the reader is referred to software reviews such as Wiechmann and Fuhs (2006) for an evaluation of their respective merits. The decision to adopt one approach and tool over the other is determined by the technical expertise available and by the scope and focus of a project, and it may well be that different corpus tools are used for the analysis of the same data.

The next section will introduce and explain, through practical examples, some types of analysis which can be carried out using some of the data retrieval and display applications just introduced. In the Tasks section some hands-on activities will be carried out using a free concordancer (*AntConc*) with a text-only version of the *Open American National Corpus* (*OANC*) available on the DVD, and the *Sketch Engine* free online trial service with the *BNC* and user-built corpora.

5.2 Analysis of corpus data

The basic staple of corpus analyses is word indexes. However, corpus analysis programs differ as regards the types of manipulation which can be carried out on basic data such as wordlists and concordances, the flexibility and complexity of the searches allowed, and the presentation and display of search results. Statistical information may be used by different applications to compute complex types of relations among words, such as collocations, colligations, word clusters and lexical profiles. Each of these techniques will now be examined in more detail, bearing in mind that these are only tools which are used to access and display information in a way that makes it easier for users to identify meaningful patterns in language, but it is still up to the analyst to interpret the data.

5.2.1 Wordlists and basic statistics

Corpus analysis software allows users to discover how many word types there are in a corpus and how often each one appears. A wordlist is in fact an index of word forms, which can be sorted according to their alphabetical order or according to their frequency. Wordlists may provide a first approach to a corpus, and help users familiarize themselves with its contents. An alphabetical list will group together all word forms beginning with the same string of characters, thus allowing the user to locate at a glance different forms of the same lemma (e.g. 'provide', 'provided', 'provides' and 'providing' will be listed one after the other) as well as words having a related root ('provider' and 'providers' will be found in the middle of the previous list). Most corpus analysis programs also allow for inverted alphabetical ordering, in which words are ordered beginning from the last letter rather than from the first. Words sharing the same suffix are thus grouped together, for instance words ending in *–ly* in English and *–mente* in Italian will probably be adverbs, while words ending in *–tion* in English and *–zione* in Italian will probably be nouns. Words beginning with a capital letter can be treated as separate types from lower case words. Thus, by listing capitalized words separately, it will be easier to identify proper names such as characters' names in a corpus of novels, or brand names in a corpus of promotional material.

A frequency list allows the user to group words on the basis of their ranking. According to Zipf's law, the distribution of word frequency is stable across corpora of different sizes, and as we saw above, the most frequent word occurs approximately twice as often as the second most frequent word, three times as often as the third most frequent word, and so on. Thus, the list head of a frequency list will be composed of very high frequency function words, while the bottom third will consist of words only occurring once (hapax legomena). While both very high and very low frequency words may be useful starting points for language and translation scholars (e.g. Kenny 2000), words in the mid-frequency range are those which usually offer the kind of information most amenable to analysis, as there are neither too few occurrences nor too many to be analyzed.

The information derived from a wordlist can be used to further manipulate other wordlists. For instance, a pre-formed wordlist (stoplist) of function words can be used as a filter to focus on the lexical content of a text or corpus. Compare the list of the 30 most frequent words in a 300,000 word corpus on 'Cosmology' created using *BootCaT* with the same list stripped of function words through a stoplist (Table 5.1). In the right-hand column the most frequent lexical words come up at the top of the list and are thus immediately available for inspection.

Wordlist			Filtered through stoplist	
1.	21517	the	1.	universe
2.	11845	of	2.	matter
3.	6096	and	3.	galaxies
4.	5980	a	4.	dark
5.	5793	to	5.	light
6.	5699	in	6.	theory
7.	4312	is	7.	space
8.	3667	that	8.	big
9.	3042	universe	9.	galaxy
10.	2172	for	10.	energy
11.	1966	as	11.	bang
12.	1937	be	12.	time
13.	1910	this	13.	years
14.	1910	matter	14.	stars
15.	1895	from	15.	mass
16.	1892	it	16.	cosmic
17.	1845	s[4]	17.	radiation
18.	1776	at	18.	new
19.	1731	are	19.	hubble
20.	1720	by	20.	gravitational
21.	1718	on	21.	gravity
22.	1698	galaxies	22.	clusters
23.	1682	with	23.	s
24.	1633	dark	24.	astronomers
25.	1517	an	25.	background
26.	1167	was	26.	gas
27.	1167	have	27.	like
28.	1118	not	28.	large
29.	1071	or	29.	earth
30.	1050	light	30.	telescope

Table 5.1: Wordlists of a 'Cosmology' corpus

[4] The 's' could be either the possessive form or the abbreviated form of the third person singular of the verb 'be'. See §4.2.3.

Plain wordlist			Lemmatized wordlist		
1.	8755	the	1.	8755	the
2.	5188	of	2.	5188	of
3.	2332	to	3.	4185	be(am 3, are 664, be 688, been 242, is 1725, m 12, was 566, were 285)
4.	2251	and	4.	2489	a (a 2080, an 409)
5.	2108	in	5.	2332	to
6.	2080	a	6.	2251	and
7.	1725	is	7.	2108	in
8.	1524	universe	8.	1543	that (that 1487, those 56)
9.	1487	that	9.	1533	universe (universe 1524, universes 9)
10.	1061	The	10.	1367	galaxy (galaxies 915, galaxy 452)
11.	915	galaxies	11.	1061	The
12.	793	matter	12.	1026	have (had 132, has 352, have 516, having 11, ve 15)
13.	778	from	13.	793	matter (matter 793)
14.	740	as	14.	778	from
15.	707	by	15.	740	as
16.	691	for	16.	724	this (these 212, this 512)
17.	688	be	17.	707	by
18.	664	are	18.	691	for
19.	650	s	19.	650	s
20.	639	Big	20.	639	Big
21.	635	with	21.	635	with
22.	605	Bang	22.	605	Bang
23.	599	it	23.	599	it
24.	597	at	24.	597	at
25.	566	was	25.	561	dark (dark 560, darker 1)
26.	560	dark	26.	518	theory (theories 49, theory 469)
27.	516	have	27.	490	star (star 160, stars 330)
28.	512	this	28.	476	on
29.	476	on	29.	466	time(time 371, times 92, timing 3)
30.	469	theory	30.	457	which

Table 5.2. Words and lemmas

A pre-established list of lemmas can be used to collate word forms and obtain alphabetical and frequency lists for lemmas rather than for types in a given corpus. This is what is done during corpus compilation in the lemmatization phase. Pre-existing wordlists can also be used with some stand-alone concordancing software. For instance, both *WordSmith Tools* and *AntConc* allow for the matching of word forms against a list of lemmas in a text file provided by the user. Such lemma lists may take the form

be --> am, are, is, was, were, being, been, be
belt --> belt, belts

in which each lemma is placed in a new line, and each base lemma is followed by its variant forms. Compare a plain wordlist with a lemmatized wordlist for the Cosmology corpus (Table 5.2).

A comparison between wordlists from different texts or corpora can also provide quite interesting data. Two (or pairs of) different translations of the same source text(s) can be compared in order to extract a list of words that are 'key' to each translated text (or corpus). These are the words whose frequency in one text (or corpus) is significantly higher than that of the same words in the other text (or corpus) (Scott 2010:online).[5] Thus, for instance, the 'keywords' of two Italian translations of a short story by Salman Rushdie ('Chekov and Zulu', 1996) derived from a reciprocal comparison reveal interesting features, which may in turn serve as starting points for further explorations (Table 5.3). Keyword lists are obtained not simply by comparing the relative frequency of the words in one list with that of the other list, but by validating the list obtained against a test of statistical significance.

Tests of statistical significance are used to assess the degree of confidence with which it can be said that the distribution of frequencies has not come about by chance. The distribution of the data are said to be statistically significant if the likelihood that it has come about accidentally is below a certain level which, by convention, is set at 5% (in statistical parlance this is expressed as $p<0.05$). There are several methods to determine whether the distribution of frequency data is statistically significant, the two most widely used being the chi-square test and the log-likelihood test. The chi-square test compares the difference between the actual frequencies in two corpora and the frequencies which would be expected if no factor other than chance were affecting the frequencies. "The greater the difference ... between the observed values and the expected values, the less likely it is that the difference is due to chance" (McEnery *et al.* 2006:55). The log-likelihood test is similar but, as opposed to the chi-square test, does not assume that the data are normally distributed, and is thus sometimes favoured in corpus-based studies (*ibid.*). Tests of statistical significance are necessary to make statistical claims about quantitative data. They can be carried out using a number of commercial or freely available statistical packages, spreadsheet applications like OpenOffice Calc and Microsof Excel, or a website performing statistical procedures online.[6]

---

[5] http://www.lexically.net/downloads/version5/HTML/?proc_compare_wordlists.htm. Accessed on 18 May 2009.

[6] For instance, Stefanowitsch (2004-2005) contains a detailed step-by-step explanation of how the chi-square test is calculated, together with an online calculator. The Centre for Computer Corpus Research on Language at the University of Lancaster (UCREL) provides an online log-likelihood calculator at http://ucrel.lancs.ac.uk/llwizard.html (accessed on 31 April 2011).

I misteri di Nuova Delhi	*Chekov e Zulu*
1 perchè	1. perché
2. perfino	2. cosi
3. sino	3. fin
4. sparviero	4. tutta
5. comunque	5. lei
6. dipty	6. ah
7. tv	7. dunque
8. tutto	8. piena
9. ti	9. preda
10. alcune	10. ahi
11. andare	11. ascolto
12. applausi	12. capisce
13. ascoltami	13. clap
14. importante	14. forte
15. patria	15. impressione
16. pensare	16. khalistan
17. ruolo	17. là
18. seduto	18. okay
19. sentire	19. persino
20. tangenziale	20. quelli
21. teletrasporto	21. stanno
22. termine	22. televisore
23. vede	23. terribile
24. nelle	24. tivù
25. successo	25. tornò
26. tuo	26. vettore
27. così	27. yaar
28. and	28. col
29. astronave	29. n
30. indiano	30. d

Table 5.3. Keyword lists of two translations of the same source text

The list on the left in Table 5.3 refers to a translation, by an anonymous translator, published in the online journal *Liberal* in 1996 with the title 'I misteri di Nuova Delhi'. The list on the right refers instead to a translation, by Vincenzo Mantovani, published in the collection of short stories *Est, Ovest* (Mondadori 1997) with the title 'Chekov e Zulu'. When comparing the two lists, a first observation regarding stylistic differences is that the first item in both lists, the word *perchè* (because), is there because it is spelt in a non-standard format in the first translation (with an acute accent on the final *é*), possibly a sign of editorial carelessness. Apart from that, the two translations differ as regards the overall frequency of 'key' subordinating conjunctions, which Mantovani uses more often than the anonymous translator (respectively, 2 *così*, 7 *dunque* and 19 *perfino* as compared to 2 *persino*, 3 *sino* and 5 *comunque*). The translation by Mantovani also contains foreign (presumably untranslated) interjections like *clap*, *okay* and *yaar*, and displays quite a few signs of an oral register (*ah*, *ahi*), which suggest that this translation is more colloquial in style than the other. These are only a few hypotheses, which would need to be further investigated by looking at parallel concordances for keywords in both translations. Other differences can be explained in terms of lexical preferences, as for example the variant *tv* in the translation by the anonymous translator and *televisore* and *tivù* in the translation by Mantovani. The word *sparviero* (hawk) features prominently in the first translation, which leads us to wonder why no similar term is apparently used in the translation by Mantovani, and what the source term is. As it turns out, the source text in this case was "(Klingon) Bird of Prey", literally translated by Mantovani as *"Uccello da preda (di Klingon)"*.

The comparison of two wordlists may not only be used to highlight consistent patterns of lexical choices in different translations of the same source text, but can also help bring to the fore linguistic features which characterize a specific text or corpus with respect to a general corpus in the same language. In this case, the larger reference wordlist may be derived either from a much larger and more balanced reference corpus, so as to obtain a more accurate keyword list with respect to the standard distribution of lexical items in general language, or from a corpus belonging to a different genre, text type and/or domain, so as to draw attention to features which relate to these dimensions. For instance, a list of keywords in Rushdie's short story obtained using as reference a frequency list derived from a 27-million-word newspaper corpus contains: proper names, non-standard and foreign words (Chekov, Zulu, Klingon, ji, bleddy, zools, Jaisingh, Dipty, etc.) as well as some function words (you, must, I, etc.). Compare this list of keywords with a wordlist created using a stoplist of function words as a filter, and with a plain frequency list for the same text (Table 5.4).

Two words, 'Chekov' and 'Zulu', are common to all list heads, albeit with a different ranking. This happens because they are both very frequent in the texts under investigation and very uncommon in the reference corpus. Other words, while not frequent in the short story, appear in the keyword list, since they are relatively more frequent than one would expect them to be on the basis of word frequencies for a larger corpus.

Stoplists, lists of lemmas, reference wordlists, and so on are sometimes included in corpus analysis packages or available on the Internet at low or no cost. For instance, reference lists (in *WordSmith Tools* compatible format) for the *BNC World Edition* and for seven years (1998-2004) of *The Guardian* newspaper are available from Mike Scott's *WordSmith Tools* website, while a lemma list for English is available online both from the *WordSmith Tools* and *AntConc* websites.[7] Far more resources are admittedly available for English than for other

[7] This is a lemma list created in 1998 by Yasumasa Someya and which "currently contains 40,569 words (tokens) in 14,762 lemma groups" (http://www.lexically.net/downloads/version4/downloading%20BNC.htm. Accessed on 20/03/11).

languages, but various types of lists can be created by the user from existing general corpora for many languages.

Keywords in *Chekov* and *Zulu*	Wordlist (using stop-words)	Wordlist (unfiltered)
1. chekov	1. zulu	1. the
2. zulu	2. chekov	2. and
3. klingon	3. said	3. a
4. ji	4. like	4. of
5. zulu's	5. know	5. to
6. you	6. old	6. in
7. bleddy	7. don't	7. zulu
8. zools	8. say	8. you
9. sahib	9. wife	9. chekov
10. jaisingh	10. ji	10. i
11. dipty	11. klingon	11. he
12. yaar	12. course	12. is
13. revolutionists	13. god	13. on
14. sulu	14. good	14. said
15. sikh	15. mrs	15. his
16. said	16. right	16. was
17. rajiv	17. asked	17. it
18. clap	18. better	18. for
19. must	19. day	19. have
20. damn	20. did	20. that
21. i	21. long	21. be
22. your	22. red	22. as
23. transporter	23. thing	23. not
24. spock	24. tv	24. with
25. kirk	25. world	25. we
26. wife	26. zulu's	26. but
27. prey	27. big	27. at
28. know	28. bleddy	28. what
29. motorway	29. can't	29. all
30. god	30. bleddy	30. been

Table 5.4. Keywords and wordlists

Wordlists obtained by filtering, comparing, or otherwise manipulating corpus data can also be used for corpus creation and compilation. For instance, the keywords obtained from a small corpus of abstracts from a journal of astrophysics can be used as seed words by the *BootCaT* system (see Chapter 3) for finding relevant documents to be included in a larger corpus on Cosmology (as was the case for the corpus used to generate the wordlist in Table 5.1). *WebBootCaT*, the version of the program used by the *Sketch Engine*, allows the user to generate a list of keywords by using as reference list a frequency list from a pre-loaded large corpus (the *BNC* or *ukWaC* for English or other large WaC corpora for other languages[8]). These keywords can be used, all or in part, as seed words which the search engine then combines in tuples, in order to collect a larger and/or more refined set of documents. A similar procedure can be followed for two or more different languages, in order to obtain comparable corpora. For example, a list of keywords extracted from a small corpus of academic publications on astrophysics in Italian can be used as a starting point to create an Italian DIY Web corpus largely comparable – at least for subject matter – to the one in English.

Some programs (e.g. *WordSmith Tools*) allow the user to create lists not only for single words or lemmas, but also for groups of two or more words (bigrams and n-grams), which can provide relevant information as regards textual genre or subject field.

Statistics provide basic measures which can be used as indicators of textual features such as lexical variety (computed as standardized type/token ratio), or of the ratio of lexical words to grammatical words as a measure of lexical density. Other statistical measures are needed in order to extract information from wordlists about the relationships between words, such as collocation and clusters of consecutive words (n-grams). Tools for the analysis of collocation and other linguistic patterns will be examined after the second main type of data provided by text analysis software, namely concordances.

5.2.2 Concordances

At its simplest, a concordance is an index of all tokens of a word type, together with their immediate linguistic context. Thus, most corpus analysis programs allow the user to click on any word in a wordlist to retrieve all its occurrences in a given corpus. A concordance can be produced not only starting from a wordlist, but also by using search functions. A basic search technique consists in simply typing the word one is looking for, but more advanced search techniques are usually also possible. Different tools have different query languages, which allow for more or less complex searches, but most tools permit a search for more than one word in the same query, as well as a search not only for 'words', i.e. fixed strings of characters, but also for regular expressions, i.e. patterns of characters.[9] This is usually done by using wildcard characters, for example a question mark '?' to represent zero or one character, and an asterisk '*' to represent any number of any characters. For instance, a search for 'lap*' will retrieve non only instances of 'lap' but also of 'lapdog', 'lapping', 'laps', 'lapse', etc., while a search for '*lap' will retrieve 'clap', 'flap', 'overlap', etc. The output is usually by default displayed in KWIC (Key Word In Context) format, that is, an index of all occurrences of the 'node' word, which is shown at the centre of the screen surrounded by one line of context. Figure 5.1 is a screenshot of *WordSmith*'s Concord Tool, showing a KWIC concordance for the search string 'lap*' in the *BNC*, in random order.

[8] See Chapter 3 for a description of these corpora.

[9] Throughout this chapter, single quotes are used for search words or patterns, e.g. 'lap' or 'lap*'. Capital letters are used for lemmas, e.g. LAP.

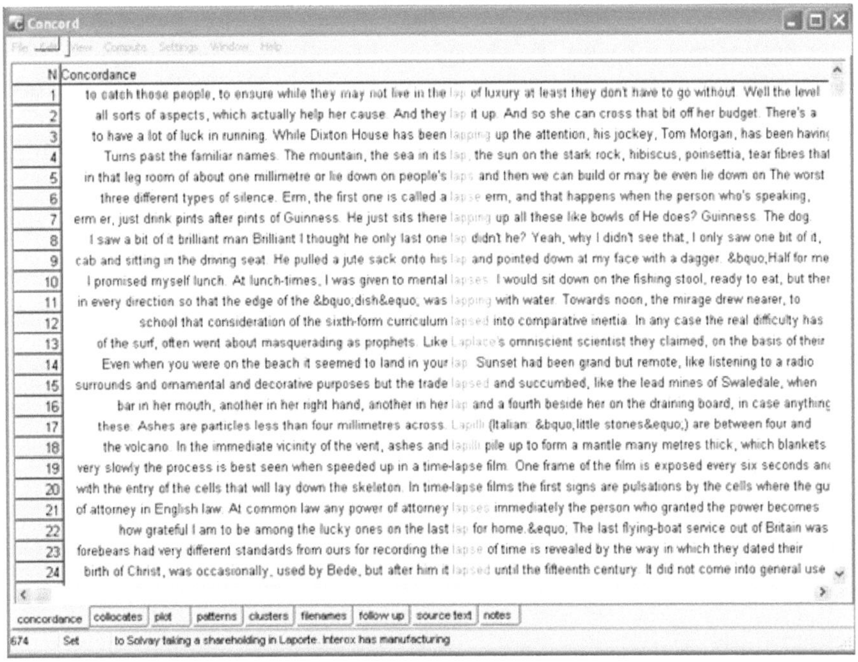

Figure 5.1. WordSmith Tools 5, *random KWIC concordance for 'lap*' in the* BNC

Some text analysis programs and query syntaxes allow very powerful 'fuzzy' phrase searches which retrieve sequences of search patterns. For example, a search for '*n @ lap', where the @ symbol is used to represent one or more words, will produce all instances of 'in his lap', 'on his lap', 'in her lap', 'on her lap'. Concordancing options usually include the possibility to specify one or more context words. For example, a search for 'lap' in the context of the word 'sit' appearing within a span ('search horizon') of five words either to the left or to the right produces the concordance in Figure 5.2. Display options are here set to show a context of one sentence rather than of one line as in a KWIC concordance view.

The search techniques described so far can rely on plain text and can thus be carried out on any corpus. Annotated corpora, on the other hand, allow the user to selectively retrieve only words or phrases which meet certain criteria, specified in textual and linguistic markup. For example, in a (sub)corpus annotated for part-of-speech it is possible to filter search results based on word classes. In other words, a user can retrieve only those instances of a word (or regular expression) which belong to a specific word class, for instance only those occurrences of the lemma LAP (i.e. lap, laps) in which this word is a noun rather than a verb. Figure 5.3 illustrates the results of a search for the string '<w NN*>lap*' in the *BNC World Edition* using *WordSmith Tools*, which will find all words (all strings beginning with '<w') which are nouns ('NN*>' finds NN1 and NN2, i.e. singular and plural forms of a noun), and begin with the string 'lap' (thus 'lap', 'laps', 'lapse'). To obtain the results shown in Figure 5.3, the query contained the specification that the word 'sit' should also be present in the immediate context of 'lap'. This way of formulating a search presupposes familiarity with the format

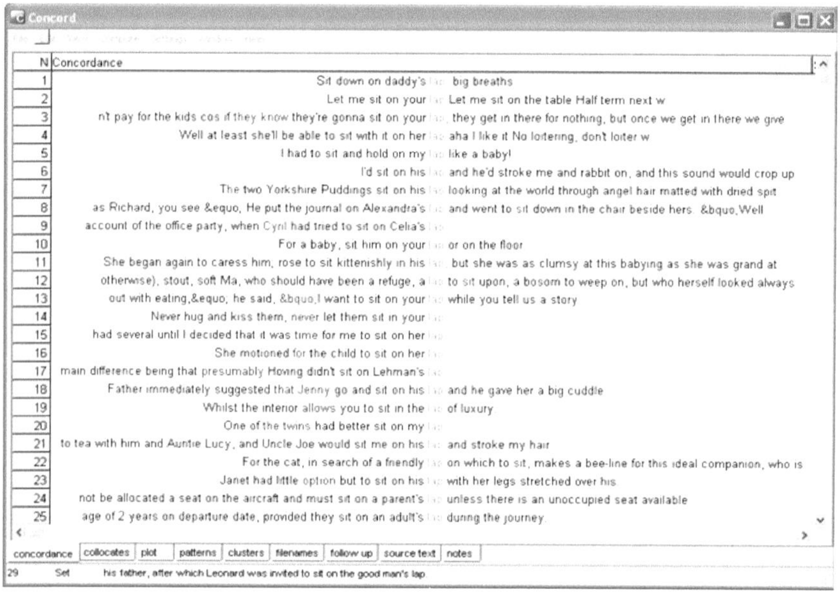

Figure 5.2. WordSmith Tools 5, *random sentence concordance for 'lap' and 'sit' in the* BNC

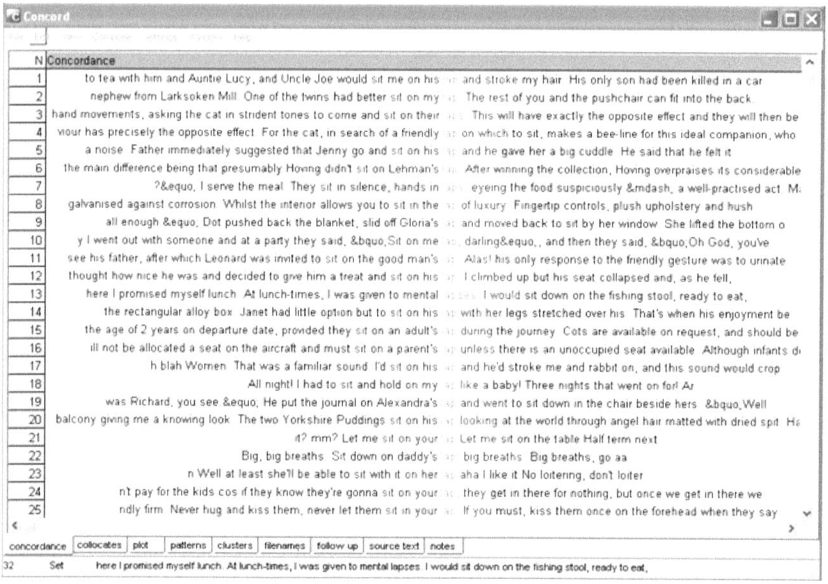

Figure 5.3. WordSmith Tools 5, *search for '<w NN*>lap*' in the context of 'sit' (5LR) in the* BNC

of annotation and the tagset used in a specific corpus, here the *BNC*. Text-based corpus analysis software such as *WordSmith Tools* and *MonoConc* Pro deal with markup as plain text, which can be searched or omitted from searches. So, in as much as markup can be specified as part of a search string, i.e. detailed in the search syntax, in principle any text-based corpus software should be capable of searching in the textual content of the tags. Annotated corpora are however best exploited by index-based software, not only because tags can considerably slow down searches in non-indexed corpora, but also because regular expression searches may be quite complex, especially in heavily annotated corpora.

As in all instances of information retrieval, the problem with concordancing is one of precision and recall, or in other words that of carefully formulating a search query. Precision means that a query should be formulated in terms wide enough to retrieve all instances of a specific feature. However, as a query will return exactly what was asked for, potentially relevant occurrences may be omitted because of a badly formulated query. This is known as 'silence': for example, a search for 'sit*' will not retrieve instances of 'sat', that is of the simple past of the verb. Recall means that a search should be formulated in terms narrow enough to retrieve only the instances of a specific feature. A badly formulated query will result in 'noise', that is more results will be obtained than was intended, as can happen with over-specified wildcards. For example, a search for 'sit*' will retrieve instances of 'sit', 'sits' and 'sitting', but also of 'site' and 'situation', while a search for 'lap*' will retrieve also instances of 'lapses' (see for instance line 13 in Figure 5.3). Noise will also be generated by homographs, for example instances of the verb rather than of the noun 'lap' (which in Figure 5.3 are excluded by the co-occurrence of 'sit'). Linguistic annotation may of course contribute to the formulation of complete and precise searches, which retrieve all and only relevant instances of the features under investigation (though some noise will derive from annotation errors).

Thus, for example, a search output similar to that in Figure 5.3 could be obtained by searching the XML *POS* tagged and lemmatized version of *BNC* using *XAIRA*'s Query Building facility (Figure 5.4).

The box in the lower part of the window contains a graphical representation of the query, which specifies a search span of 5 words, within which two 'words' (i.e. lemmas) must occur, LAP and SIT. The content of each rectangle inside the Query Builder window is expressed in CQL query language, but is specified by the user through a dialog box like the one in the upper corner of the screen. This is the query for the lemma LAP: within this search window, all the different lemmas related to forms of the word 'lap' are listed next to their *POS* tag and frequency. There are three different lemmas for the word 'lap' itself, one SUBST (noun) with 1,479 occurrences, one verb (with 238 occurrences) and one UNC (unclassified item). The unique form sub-window lists all the different forms of the highlighted lemma LAP as a noun, which include both singular (NN1) and plural (NN2) forms. Also included are ambiguous cases, for which a double tag is given.

The same search can be carried out in an even simpler way using the online *Sketch Engine* query interface, which allows the user not only to specify search and

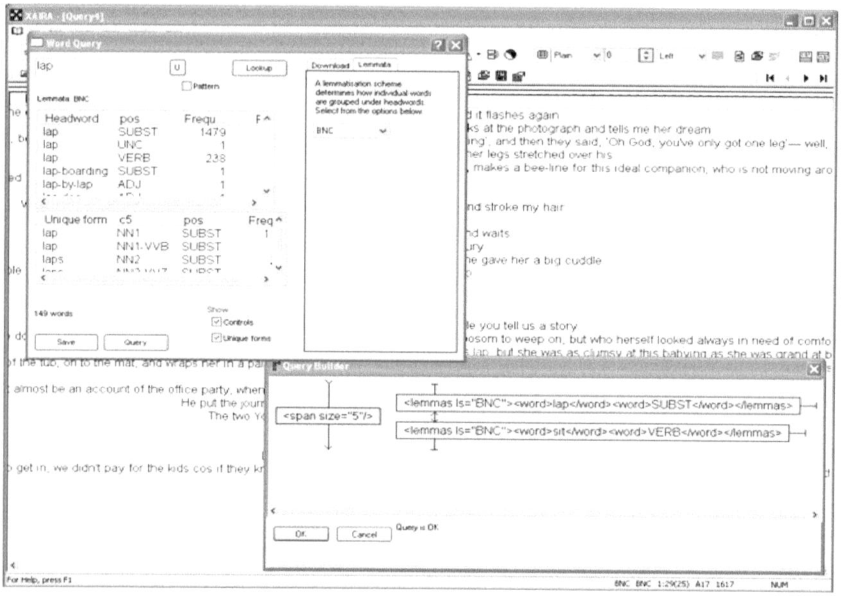

Figure 5.4. XAIRA, *a query for LAP (as a noun) and SIT (as a verb)*

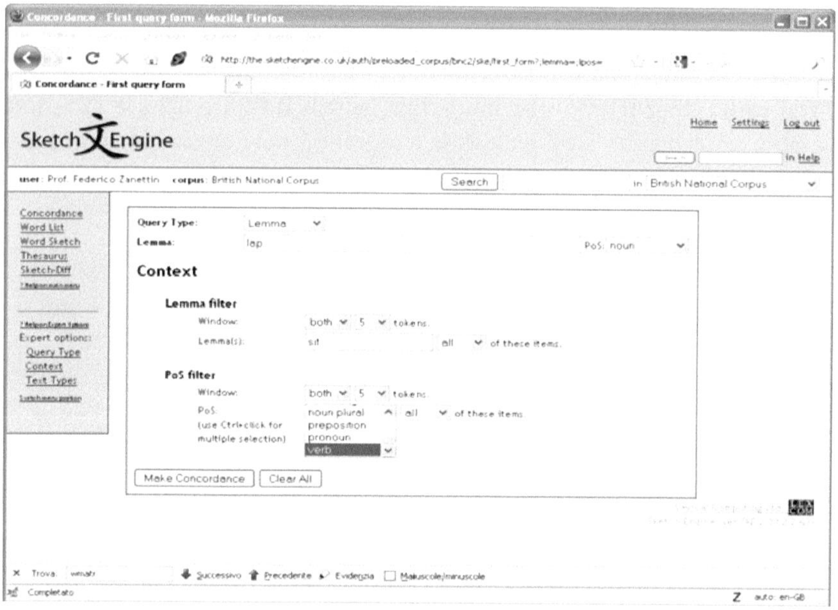

Figure 5.5. The Sketch Engine, *a query for LAP (as a noun) and SIT (as a verb)*

context words but also to select *POS* and *lemma* values from a pull down menu (Figure 5.5). The query in Figure 5.5 will produce a concordance of those instances of nominal forms of the lemma LAP which occur together with verbal forms of the lemma SIT, in a context of 5 words either to the left or to the right of LAP. Once a query has been formulated, corpus analysis software allows the user to manipulate the output of a concordance in order to display a convenient layout for studying the usage of a word in context. Some software interfaces allow the user to randomly retrieve concordance lines every given number of occurrences, to filter out occurrences matching a given search pattern, to manually delete and classify results, and to order them according to different sorting options. The output can also be manipulated by selectively showing text and/or annotation, by colour-coding words on the basis of sorting order or tag type, and so on.

Figure 5.6 shows the results of the query in Figure 5.5. The output shows 25 occurrences of the search combination randomly selected (out of 77) from the *BNC*, and results have been sorted so that concordance lines are ordered first according to the word-class of the second word to the left of the node word (LAP), so that adjectives and nouns come before the prepositions 'in', 'on' and 'to'. Results are also arranged according to a second-level sort order, that is, according to the first word to the left of the node word, so that 'in his lap' comes before 'in my lap', and 'on my lap' comes before 'on the lap'. This sorting order makes it possible to see that when LAP appears following SIT it is usually preceded by a possessive form, most commonly an adjective, itself usually preceded by a preposition, either 'in' or, more commonly, 'on'.

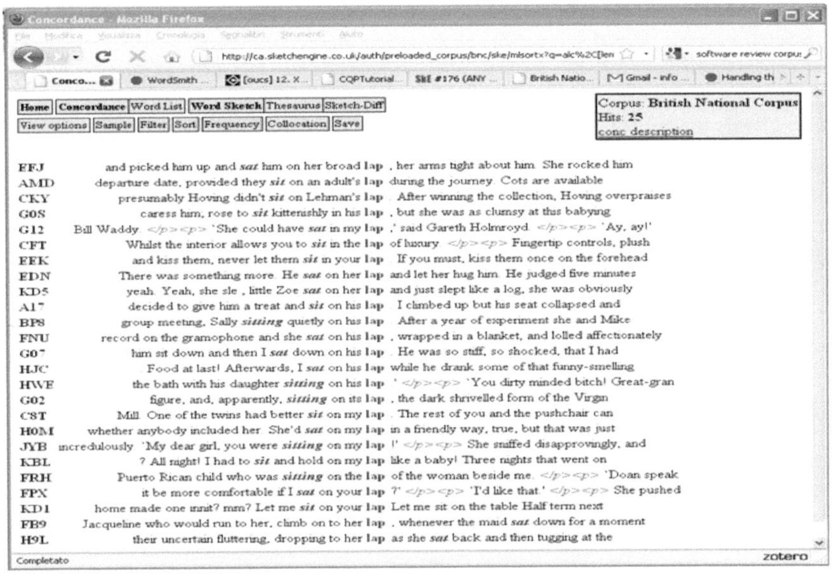

Figure 5.6. The Sketch Engine, *results for LAP sorted first according to the first word class of the word preceding the node by 2 positions, then according to the word to the left of the node*

A concordancer is a powerful tool which affords unprecedented access to linguistic and textual information. A corpus provides empirical evidence which allows the user to discern more easily patterns of linguistic and textual behaviour and verify or overrule intuition. By retrieving and sorting concordances the user (student, researcher or translator) can gather information about the lexical environment of a word, that is to say about its collocational profile.

5.2.3 Collocations, clusters and clouds

Collocation has been metaphorically described as "the company a word keeps" (Firth 1957:11), or the way words 'hang around' together. In corpus linguistics literature, collocations are identified through a statistical approach and have been defined as "the patterns of combinations of words in a text" (Barnbrook 1996:167 and "the characteristic co-occurrence patterns of words" (McEnery and Wilson 1996:7). The relevance of a collocational pattern can be computed by comparing "the actual co-occurrence patterns of words against the patterns that would have been expected if the two words were randomly distributed throughout the text" (Bowker 2002a:67). Collocation generators used by corpus-analysis software rely on statistical formulas such as Mutual Information (MI), Z-score, T-score and log-likelihood, which measure collocational salience between word pairs. Figure 5.7 and Figure 5.8 contain a list of collocates of the word 'lap', ordered according to T-score (Figure 5.7) and MI score (Figure 5.8), respectively. As can be seen by comparing the frequency columns in the two images, T-score

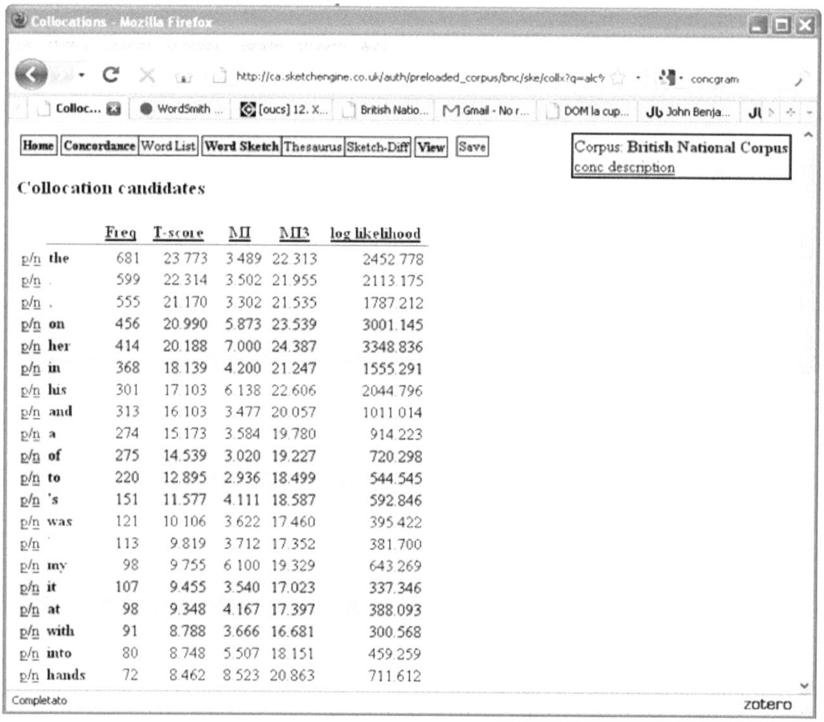

		Freq	T-score	MI	MI3	log likelihood
p/n	the	681	23.773	3.489	22.313	2452.778
p/n	.	599	22.314	3.502	21.955	2113.175
p/n	,	555	21.170	3.302	21.535	1787.212
p/n	on	456	20.990	5.873	23.539	3001.145
p/n	her	414	20.188	7.000	24.387	3348.836
p/n	in	368	18.139	4.200	21.247	1555.291
p/n	his	301	17.103	6.138	22.606	2044.796
p/n	and	313	16.103	3.477	20.057	1011.014
p/n	a	274	15.173	3.584	19.780	914.223
p/n	of	275	14.539	3.020	19.227	720.298
p/n	to	220	12.895	2.936	18.499	544.545
p/n	's	151	11.577	4.111	18.587	592.846
p/n	was	121	10.106	3.622	17.460	395.422
p/n	'	113	9.819	3.712	17.352	381.700
p/n	my	98	9.755	6.100	19.329	643.269
p/n	it	107	9.455	3.540	17.023	337.346
p/n	at	98	9.348	4.167	17.397	388.093
p/n	with	91	8.788	3.666	16.681	300.568
p/n	into	80	8.748	5.507	18.151	459.259
p/n	hands	72	8.462	8.523	20.863	711.612

Figure 5.7. The Sketch Engine, *list of collocates for 'lap' in the BNC, ordered according to T-score*

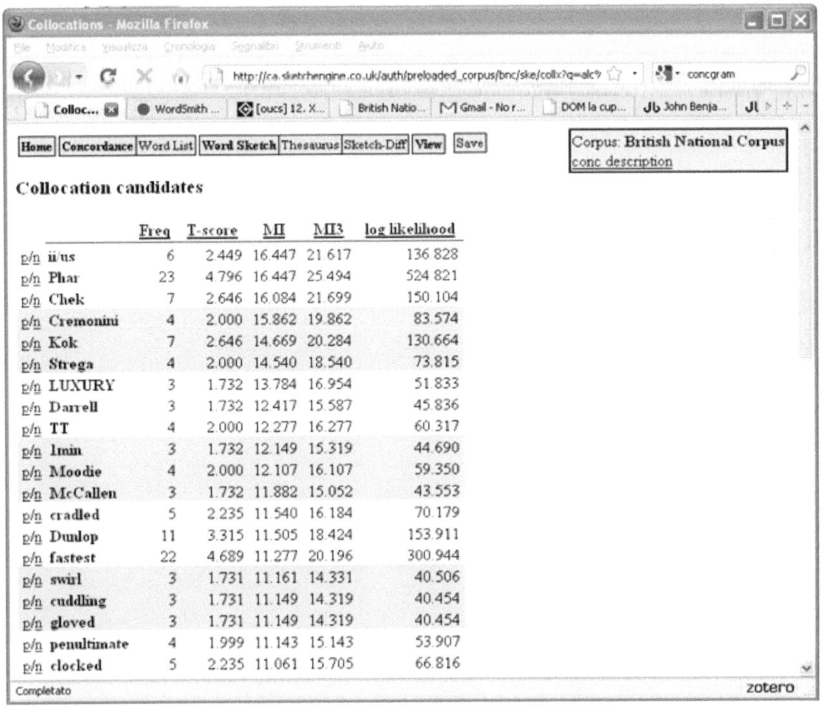

	Freq	T-score	MI	MI3	log likelihood
p/n ii/us	6	2.449	16.447	21.617	136.828
p/n Phar	23	4.796	16.447	25.494	524.821
p/n Chek	7	2.646	16.084	21.699	150.104
p/n Cremonini	4	2.000	15.862	19.862	83.574
p/n Kok	7	2.646	14.669	20.284	130.664
p/n Strega	4	2.000	14.540	18.540	73.815
p/n LUXURY	3	1.732	13.784	16.954	51.833
p/n Darrell	3	1.732	12.417	15.587	45.836
p/n TT	4	2.000	12.277	16.277	60.317
p/n 1min	3	1.732	12.149	15.319	44.690
p/n Moodie	4	2.000	12.107	16.107	59.350
p/n McCallen	3	1.732	11.882	15.052	43.553
p/n cradled	5	2.235	11.540	16.184	70.179
p/n Dunlop	11	3.315	11.505	18.424	153.911
p/n fastest	22	4.689	11.277	20.196	300.944
p/n swirl	3	1.731	11.161	14.331	40.506
p/n cuddling	3	1.731	11.149	14.319	40.454
p/n gloved	3	1.731	11.149	14.319	40.454
p/n penultimate	4	1.999	11.143	15.143	53.907
p/n clocked	5	2.235	11.061	15.705	66.816

Figure 5.8. The Sketch Engine, *list of collocates for 'lap' in the BNC, ordered according to MI-score*

favours high frequency items whereas MI brings up as collocation candidates words which have a very low frequency, but which exclusively or almost exclusively occur together with 'lap'. For example, the word 'Phar' occurs 23 times in the *BNC*, always next to the word 'lap' since it is the name of a horse, as in "The colt was named *Phar* Lap, Sinhalese for 'lightning'") (all instances come from a book on horse racing). Whereas Mutual Information computes collocation strength, the T- test measures "the confidence with which we can claim that there is some association between two words" (McEnery *et al.* 2006:57). Other statistical tests provide still different outputs based on the implementation of a number of statistical considerations (see McEnery *et al.* 2006 for an explanation of the difference among the various tests).

Some tools offer alternative visualizations of collocational data. For instance, *WordSmith*'s *Concord* tool can not only generate concordances but also give access to information about *Collocates*, *Plots* (the dispersion of a word in the corpus files), *Patterns* and *Clusters*. The *Patterns* view (Figure 5.9) shows collocates visually organized in terms of frequency, each column having at the top the word most frequently found in that position. By double-clicking on a collocate, the concordance lines containing that collocate in that position are highlighted and grouped together in the concordance tab.

By clicking on the tabs in the lower part of the window, the user can switch

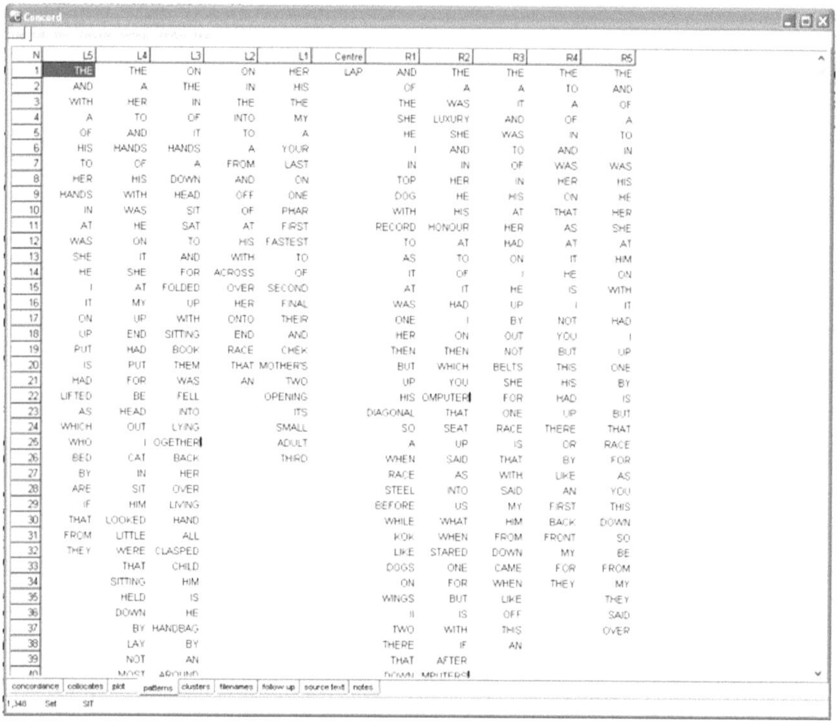

Figure 5.9. WordSmith's Concord tool, *Patterns view for 'lap'*

view. The tab next to Patterns is called Clusters (Figure 5.10). The software can compute and display all recurrent groups of words which appear more frequently in the context of the search word or expression. Frequency settings can be adjusted by the user. For example, the output in Figure 5.10 was obtained by selecting clusters of between 3 and 6 words, with a frequency of at least 5 occurrences. Two quite long patterns of 6 words, relating to the two senses of the noun (or to the two homographs) can be seen, "the end of the first lap" and "living in the lap of luxury". The 'Related' column shows all the shorter clusters contained in the longer ones.

Corpora and corpus analysis tools bring to the fore the patterned nature of language, in which orthographical words are often parts of longer sequences co-occurring with other words in variable combinations. While *WordSmith Concord Patterns* and *Clusters* views offer summaries of the combinatorial patterns in the results of a search, it is also possible to obtain similar automatic summaries for a whole corpus. In order to do so, a corpus needs first to be indexed, so that frequency and positional data can be computed together. *WordSmith Tools* allows for the creation of an index which can be used to generate frequency and alphabetical lists of all clusters in a corpus within a given word span and frequency range. Furthermore, it is possible to compute not only clusters of consecutive words (n-grams) but also instances of the co-occurrence of two or more words, though not at all times in the same order or in the same position ('completed'

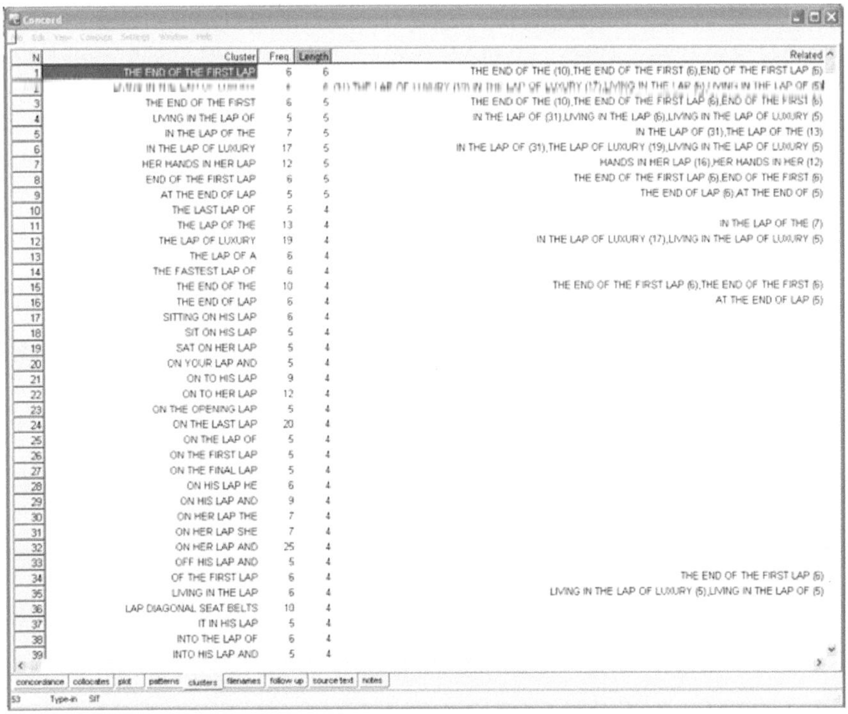

Figure 5.10. WordSmith's Concord tool, *Clusters view for 'lap'*

may precede or follow 'lap', with one or more intervening words). Such items, which are candidates for phraseological units, have been called 'concgrams' and can be generated automatically by a program such as *ConcGram* (Greaves 2009) or by the *WordSmith Tools*' ConcGram utility. *CongCgram* was in fact created to be a program which could specifically "identify all of the co-occurrences of two or more words irrespective of constituency and/or positional variation in order to account for phraseological variation and provide the raw data for identifying lexical items and other forms of phraseology" (Warren 2009:2). *ConcGram*'s concordance viewer displays concordance lines with all the words in a concgram equally highlighted (Figure 5.11), and concordance output can be sorted and centred alternatively around any of these words.

KWIC or sentence view, collocate lists, clusters, and concgrams are different ways to display the data, each providing a specific graphical presentation. The interpretation of data relies on the observation of the way they are presented, and different tools may provide different means for highlighting lexical patterns, by making use of visual aids such as colour coding and sorting.

Alternative ways of displaying collocational data, which rely to an even greater extent on visual and graphical features, have also been implemented. These include 'collocate clouds' and 'concordance trees'. In a collocate cloud, collocates are listed alphabetically, while frequency information is displayed as font size and collocational strength as text brightness. Figure 5.12 shows a collocate cloud for the word 'lap' in the *BNC*, generated using the interface developed by the SCOTS project[10] (Anderson *et al.* 2007). Each collocate in the cloud can be selected as a new node, and the user can navigate the corpus by clicking on the words listed.

Figure 5.11. A concgram search for 'people/different'

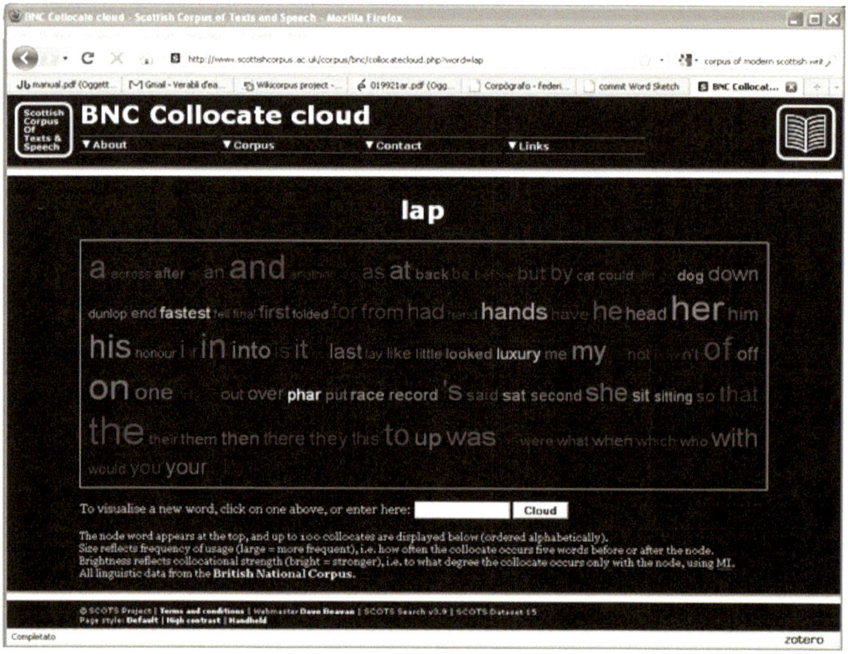

Figure 5.12. Collocate cloud for 'lap' in the BNC

[10] This explains the reference to the Scottish Corpus in the screenshot.

Figure 5.13 shows instead a concordance tree for the word 'lap' in the *TEC*, generated by a modular component of the *MODNLP-tec* software suite (Luz 2000). As can be seen from the image, the collocates of 'lap' are shown in their positional relation, so that collocational patterns can be made out using word position and font size and type as indicators of frequency and collocational strength. The concordance tree can be shown either to the left or right of the node word, and the user can zoom in and out to focus on given patterns. The *Prune tree* button can be used to remove lines with less significant collocates, thus showing the main patterns more clearly.

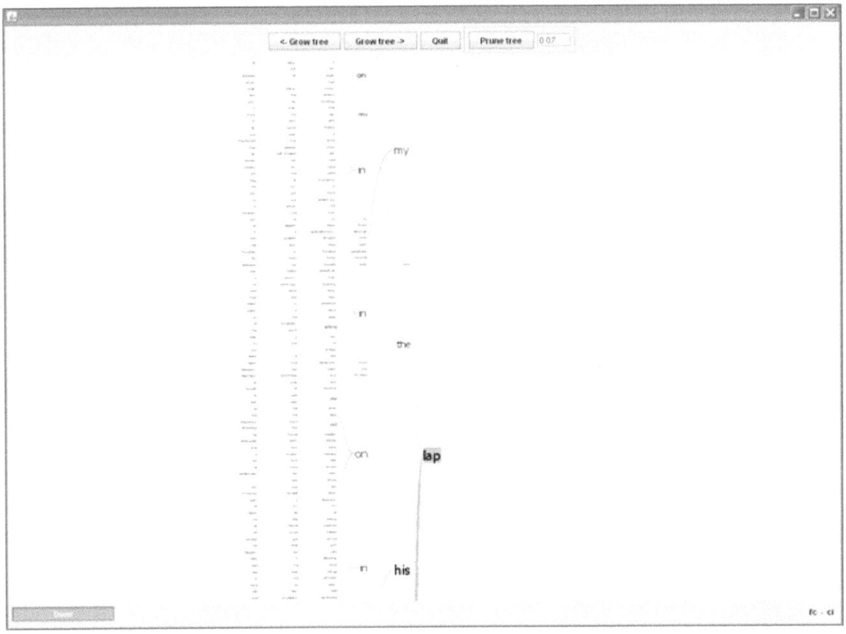

Figure 5.13. MODNLP-tec *concordance browser, Concordance tree viewer display for 'lap'*

5.2.4 *Colligations and word profiles*

While patterns of co-occurrence are generally referred to as collocations, a distinction is usually made between the simple collocation of word forms and colligation, or "[t]he occurrence of a grammatical class or structural pattern with another one, or with a word or phrase" (Sinclair 2003:173). An example of colligation is that exemplified in Figure 5.6, in which 'lap' has the meaning sense of part of the human body or posture that is made when sitting on a chair, and regularly co-selects a possessive expression (adj, pron, NP) to its left, preceded by a preposition. As Sinclair demonstrates, and as again Figure 5.6 exemplifies, this colligational pattern of 'lap' also often occurs in sentence/clause final position. Colligational relations can be difficult or impossible to observe when presented with large amounts of data, and 'clusters' or 'cloud' collocation summaries offer a visual approach to data which may help focus the researcher's attention. For instance, the colligational pattern of 'lap' just referred to is immediately apparent from the clusters in Figure 5.10, since the various forms of the lemma SIT account for different collocational patterns. Colligational relations can be extracted automatically only from a lemmatized and *POS*-tagged corpus, using index-based software which computes measures of relations between word forms, lemmas and word classes, as well as of any other type of annotation encoded in a corpus. This is the approach taken by the *Sketch Engine*, whose most specific feature is the *Word Sketch*, defined as an "automatic, corpus-based summar[y] of a word's grammatical and collocational behaviour" (Kilgarriff *et al.* 2004:105). Figure 5.14 shows a *Word Sketch* for LAP (as a noun) in the *BNC*.

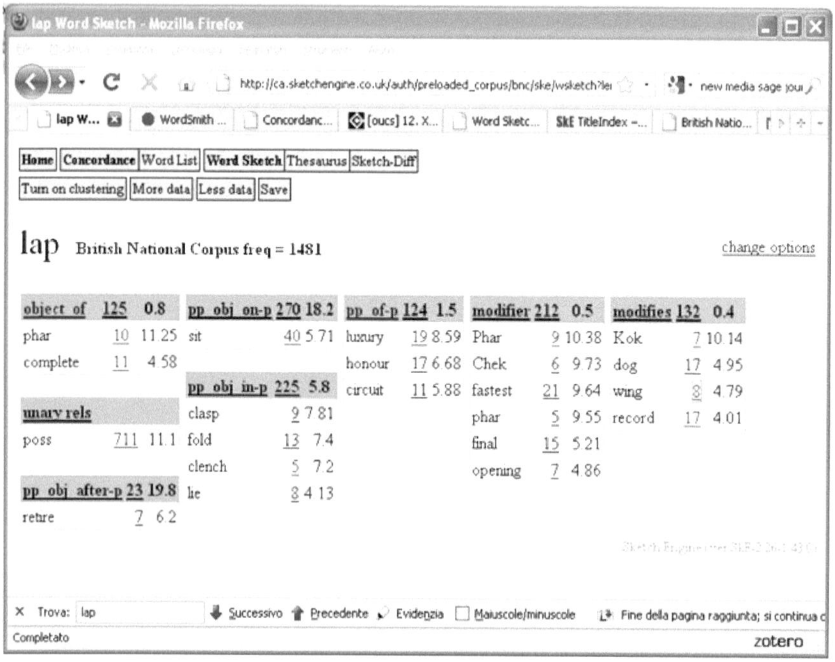

Figure 5.14. The Sketch Engine, *a Word Sketch of 'lap' in the BNC*

A *Word Sketch* provides a synthetic lexical profile of a word (or rather, of a lemma) and of the lemmas which typically combine with it, grouped according to the particular grammatical relation that links them. Each box inside the picture contains a list of lemmas collocating with LAP, showing how LAP can often be found as the object of PHAR (see previous section) and COMPLETE, the object of SIT ON, RETIRE AFTER, CLASP IN, the head of a Noun Phrase postmodified by a Prepositional Phrase headed by OF (e.g. 'lap of luxury', 'lap of the town circuit'), as a modifier of KOK, DOG, etc. The *unary rels* category refers to a colligational relation, that of LAP with the class of possessive forms. Lemmas are listed inside each box in order of saliency rather than raw frequency.[11] CLASP is shown to have a stronger collocational link with LAP than FOLD does, even though FOLD is more frequent as a collocate of LAP. Clicking on the number next to each word generates a concordance of all sentences containing both words within a span of 5 words to each side of the 'node' word. Grammatical relations are computed through a 'grammar' consisting of rules formulated in the CQP query language supported by the *CWB* using regular expression over *POS* tags. For example the formalism which identifies COMPLETE as a lexical verb (V) which has LAP as its object can be expressed as follows:

```
1:"V" "(DET|NUM|ADJ|ADV|N)"* 2:"N"
```

As Kilgarriff *et al.* (2004:110) explain, this expresses a combination between "a verb and the last noun in any intervening sequence of adverbs, determiners, numbers, adjectives and nouns". The *Sketch Engine* formalism can be glossed as follows:

> "The 1: and 2: mark the words to be extracted as the first and second arguments of the grammatical relation. |, (), and * are standard regular expression metacharacters. | is for disjunction and * indicates that the preceding term (here, the bracketed disjunction) occurs zero or more times" (*ibid.*)

All sentences which contain the combination of COMPLETE and LAP within a given word range which match this definition for a "verb-object" pair will be included in the frequency count used to determine collocational strength. By clicking on the number next to COMPLETE (11) a concordance showing instances of LAP as a direct object of COMPLETE is displayed (Figure 5.15).

As can be seen in Figure 5.15, a number of results stand out as possible errors. 'Phar' (also spelt with initial lower case), 'Chek' and 'Kok' (all of them scoring high in the MI test) are listed either as verb, modifier or modified. This happens because the *Word Sketch* took into account also all instances of 'lap' as part of two non-English compound names (Phar Lap and Chek Lap Kok, a Chinese place name), which were often annotated in the corpus with incorrect *POS* tags (see Chapter 4). Some level of noise may also depend on rare or complex structures, but the author claims that the system can catch the most frequent relations and can therefore provide reliable automatic summaries from large amounts of data. The *Sketch Engine* provides preloaded 'sketch grammars' for English (each comprising one or more formalisms) and other languages, but the 'grammar rules' which define the grammatical relations used to create word sketches can also be provided by the user (see the *Sketch Engine* online help for more information). The *Sketch Engine* features also a Thesaurus function, which compiles a list of candidates for near synonymity by comparing the similarity of collocational and

---

[11] Settings for word range and statistical significance can be adjusted by the user. In the case of Figure 11, values were tuned to select only relations within a word span of 5 words defined by a high MI index (more than 5%).

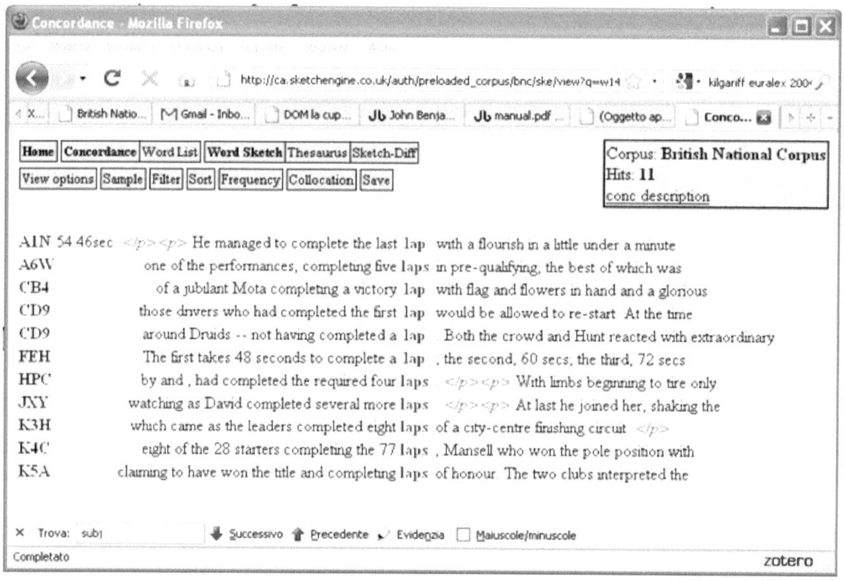

Figure 5.15 The Sketch Engine*, a concordance of LAP as a direct object of COMPLETE in the* BNC

colligational behaviour of different lemmas, and the Sketch-Diff function, which shows overlapping and distinct patterns between two given lemmas.

Structurally annotated documentary information can be used to select appropriate subcorpora or to show the distribution of a given feature across corpus-internal textual categories. Figure 5.16, for instance, illustrates the distribution of LAP within *BNC* text classes. Almost half of the occurrences come from *Fiction and verse*, while another half is almost equally subdivided between *Other unpublished written material* and *Newspapers*, presumably related to the occurrence of LAP in the +sense of "circuit of a race course" in the sports section. An analysis of the distribution of the results of a search for the SIT – LAP combination, which presumably selects the other sense of the noun LAP, shows in fact no occurrences in newspapers.

5.2.5 *Semantic associations*

Various concepts have been used to define the different types of associations which can be established among words or word patterns. Collocation is the most general term which designates a relation of habitual frequency between word forms, while colligation represents one more level of abstraction as it relates single word forms or groups of words to other groups of words sharing the same word class. According to Sinclair, two further levels of abstraction can be posited when describing the types of associations which derive from recurrent patterns of occurrence, that is, semantic preference and semantic prosody.

Semantic preference is defined as the relation between one (or more) word(s) and a group of its co-occurrences based on semantic rather than syntactic similarity among these co-occurrences. As Sinclair (2003:78) puts it,

> Sometimes in the structure of a phrase there is clear preference for words of a particular meaning. The word class is not important, and any word with the appropriate meaning will do (though there are often collocational patterns with semantic preferences).

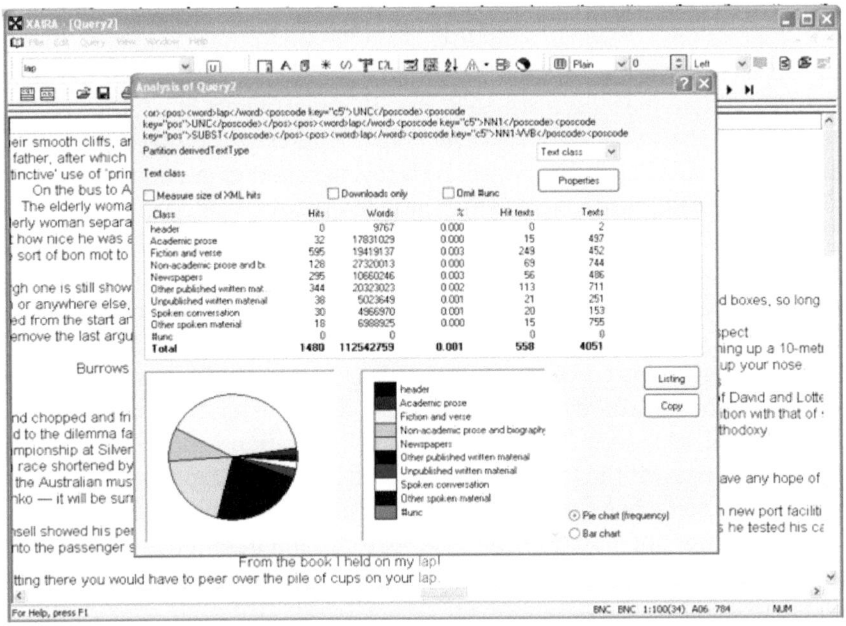

Figure 5.16 XAIRA, *distribution of LAP within text classes in the* BNC

A classic example of semantic preference is that of the phrase 'with/to the naked eye', which tends to collocate with 'expressions of visibility'. Common examples include "visible to the naked eye", "you can see with the naked eye", and "look at with the naked eye".

Semantic prosody requires an interpretative effort on the part of the analyst, since here "words [group] together to make special meanings that relate not so much to their dictionary meanings as to the reasons why their were chosen together" (Sinclair 2004:178). Semantic prosody has variously been described as 'attitudinal', 'pragmatic', 'interpersonal', or 'connotational' meaning, in that it contains an evaluation about things, people and events. A semantic prosody is a favourable or unfavourable connotation which a word is assumed to be 'coloured' with because of its semantic preferences. By virtue of 'keeping good or bad company', words can begin to signal a certain attitude. For example, the word 'commit' is said to have an unfavourable semantic prosody because it collocates with words such as 'suicide', 'offence', 'crime' and 'murder'; the association between these words and the verb 'commit' is also a colligational one, since they all belong to the same word class and are in the same grammatical relation as direct objects of 'commit'.

A divergence from expected semantic profiles is likely to be perceived as highly marked, since once 'imbued' with a negative prosody, a word cannot, in normal circumstances, be used in a favourable environment (and vice versa). One of the most quoted examples of semantic prosody is offered in an essay by Bill Louw (1993), where the term is first introduced. He argues that the expression 'symptomatic of' has a negative semantic prosody in that it consistently occurs with expressions referring to diseases, illnesses and other problems. Thus the sentence "it is symptomatic of the University of Zimbabwe, which has such a high reputation, that there are 15 links with departments in ...", uttered by an institutional speaker at an official event may be perceived as marking a distance between the speaker and the words he is saying, whether intentionally and thus ironically, or unintentionally and thus insincerely.

While semantic preference can be analyzed more efficiently using corpora since it relies on the observation of recurrent patterns of use, semantic prosody is a phenomenon more deeply entrenched in the realm of pragmatics, hence it is more difficult to disentangle solely on the basis of corpus data (Stewart 2010). Much has been written on semantic prosody and related terms and concepts such as 'discourse prosody' (Stubbs 2001:65), 'semantic association' (Hoey 2005) 'collocational resonance' (Williams 2008) and 'collocational connotation' (Francis 2011:69). Whatever the terminology adopted and one's stand on the subject, it seems clear that while corpus data and tools make the empirical observation of language patterning possible, semantic features and descriptive categories are interpretative constructions, and the weight of interpretation ultimately rests on the researcher.

5.3 Conclusions

This chapter has shown how various tools for corpus creation and analysis can lead to the observation of linguistic regularities in corpora from different angles. It has also illustrated how statistics, visualization formats and linguistic annotation can be used to derive information from corpora. The overview of data retrieval and display techniques has focused on lexicogrammatical features related to language patterning in monolingual corpora. Other types of analysis are of course possible, based on both deep and shallow annotated corpora. For instance, Olohan (2004:148-149) suggests that a comparison between the lexical and grammatical patterns in a corpus of translations and those in a reference monolingual corpus can help uncover the ideological positions of translators. Moreover, Bowker and Pearson (2002:215) argue that since a corpus allows the user to search terms in context, the analysis of these contexts can help "to identify other terms and expressions that can be used to construct a metaphor", and various methods and techniques have been proposed for the corpus-based investigation of figurative language (Stefanowitsch and Gries 2006), which could be applied to the study of translation-driven corpora.

In the Tasks section some data retrieval and display options are illustrated, using a free concordancer (*AntConc*) and the trial service of the *Sketch Engine* corpus tools.

5.4 Tasks

5.4.1 *Wordlists*

In this task you will use *AntConc* to create two wordlists from the bilingual comparable corpus you created in Chapter 3 with the help of the *BootCaT* graphical interface.

1. Copy *AntConc* from the DVD or download it from: http://www.antlab.sci.waseda.ac.jp/software.html, then install the program and launch it.

2. From the *File* menu select *Open file(s)…*, then select the file containing the English corpus you created in task 3.6.3. For ease of access, a copy of a corpus of about 130,000 words on Cosmology, created as described in that task, is available on the DVD. The corpus in contained in one file, *cosm_en.txt*.

3. Click on the *Wordlist* tab, then on the blue *Start* button. This will generate a list of all word forms in your corpus. The results can be displayed in order of frequency, in alphabetical order, or in reverse alphabetical order. You may also decide whether to treat words beginning with capital letters as different word types, and you can use the search box to locate a word in the list. To obtain the type/token ratio for the corpus, simply divide the number of types by the number of tokens (these are displayed at the top of the table). Note, however, that since texts are of different lengths the conventional T/T ratio is not very informative. For this reason, programs such as *WordSmith Tools* use a measure of standardized type/token ratio (STTR), which is a running average based (by default) on consecutive 1,000-word chunks of text.

4. Create a Wordlist for the comparable corpus in the other language you created in task 3.6.3. For ease of access, a copy of an Italian corpus on Cosmology of about 140,000 words, created as described in that task, is available on the DVD. The corpus consists of one file, *cosm_it.txt*. Depending on the language of the corpus you may want to change tokenization settings. To do so, click on the *Global Settings* menu entry and select the *Token (word) definition* category.

5.4.2 *Lists of lemmas*

In this task you will lemmatize the corpus using the *Lemma List for English* by Yasumasa Someya.

1. Download the *Lemma List for English* from http://www.lexically.net/downloads/e_lemma.zip and unzip it into your working folder. A copy of the lemma list is also contained on the DVD.

2. After you have generated a wordlist of your corpus in *AntConc*, click on the *Tool Preferences* menu entry and select the *Wordlist* category. Under *Lemma list options*, tick the *Use lemma list file* checkbox, then click on the *Open* button and select the lemma list file (e_lemma.txt) in your working directory.

3. Click on *Load*, then on *OK* in the dialog box, then on *Apply*. You will be brought back to the main *Wordlist* screen.

4. Click on the blue *Start* button and you will get a list of lemmas rather than of word forms as in the previous task. The frequency in the second column refers to the cumulative frequency of all forms of the lemma listed in the third column, followed by all its forms with their individual frequency. The number of types shown at the top of the table really refers to the number of lemmas, so that you can also compute the lemma/token ratio for the corpus.

5.4.3 Keywords

In this task you will create a list of key tokens in your corpus. In order to do this, you need to compare the frequency list of your corpus with a frequency list from another corpus. You will use as a reference the 14-million-word *Open American National Corpus (OANC)*, a subset of the ANC available with no copyright restrictions and which contains a variety of texts from various genres, both written and spoken.[12] A text-only version of the corpus is contained on the DVD in the *OANC* directory, which should be copied into your working folder.

1. Generate a wordlist of your corpus in *AntConc*, then click on the *Tool Preferences* menu entry and select the *Wordlist* category. Untick the *Lemma list options* checkbox, then select the *Keyword* category. Under *Reference corpus options* click on *Add directory*, and select the *OANC* directory in your working folder. All text files should appear in the box. Leave default values for all other options, then click on *Apply*.

2. In the main *AntConc* window, select the *Keyword List* tab. Check that the *Reference corpus* is loaded, then click on *Start*. The resulting list of

[12] For information on the composition of the *OANC*, see http://www.anc.org/OANC/. Accessed on 30 March 2011.

keywords can be sorted according to keyness, frequency, and alphabetical order. If you use a lemmatized wordlist, you will get as a result a list of key lemmas.

Keywords are 'key' not because they are the most frequent but because they are unusually frequent in your corpus as compared to their frequency in the corpus you used as the reference. The words at the top of the list will in fact probably be those that you used as *seeds* when building your corpus with *BootCaT*.

5.4.4 *Concordances*

For this task you will be using the *OANC*. The activity is based on Sinclair's *Reading concordances* (2003:83-90).

1. Open *AntConc*, and from the *File* menu select *Open dir…*, then select the *OANC* directory in your working folder. All 119 files should appear in the *Corpus files* window.

2. Click on the *Tool Preferences* menu entry and select the *Concordance* category. Leave all *Display options* selected and tick the *Treat case in sort* checkbox under *Other options*. Then click on *Apply*.

3. In the main *AntConc* window, click on the *Concordance* tab, then on the *Advanced* button.

4. In the *Advanced search* window tick the *Use search term(s) from list below* checkbox, then type the words *budge*, *budged*, *budges* and *budging*, each as a new line. Click on *Apply*.

5. Click on *Start*, and wait until *AntConc* runs through the corpus and produces a KWIC concordance. You should get 17 results, including some spurious instances (a duplicated line, an occurrence of the word *Budge* as a proper noun rather than as a verb form, and a typo.

6. Analyze the remaining concordance lines. In order to get a clearer view of linguistic patterns, sort the results. For instance, to sort concordance lines according to the first word to the left of the node word, then according to the second word to the left, tick the *level 1* checkbox of the *Quick sort* menu and set the value at *L1*, then tick the *level 2* checkbox and set the value at *L2*. Then click on *Sort*.

7. Sinclair claims that about 25-30 random concordance lines should be enough to derive a profile for most words. After a very detailed analysis of 31 random occurrences of forms of the verb *budge* from a general

corpus (Sinclair 2003:83-90), he presents the following "outline of [his] dictionary entry for budge: "Budge, verb. This word is always used with a negative of some sort, whether grammatical or lexical. Normally there is also a modal of (a) ability ... [or] (b) determination ....".

Look at the results of your search. Are there any repeated words, expressions, or grammatical categories? Can you spot any collocations, colligations and semantic preferences? Do your data support Sinclair's claim that the word *budge* has a semantic preference for a related group of words and expressions, and an overall negative semantic prosody? Are there any occurrences of BUDGE which seem to contradict the overall collocational profile of the word? If so, can you provide an explanation?

8. Look up in the *OANC* one or more words from the following list: *rife*, *caused*, *provided*, *persisted*, *utter*, *sheer*, *dealings*, *peddle* and *habitual*. Sort results both to the left and to the right to identify regular patterns and see whether you can infer a clear positive or negative semantic prosody.

5.4.5 Collocations and clusters

In this task you will create tables of clusters and collocates for a given word or regular expression.

1. To create a table of collocates, click on *AntConc*'s *Collocates* tab and provide query settings. For instance, you can type *budg** in the search box, set the search window at 2L and 2R, the minimal collocate frequency at 10, and sort by frequency. Then click on *Start*. You will be able to change sorting order after *AntConc* has processed the data. Collocational strength is computed by default by using Mutual Information (MI) scores. For example, if *problem* is often found with *solve*, they may have a high mutual information score. The procedure for calculating Mutual Information takes into account not just the most frequent words found near the word in question, but also whether each word is often found elsewhere, well away from the word in question. For example, while *the* is found near *problem* much more often than *solve*, it is also found very often far away from *problem*. Therefore the combination of *the* and *problem* will get a low MI score. Under *Tools Preferences* you can also set the method for computing the strength of collocational associations to T-score, which tends to rank frequent collocates higher than uncommon ones.

2. To create a table of clusters, click on the *Clusters* tab and provide query settings. For instance, to look for clusters containing the word *caused* set *Cluster Size* at between 4 and 6 words, and *Minimum Cluster Frequency* at 4. In the search dialog box type *caused* as search word, then click on *Start*.

5.4.6 Word profiles

While the activities in the previous tasks were based on plain text corpora, more advanced queries can be carried out taking advantage of annotation, as seen for example in task 4.6.6. In this task you will use the online corpus compilation and query system *Sketch Engine* to look at collocational and colligational profiles ('word sketches').

1. Go to: http://www.sketchengine.co.uk/ and register for the free trial account, which gives full access to the *Sketch Engine* for one month. You should immediately receive an account name and password in your email (save your account details for later access).

2. To produce a *Word Sketch* of the word *budge* in the *BNC*, follow the steps below:

- Log into the *Sketch Engine* and click on *British National Corpus* in the list of pre-loaded corpora.
- Click on *Word Sketch* in the left hand side column.
- Type *budge* in the *lemma* box and select *verb* as *part of speech*. Then click on *Show word sketch*.

Is the information consistent with Sinclair's observations reported in § 5.2.5?

3. Next, compare the word sketches of two words that are 'similar' in form (e.g. cognates) or content (e.g. prima-facie dictionary equivalents) across languages, in a bilingual comparable corpus. You can either use the comparable corpus you created in task 3.6.3, or create a new one using the *WebBootCaT* interface integrated in the *Sketch Engine* and following the procedure outlined in task 3.6.3 in relation to the stand-alone *BootCaT* graphical interface. For ease of access, a copy of a comparable English-Italian corpus on Retinopathy is available on the DVD. The corpus consists of two files, *ret_en.txt* and *ret_it.txt*, each of about 90,000 words.

To create a new corpus from scratch, click on *WebBootCat* on the left hand side menu. To annotate and compile an existing plain text corpus, click on *Create corpus*.

4. If you clicked on *Create corpus*, provide a corpus ID, name and language in the first step, then leave default options in the following steps concerning the selection of a tagging scheme (configuration template) and phrase-level rules (sketch grammar). Once you have provided the general settings for the corpus, click on *Upload file*, and upload the English corpus file from your computer. After the file has been uploaded, click on *Compile corpus*.

If you clicked on *WebBootCaT*, the procedure described is integrated in the *BootCaT* procedure (see task 3.6.3).

5. Once your English (sub)corpus is compiled, upload or create a comparable (sub)corpus in another language following the procedure just described.

6. For each subcorpus produce and compare the word sketches of two related words, for example the homographs *glaucoma* in the English-Italian bilingual comparable corpus on Retinopathy.

5.5 Further reading and software

Corpus-based studies textbooks usually contain an introduction to basic corpus processing tools (e.g. Bowker and Pearson 2002, Hunston 2002). A more detailed presentation can be found in Geoff Barnbrook's *Language and Computers* (1996). Sinclair's classic *Corpus, Concordance, Collocation* (1991) and the more pedagogically oriented *Reading Concordances* (2003) are excellent introductions to the analysis of concordances, while *The BNC Handbook* (Aston and Burnard 1998) provides clear and detailed guidelines for the exploration of annotated corpora. McEnery *et al.* (2006) contains an introduction to statistical tests and measures, while Oakes (1998) is a more in-depth treatment of statistics for corpus linguistics. For an extensive discussion of semantic prosody see Dominic Stewart's *Semantic Prosody: A Critical Evaluation* (2010).

Most software programs cited in this Chapter provide extensive documentation, including comprehensive instruction manuals and online help, which often contain useful examples (see for instance Mike Scott's excellent *WordSmith Tools'* help site). Software authors or publishers usually also provide bibliographic information concerning research conducted using the software distributed through the site.

Various pages devoted to listing corpus tools and resources are available on the Web, see for instance 'Corpora and Corpus Annotation Tools on the WWW' by Markus Dickinson and Detmar Meurers (2002) at http://www.ling.ohio-state.edu/~dickinso/corpus.html, and 'Software, Tools, Frequency Lists, etc.' by David Lee (2010) at http://www.uow.edu.au/~dlee/software.htm. A good place to ask for advice on both hardware and software is the *Corpora List*, which can be joined at http://www.hit.uib.no/corpora/. The entire list can be consulted at http://listserv.linguistlist.org/archives/corpora.html.

Format conversion software

Java XML Converter (JXC), tool for converting XML from one form to another, freeware, at http://jxc.sourceforge.net/.
rtf2xml, converts from Microsoft Word RFT to XML, freeware, at http://rtf2xml.sourceforge.net/.
XSlicer, XML to CSV (Comma-separated values) conversion tool, freeware, at http://xslicer.sourceforge.net/.

XML editors

<Oxygen/> XML editor, commercial software, at http://www.oxygenxml.com/.
Altova XMLSpy®, commercial software, at http://www.altova.com/xml-editor/.
MMax2 - Multi-Modal Annotation in XML, open source annotation tools that allows stand-off annotation, at *http://mmax2.sourceforge.net/.*
Rinzo XML editor, shareware, at http://editorxml.sourceforge.net/m.
XML Copy Editor, shareware, at http://xml-copy-editor.sourceforge.net/.
XML Marker, shareware, at http://download.cnet.com/XML-Marker/3000-7241_4-10202365.html.
XML Pad, shareware, at http://download.cnet.com/XmlPad/3000-7241_4-10252051.html.

Parsers and Taggers

CLAWS – Constituent Likelihood Automatic Word-tagging System, part-of-speech tagger for English, licenses and services available at http://ucrel.lancs.ac.uk/claws/.
TnT, a tool for Statistical Part-Of-Speech Tagging, freeware, at http://www.coli.uni-saarland.de/~thorsten/tnt/.
Tree Tagger, a language independent part-of-speech tagger, freeware, at http://www.ims.uni-stuttgart.de/projekte/corplex/TreeTagger/DecisionTreeTagger.html.

Corpus management and query systems

IMS Open Corpus Workbench (CWB), open source tools for managing and querying large text corpora with linguistic annotations, at http://cwb.sourceforge.net/.
Manetee/Bonito, a corpus manager software tool for a text processing similar to the CWB, at http://www.textforge.cz/products.
MODNLP-tec, open source corpus management suite containing an indexer, a server side application and a client corpus/concordance browser, at http://modnlp.berlios.de/tec-tools.html.
Poliqarp, a free, open source suite of utilities for processing and searching large annotated corpora, at http://poliqarp.sourceforge.net/.
XAIRA – XML Aware Indexing and Retrieval Architecture, open source software package which supports indexing and analysis of large XML corpora, at http://xaira.sourceforge.net/.

Concordancers

AntConc, version 3.2.om (Lawrence Anthony, freeware 2010, at http://www.antlab.sci.waseda.ac.jp/antconc_index.html).

ConcGram, version 1.0 (Chris Greaves, John Benjamins 2009, at http://www.benjamins.com/cgi-bin/t_bookview.cgi?bookid=cls%201).

Concordance, version 3.3 (R. J. C. Watt, commercial software 2010, at http://www.concordancesoftware.co.uk/).

MonoConc Pro, version 2.2 (Mike Barlow, Athelstan 2004, at http://www.athel.com/mono.html).

Multi Language Corpus Tool (*MLCT*) (Scott Piao, freeware 2010, at https://sites.google.com/site/scottpiaosite/software/mlct).

Simple Concordance Program, version 4.0.9 (Alan Reed, freeware 2010, at http://www.textworld.eu/scp/index.html).

TextSTAT, version 2.8 (Matthias Hüning, freeware 2010, at http://neon.niederlandistik.fu-berlin.de/textstat/).

WordSmith Tools, version 5 (Mike Scott, Oxford University Press 1996-2011, at http://www.lexically.net/wordsmith/).

6. Creating multilingual corpora

In the typology of translation-driven corpora presented in Chapter 2, bilingual and multilingual corpora were classified as either comparable or parallel. However, the terminology used is somewhat contradictory and overlapping, and the difference between the two types is not always clear-cut. Some scholars use the term 'parallel texts' to refer to texts originally composed in the respective languages in "comparable situations" (Snell-Hornby 2006:127, see also Schäffner 1998:84), for instance collections of laws in French and Danish (Dyrberg and Tournay 1990), public signs from various English- and German-speaking countries (Snell-Hornby 1988), or English and German party political texts (Laffling 1992). Research using parallel corpora builds on the tradition of studying parallel texts but, as argued by Olohan (2004:33), "the advantage offered by an electronic corpus and corpus tools [over parallel texts on paper] ... is in locating and counting instances for analysis... [and] once held electronically, [parallel] texts could be used for an almost unlimited number of studies and analyses".

Laffling (1992:20) uses the term "globally parallel corpora", to define collections of "texts which, though composed independently in the respective language communities, have the same communicative function" (*ibid.*). These corpora are "typically unrelated except by the analyst's recognition that the original circumstances that led to the creation of the two [sets of] texts have produced accidental similarities" (Hartmann 1980:38). Bi- or multi-lingual corpora whose features are compared on the basis of an assumed production similarity are, however, more commonly referred to as 'comparable corpora', as opposed to 'parallel corpora', which are instead defined as collections of "texts which translate one another" (Leech and Fligelstone 1992:124). This second type of corpora has also been called 'translation corpora' (e.g. Granger 1996:38, Johansson 1998:4) but, to further complicate the matter, not all corpora which are called 'parallel' as opposed to 'comparable' do in fact contain source texts and their translations, as will be discussed below.

In order to bring some clarity, it may be useful to distinguish between two different issues, each of which does not presuppose a binary but rather a gradable opposition: on the one hand, two (or more) subcorpora in different languages may be taken to have different degrees of comparability, going from a rather loose and general similarity of content to more stringent requirements. On the other hand, the term 'parallel corpora' may be taken to refer to similarity of structure rather than of content, meaning that two (or more) subcorpora in different languages may be 'aligned' together as a series of bi-textual translation units. Parallel corpora may also exhibit various degrees of 'parallelism', going from correspondence at the level of text pairs to correspondence at the level of words.

This chapter focuses on the creation of multilingual corpora, and in particular on the issues involved in the acquisition and alignment of parallel corpora, while Chapter 7 focuses on tools and techniques for their analysis. As a multilingual corpus may show quite intricate relationships among its subcorpora as more languages are added, all examples in this chapter concern bilingual corpora. However, the issues discussed can be extended to corpora involving more than two languages.

6.1 Corpus acquisition

As with monolingual corpora, the different stages involved in the creation of multilingual corpora go from corpus design and acquisition to corpus encoding, annotation and indexing. A number of additional issues are involved in the creation of multilingual corpora. These include the availability of texts to be included and the alignment of text pairs in parallel corpora.

6.1.1 Comparable corpora

The scope and size of comparable corpora may vary considerably. According to McEnery *et al.* (2006:49), comparability between two subcorpora in different languages is ensured by similarity of "sampling techniques" and "balance and representativeness", and applies both to large, reference corpora and smaller, specialized corpora. So, "as the Korean National Corpus, the Chinese National Corpus ... and the Polish National Corpus have adopted a sampling frame quite similar to that of the *BNC* ... these corpora can form a balanced comparable corpus" (*ibid.*). In a similar way, the '*WaC*' corpus series (Baroni *et al.* 2009, Ferraresi *et al.* 2010) can be said to contain comparable corpora in different languages (British English, Italian, German, French, etc.) in as much as these corpora were created using the same procedure for different languages, that is by using the *BootCaT* system to harvest Internet texts containing tuples generated from middle frequency range words for all languages. Large monolingual corpora created according to similar design criteria can be defined as 'globally comparable', and can serve as useful reference resources for comparing languages at a general level. At the other end of the spectrum we find specialized comparable corpora, in which comparability is established on the basis of more fine-grained sampling criteria, including not only a loosely defined similarity of content and communicative function, but also aspects such as medium, text type, authorship, language and publication date (see Chapter 3).[1]

Large 'representative' monolingual corpora in different languages may also function as sources from which to extract material for smaller but more focused comparable corpora. Thus, for instance, in order to create a comparable corpus of English and Chinese newspaper texts one could select newspaper texts from the written component of the *BNC* and combine them with the corresponding newspaper component from the *Chinese National Corpus*. Large 'balanced and

[1] In this sense then, corpora containing translations and their source texts could also be considered a specific type of comparable corpora comprising texts which, while not being both the result of 'original' production in both languages, are very similar along all or most other criteria.

representative' general monolingual corpora compiled according to similar sampling criteria are however only available for a few languages, and even fewer are created according to the same sampling framework – in fact, the *BNC* seems to stand unchallenged as a model of 'national corpus'. Furthermore, even when 'globally' comparable source monolingual corpora are available, it may be difficult to extract comparable subcorpora from them since increasing delicacy in categorization criteria as far as comparability is concerned may conflict with criteria for representativeness (see discussion in Chapter 3).

Other sources of potentially comparable multilingual data include collections of texts from multilingual news reporting agencies like AFP, Xinhua, Al-Jazeera and the BBC, and from commercial language resource repositories such as the Linguistic Data Consortium (LDC) and the European Language Resources Association (ELRA). Perhaps the most easily accessible source of multilingual comparable corpora is the multilingual Wikipedia, since its contents are in the common domain and are freely distributed as XML text file dumps by the Wikipedia Foundation itself.[2] Wikipedia is currently being explored as a source of multilingual corpora (e.g. Fissaha Adafre and de Rijke 2006, Gamallo Otero and González López 2010, Bernardini and Ferraresi forthcoming). Such corpora have already been created and are available in some languages as part of the INEX project[3] (Denoyer and Gallinari 2006).

Wikipedia corpora are an interesting case of 'comparable-cum-parallel' corpora, as the difference between comparable and parallel corpora becomes fuzzy when considering hybrid texts where translation as a production mode blurs with 'original' writing. In fact, while some Wikipedia articles are created anew, others are translations of 'parallel' articles in another language, and more often than not they are the result of a combination of production modes and authors. Thus, an entry may initially start as a translation of a corresponding entry in another language, but then the content is independently developed through collaborative and interactive writing. A bilingual corpus consisting of pairs of Wikipedia articles dealing with the 'same' entries in different languages (i.e. cross-linked articles) can be seen as a rather specialized comparable corpus, since it contains texts which are usually very similar in terms of medium, text type, topic, etc. It can also be seen as a parallel corpus containing the same number of texts in two languages, though no clear correspondence may be detectable below the level of whole texts, between units such as blocks, paragraphs and sentences – each of which may or may not consist of translated text.

Large comparable corpora such as those just described are mostly created and used for NLP-related tasks such as text classification, clustering, information retrieval, multimedia retrieval and machine translation. For instance, Pekar *et al.* (2006) use newspaper texts in 5 languages (the *Wall Street Journal* (1987-89) for English, *Le Monde* (1994-96) for French, *Die Tageszeitung* (1987-89 and 1994-98) for German, and *EFE* (1994-95) for Spanish) to extract 'translation equivalents' based on similar distributions of low-frequency words in different language

[2] At http://download.wikipedia.org. Accessed on 20 March 2011.

[3] At http://www-connex.lip6.fr/~denoyer/wikipediaXML/. Accessed on 20 March 2011.

corpora. Kaji and Morimoto (2002) use comparable newspaper corpora in English and Japanese for automatic word sense disambiguation (see § 6.5 below).

As discussed in Chapter 3, both external and internal criteria can be used to create corpora from existing electronic sources. External criteria presuppose the acquisition of texts selected after a survey has been carried out of the textual population to be sampled. Internal criteria rely on the automated retrieval of texts on the basis of linguistic features posited to be representative of a given domain, text type or genre, and text classification can only happen *post-hoc* (see Chapter 3). The automatic creation of comparable corpora is the main focus of the BUCC (Building and Using Comparable Corpora) ongoing series of workshops (Zweigenbaum *et al.* 2008, Fung *et al.* 2009, Rapp *et al.* 2010, Sharoff *et al.* forthcoming), which aims at bringing together researchers in language engineering and linguistics. The interest on the part of the NLP community is chiefly motivated by the scarcity of large parallel corpora beyond a few language pairs and domains, despite the creation of automated methods to collect parallel corpora from the Web (see below). Language engineers have thus turned their attention to comparable corpora as sources of training data for applications such as statistical machine translation or for building or extending bilingual lexicons and terminology databanks.

Topics investigated include ways of creating multilingual corpora in comparable domains from the Web starting from translated wordlists (Kilgarriff 2010a, forthcoming, Sharoff forthcoming), word association measures (Rapp forthcoming), or both linguistic and structural similarities across languages. For example, Goeuriot *et al.* (2009) describe a methodology and a system for the creation of specialized comparable corpora of medical discourse in French and Japanese. They suggest that a Web crawl based on a mix of both structural and linguistic features can generate a pool of highly comparable documents in the two languages, which after further screening can ensure an even higher level of comparability. Structural features consist of implementing pattern matching searches which restrict the range of URLs to, for example, those belonging to universities and hospitals. Linguistic features may consist not only of using as search words specialized 'equivalent' terminology in the two languages, but also of 'pragmatically equivalent' features such as modality markers (e.g. pronouns and politeness forms in French and Japanese).

The manual and semi-automated construction of comparable corpora may be daunting and require intensive work as more user control is exerted over the selection of texts. However, corpus size requirements may be greatly reduced if the aim is to create a specialized corpus of texts belonging to a very specific domain, text type and topic, as is the case with the corpus of Travel Insurance documents in English and Spanish described in Seghiri and Corpas Pastor (2009).

6.1.2 Parallel corpora

In a parallel corpus the relationship between two (or more) subcorpora is established at the level of structural composition. That is to say, a bilingual parallel corpus is a 'bi-text' (Harris 1988) in which segments in one language are directly linked to segments in another language, regardless of mode of production, translation status and directionality. A parallel corpus may contain, for instance, text pairs which are not or are only partially translations of each other, that is, texts which were created or developed independently in each language but which have a common textual or ideational source. For instance, a parallel corpus may contain authoritative multilingual versions of legal texts or closely related text pairs such as promotional literature about industrial products or tourist brochures independently composed or simultaneously formulated in different languages (Hartmann 1988:38 calls them 'adaptations').

Usually each text pair in a parallel corpus can be further subdivided into lower textual unit pairs such as parts, chapters, paragraphs and sentences. Again, even in this case a direct translational relationship does not have to exist between unit pairs, since units in a pair can come from texts translated from a third source text, as is the case with many multilingual EU documents. For instance, the *Europarl* parallel corpus (Koehn 2005) contains many text pairs which are not in fact translations of each other. A text contained in a subcorpus in any given language may be either a transcription of a speech originally delivered in that language or a translation into that language of a speech given in one of the other 10 EU official languages. Thus, each text pair in a given bilingual *Europarl* subcorpus may comprise a source text and its translation, or two texts which are both translations of a third text produced in another language.

The creation and alignment of parallel corpora has long been a concern for researchers aiming at creating suitable resources for practical applications such as machine translation, bilingual lexicography retrieval and translation memories. Machine translation research has found in large quantities of parallel corpora a basis to implement a statistical approach which is currently complementing if not superseding the more traditional rule-based approach (Och 2006, Shen 2010). Bilingual and multilingual lexicology has looked into both parallel and comparable corpora as an unprecedented source of data, and translation memory systems have profited from the availability of translation memories compiled from existing parallel corpora. Parallel corpora have also been used in language teaching (e.g. Barlow 2000, Lawson 2001, King 2003), and in corpus-based descriptive studies and translator education research (see Chapter 2).

Existing parallel corpora can be largely divided into two categories. On the one hand there are very substantial parallel corpora, usually derived from multilingual texts created within institutions or private companies. The largest parallel corpus available is possibly the multilingual parallel corpus of the *Acquis Communautaire* (JRC-Acquis), comprising the total body of European Union law and consisting of texts in 22 languages totalling over one billion words and 231 language pairs (Steinberger *et al.* 2006). Hansard proceedings, i.e. the transcriptions of parliamentary debates, are also a source of parallel corpora. Besides the already mentioned *Europarl* corpus, containing the proceeding of the European Parliament from 1996 to 2009, other Hansard corpora include the Canadian French-English parallel corpus (Roukos *et al.* 1995), the English-Inuktitut parallel corpus created from the Canadian territorial Legislative Assembly of Nunavut (Martin *et al.* 2003), and the Hong-Kong English-Chinese parallel corpus (Ma

2000). These and other parallel corpus resources such as localized versions of software manuals have been heavily exploited as a testbed for cross-lingual information retrieval and machine translation applications, while their use in descriptive translation studies and language learning is less documented.

Given the scarcity of easily available sources of parallel corpora beyond a few domains and text types, researchers have turned their attention to the Web in an attempt to devise automatic or semi-automatic procedures to harvest parallel text. For instance, Resnik and Smith (2003) describe the STRAND system for mining pairs of parallel texts from the Web. The system is based on the observation that translated Web pages tend to exhibit a structure similar to that of parallel source texts, thus permitting their identification even without looking at their content. Thus, using strategies such as pattern matching (i.e. rules that generate pairs of URLs which may point to parallel documents) and document length statistics, it is possible to locate pages that might be translations of each other, and then filter out document pairs whose page structures diverge too much. Databases of URL pairs acquired by STRAND for five language pairs (English and one of Chinese, Japanese, Arabic, Basque and French) are available from Philip Resnik's website.[4] Similar methods are applied by Shi *et al.* (2006) for Chinese and English, and by Utiyama *et al.* (2009), who attempt to derive parallel texts from pages containing mixed-language text for English and Japanese.

A second type of parallel corpora consists of 'belletristic' material, belonging either to fictional and non-fictional genres, or to both. These corpora, which are typically created and used for studies of language or translation, are often manually built and may range in size from a single book and its translation to text collections totalling a few million words. Examples include the heavily annotated *Multext-East "1984"* corpus, i.e. the novel by George Orwell in English and its translations in six Eastern European languages (Erjavec 2010), parallel versions of the Bible in many languages[5], the parallel corpus of texts in Slavic and other languages called *ParaSol* (von Waldenfels 2006), the already mentioned *COMPARA* bilingual parallel corpus and the *OSLO multilingual parallel corpus* (see Chapter 2 and Chapter 7).

Some projects, such as the *ENPC*, have created their own software applications for building and using parallel corpora (see §6.2.2 and §7.2), while others have largely relied on freely available or commercial tools. The rest of this chapter will focus on tools and techniques for the alignment of parallel corpora, while Chapter 7 will consider tools and techniques for their analysis. Translation memories, which can also be seen as a special kind of parallel corpus, are briefly discussed in §6.4.

6.2 Alignment

While a number of investigations can be carried out using non-aligned parallel corpora (e.g. Kenny 2000, Zanettin 2001b), parallel corpora can best be exploited

---

[4] http://www.umiacs.umd.edu/~resnik/strand/. Accessed on 10 October 2010.

[5] See e.g. http://bible.cc/. Accessed on 10 October 2010.

when accessed through parallel concordancing software which displays paired segments. For this, alignment is a prerequisite.

According to Kraif (2002:273) "[a]lignment consists in finding correspondences, in bilingual parallel corpora, between textual segments that are translation equivalents". Such correspondences hold first between texts, then between shorter segments within texts, in what is called 'translational compositionality' (*ibid.*). Thus alignment involves the parallel segmentation of text pairs "into smaller logical units (paragraphs, sentences, phrases) in such a way that the nth segment of source text and the nth segment of target text are mutual translations" (Kraif 2002:275). It ultimately consists in creating a bi-textual map of anchor points referring to "precise locations in the source and the target text that denote portions of text corresponding to one another" (Kraif *ibid.*). More specifically, alignment is usually understood to hold between 'sentences'.

What exactly is a sentence from a theoretical as well as a practical and computational point of view is of course one of the problems of alignment. Before examining how the process of sentence alignment is carried out and what software resources are available, it should be pointed out that the term 'alignment' can also be used to refer to the alignment of incrementally longer segments, up to full text pairs, or of shorter ones, down to the word. Alignment below the level of sentence, including 'alignment' of phrases or other groups of words in bilingual comparable corpora will be dealt with in § 6.5.

6.2.1 *Paragraphs and sentences*

Parallel text pairs can in principle be aligned using one of the available alignment programs or utilities. In order to ensure successful results, however, parallel texts may have to be pre-processed, since some "alignment programs ... assume that source texts and translations have the same number of paragraphs and preferably the same number of sentences" (Bowker and Pearson 2002:96).

Some text types are better suited to automatic alignment than others. Typically, parallel collections of technical, legal or otherwise official documents such as transcriptions of parliamentary proceedings, especially in related languages, are, in this respect, much better material than journalistic and fictional texts. While the former usually present the same formal structure and contain the same number of paragraphs and sentences as well as fixed and standard punctuation, the latter often score low on these features. For instance, translated versions of newspaper articles may omit one or more paragraphs, while a translated novel may also contain additional paragraphs in the form of translator's notes. Thus, literary texts are often difficult to align and according to Mikhail Mikhailov (2002:87), "paragraphs and larger text units are the only elements of formal text structure which can be used for comparing literary parallel texts".

Manual alignment at paragraph level is thus often a prerequisite for further processing, since misalignment at paragraph level will result in misalignment at lower levels. Frankenberg-Garcia *et al.* (2008) detail the procedure used for the alignment of the *COMPARA* parallel corpus of literary texts. They explain how paragraph markup was manually inserted using a word processor, following the paragraph divisions in the source texts, then how paragraph breaks were either removed or inserted into translations to obtain the same number of paragraphs in text pairs. In some cases entire paragraphs were either absent from or added to translated texts. This led to the decision to remove from the corpus the corresponding paragraphs from either the source texts or the translations. Frankenberg-Garcia *et al.* (2008:online) argue that this procedure, which precludes the study of paragraph omissions in translated texts, "does not compromise the spirit in which the corpus was created, since the basic alignment unit of *COMPARA* is the sentence and not entire texts". Certainly this choice, while not being the only possible one, allows for smoother alignment at sentence level.

Below the paragraph, alignment is usually carried out using punctuation marks as sentence delimiters. Again, this is not always a straightforward procedure, at least as far as most fictional texts are concerned. For example, the two paragraphs below, the first taken from an English novel (*Shame*, by Salman Rushdie) and the second from its Italian published translation (*Vergogna*, by Ettore Capriolo) could be broken up in different ways.

1) 'A jewel,' he said, honking into a handkerchief, 'Sir and Madam, your daughter is a jewel. I am humbled, absolutely. Darn humbled. She has proved to me that a golden voice is preferable even to golden teeth.'
2) «Un gioiello», disse, strombettando nel suo fazzoletto. «Signore, signora, vostra figlia è un gioiello. Sono mortificato. Assolutamente mortificato. Mi ha dimostrato che una voce d'oro è preferibile persino ai denti d'oro».

Because of different punctuation conventions in the rendering of direct speech in English and Italian, the translated text appears to contain 5 sentences, while the source text only 4 (Table 6.1).

1. 'A jewel,' he said, honking into a handkerchief, 'Sir and Madam, your daughter is a jewel. 2. I am humbled, absolutely. 3. Darn humbled. 4. She has proved to me that a golden voice is preferable even to golden teeth.'	1. «Un gioiello», disse, strombettando nel suo fazzoletto. 2. «Signore, signora, vostra figlia è un gioiello. 3. Sono mortificato. 4. Assolutamente mortificato. 5. Mi ha dimostrato che una voce d'oro è preferibile persino ai denti d'oro».

Table 6.1. Segmentation into sentences

This, at least, is the kind of segmentation which can be expected from the automatic alignment of the two paragraphs based on punctuation marks, without considering the different devices used in the two languages to signal the start and end of direct speech. The segmentation of the paragraph is also problematic from a syntactic point of view since it can be noted that the third 'sentence' in the English source text hardly meets the traditional requirements of a sentence, that of consisting of a subject and a predicate (Wales 1989:418).

In order to have the same number of textual segments in both source and target texts, two options are available. The first option consists in joining the first two Italian sentences, in order to reproduce the segmentation of the English text (Table 6.2).

1. 'A jewel,' he said, honking into a handkerchief, 'Sir and Madam, your daughter is a jewel. 2. I am humbled, absolutely. 3. Darn humbled. 4. She has proved to me that a golden voice is preferable even to golden teeth.'	1. «Un gioiello», disse, strombettando nel suo fazzoletto. «Signore, signora, vostra figlia è un gioiello. 2. Sono mortificato. 3. Assolutamente mortificato. 4, Mi ha dimostrato che una voce d'oro è preferibile persino ai denti d'oro».

Table 6.2. Joining two Italian sentences

The second option consists in splitting the first English sentence into two smaller segments, in order to reproduce the segmentation of the Italian text. As can be seen in Table 6.3, the second and third 'sentence' of the original English text (as well as the corresponding Italian ones) have also been joined together as one unit, in order to avoid very short paired segments (for this type of approach to segmentation, see Simon and Osenova 2004).

1. 'A jewel,' he said, honking into a handkerchief, 2. 'Sir and Madam, your daughter is a jewel. 3. I am humbled, absolutely. Darn humbled. 4. She has proved to me that a golden voice is preferable even to golden teeth.'	1. «Un gioiello», disse, strombettando nel suo fazzoletto. 2. «Signore, signora, vostra figlia è un gioiello. 3. Sono mortificato. Assolutamente mortificato. 4. Mi ha dimostrato che una voce d'oro è preferibile persino ai denti d'oro».

Table 6.3. Splitting one English sentence

Whatever the solution adopted, it is clear that aligned segments, or 'S-units', do not necessarily coincide with sentences, however these are defined.

Given the often ambiguous use of punctuation marks and the fact that 'S-units' may or may not correspond to 'sentences', different types of correspondence between source and target S-units may be found in an aligned parallel corpus.

- One-to-one correspondences (1-1), which generally make up in the majority of cases;
- One-to-zero correspondence (1-0), when an S-unit in the source text is omitted in translation;
- Zero-to-one correspondence (0-1), when an S-unit is present in the translation but not in the source text;
- One-to-many correspondence (1-n), when one S-unit in the source text is translated with two or more S-units in the target text;
- Many-to-one correspondence (n-1), when two or more S-units in the source text have been condensed in one S-unit in the translation;
- Two-to-three correspondence (2-3), when two S-units in the source text correspond to three S-units in the translation, none of which exactly corresponds to a single S-unit in the source text;
- Three-to-two correspondence (3-2), when three S-units in the source text correspond to two S-units in the translation, none of which exactly corresponds to a single S-unit in the source text;
- Other combinations (3-4, 4-3, etc.) are also possible, though relatively rare.

In the *COMPARA* corpus, paragraph alignment was followed by sentence alignment, which was first carried out automatically using an alignment program (see §6.2.2), and then manually checked and revised with the help of a word processor. The output of automatic alignment was edited to obtain alignment units in which each sentence in the source text was aligned with the corresponding segment in the translation, containing either one, more than one or only part of a sentence. Sentences that had not been translated were aligned with empty units, while sentences added to a translation without any corresponding segment in the source text were "marked <add> and fitted into the immediately preceding alignment unit" (Frankenberg-Garcia *et al.* 2008:online).

6.2.2 Approaches and tools

A first approach to the alignment of parallel corpora consists in creating a bitext in which each S-unit from the source text is followed by a corresponding S-unit in the target text, thus creating a new bilingual document consisting of interspersed S-units. This is the approach adopted by *WordSmith Tools' Viewer and Aligner* utility (Figure 6.1).

After two or more files in different languages have been loaded into the program, the utility splits each file into 'sentences'. The following definition of sentence is provided by *WordSmith Tools'* Online Help (Scott 2010):

> A sentence ends if a full-stop, question-mark or exclamation-mark (.?!) is immediately followed by one or more word separators and if the next non-punctuation symbol is a capital letter A..Z or an accented capital letter, a number or a currency symbol.

This type of segmentation will only work if source and target texts contain the same number of 'sentences', since the first non one-to-one correspondence

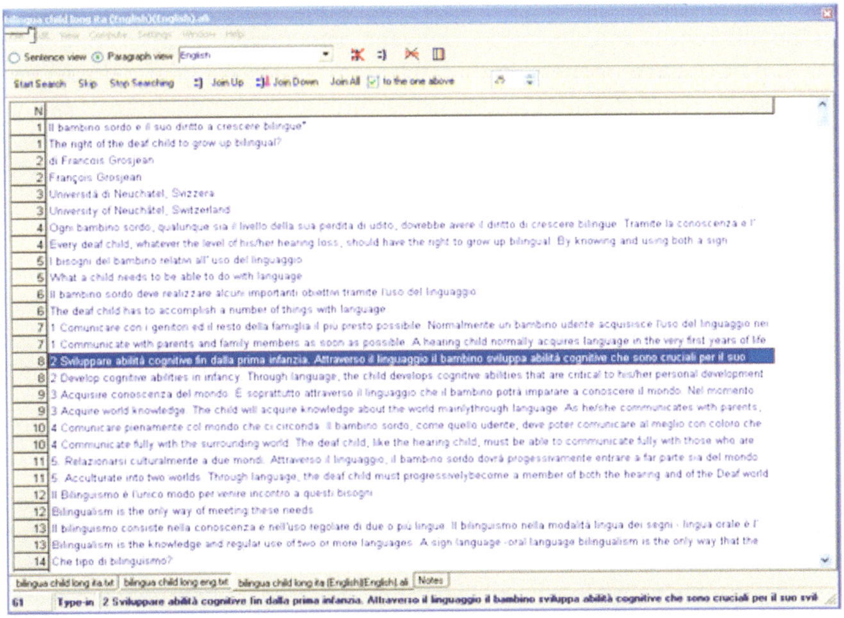

Figure 6.1. WordSmith Tools' Viewer and Aligner

will cause the rest of the alignment to go wrong. *WordSmith Tools' Viewer and Aligner* utility allows the user to edit the bilingual file by manually splitting or joining sentences after automatic segmentation and alignment, but this process is clearly rather impracticable if a large quantity of parallel texts are involved. Researchers in computational linguistics have however developed a number of more refined alignment techniques, which have resulted in the creation of both very large aligned parallel corpora and more reliable alignment tools.

Alignment methodologies belong usually to one of two types, those based on length and those based on content. Length-based alignment relies on the computation of the number of characters, words and sentences in text pairs and their interrelation through statistical techniques. At the beginning of the 1990s William Gale and Kenneth Church (1993:78) devised a method and a program (*align*) for aligning sentences based on a simple statistical model of character lengths. The program uses the fact that longer sentences in one language tend to be translated into longer sentences in the other language, and that shorter sentences tend to be translated into shorter sentences. A probabilistic score is assigned to each proposed correspondence of sentences, based on the scaled difference of lengths of the two sentences (in characters) and the variance of this difference. This probabilistic score is used in a dynamic programming framework to find the maximum likelihood alignment of sentences. Similar methods were developed in the same years by other researchers, for instance a statistical model based on word length rather than character length is described in Brown *et al.* (1991).

A second type of approach is based on 'types' rather than on 'tokens', i.e. on the differences and similarities between pairs or sets of words rather than on word or character counts. In this approach a bi-textual map is drawn up by reference to 'anchor points', established through a corpus-external bilingual dictionary or lexicon and/or the identification of 'cognate' words. These are words which display a formal measure of resemblance, for instance words which share a certain number of characters in the same or similar sequence (i.e. in word initial position), as well as numbers and symbols (Simard *et al.* 1992). One specific type of anchor point is structural markup in annotated corpora. Romary and Bonhomme (2000), for instance, explain how to take advantage of structural annotation in corpora annotated according to TEI/CES guidelines.

While the Gale and Church (1993) algorithm as well as methods based on formal similarities (e.g. cognate words) seem to perform well with corpora in closely related language pairs and for 'well-behaved' texts, that is texts where most alignments are 1-1, problems arise with distant language pairs such as Chinese, Arabic and European languages and more in general with translated texts which contain many omitted or inserted segments compared to the source texts. Alternative techniques for alignment have thus been developed especially for dealing with 'noisy' text pairs. Fung and McKeown (1994) suggest a method based on 'positional difference vectors', that is, correspondences between a word and its translated counterpart in frequency position and recency (the interval between occurrences). The authors propose to derive alignment from a set of anchor points, a small 'lexicon' created by matching word pairs on the basis of a 'Dynamic K vector' (DK-vec) algorithm. This is "based on the assumption that if two words are translations of each other, they are more likely to occur in the same segments than two words which are not" (Fung and McKeown 1994:82). The alignment procedure uses frequency, position and recency information as features for pattern matching.

One of the first implementations of the Gale and Church (1993) algorithm was the *Vanilla aligner* (Danielsson and Ridings 1997), a series of simple tools which perform automatic sentence alignment. The *Vanilla aligner*, which operates in a Unix environment, requires two input files in plain text, one for each language, containing only one word per line. The output of the alignment process is a file consisting of a series of three lines, the first of which provides information about the relationship between the units, followed by one line of text for each language. The aligner is limited to 1-1, 0-1, 1-0, 2-1, 1-2 and 2-2 correspondences and fails in some cases of 1-0 or 0-1 alignments. The authors report a success rate of over 95%, and indicate that some partially automated proofreading is required at the end of the alignment process. A GUI (Graphical User Interface) is provided as a front end to display the alignment. A Unix based front end for the *Vanilla aligner* is also included in the *NATools* workbench for parallel corpora processing (Simões and Almeida 2003). The *Vanilla aligner* has been used to process, among others, the *JRC-Acquis Multilingual corpus*. The Gale and Church algorithm is also implemented in most alignment programs, including *EasyAlign 1.0*, the aligner incorporated in the *CWB* system (see Chapter 5) which was used, among others, for the automatic alignment of the *COMPARA* corpus.

The *Champollion Tool Kit* (*CTK*) is a freely available "lexicon-based parallel text sentence aligner" (Ma 2006:online) distributed as source code written in the programming language Perl. The toolkit, which aims to provide "ready-to-use parallel text sentence alignment tools for as many language pairs as possible" (*ibid.*) was specifically designed for aligning noisy parallel texts. It was tested on an English-Chinese parallel corpus, relying on a bilingual lexicon "created by combining a few bilingual English – Chinese dictionaries collected from the Internet" (*ibid.*). Content and statistical information are both considered and weighed: lexical matches of less frequent words are considered a strong indication that two segments translate each other, while sentence length information is used to filter out wrong alignments.

Another program which presupposes noise in the input is the *Geometric Mapping and Alignment* (*GMA*) software package. *GMA*, which is also freely distributed as source files written in the programming language Java, was tested on a Unix environment. Like *Champollion*, the system relies on language-specific resources "such as seed translation lexicons and lists of stop words" [6] which are used to generate anchor points, which in turn are used to align sentences (Melamed 1999). A further freely available program is *hunalign* (Varga *et al.* 2007) which uses a mix of content- and length-based methods:

> In the presence of a dictionary, *hunalign* uses it, combining this information with Gale-Church sentence-length information. In the absence of a dictionary, it first falls back to sentence-length information, and then builds an automatic dictionary based on this alignment. Then it realigns the text in a second pass, using the automatic dictionary.[7]

Trushkina *et al.* (2008) suggest that precision in the alignment can considerably improve by combining different aligning methods. They describe how to assist manual verification of the sentence alignment task for the 10 million word *Dutch Parallel Corpus* in Dutch, English and French using automatic control procedures. The output of three different aligning programs was compared, and manual verification was restricted to alignments which were not recognized by at least two aligners. This reduced the percentage of alignments to be verified to 6% of total alignments, and resulted in almost 100% accuracy.

The methodologies and tools described above require considerable computational expertise, which most researchers in descriptive translation studies and translators probably do not possess. Furthermore, while the integration of increasingly more refined alignment methods and procedures can produce very good results even for 'noisy' texts, manual intervention cannot be bypassed completely if the desired outcome is accurate alignment. There is a trade-off between the time and effort needed for manual verification of alignment and

---

[6] Frequently Asked Questions List for GMA, at http://nlp.cs.nyu.edu/GMA/docs/FAQ.list.htm#3.1. Accessed on 12/12/10, last updated on 17 May 2004.

[7] http://mokk.bme.hu/resources/hunalign. Accessed on 10 January 2011.

the shortcomings of imperfect alignment. For large parallel corpora such as those required for machine translation and terminology retrieval purposes, quantity may make up for precision, so that a percentage of wrong alignments may be statistically tolerable. On the other hand, for smaller parallel corpora to be used in descriptive research it may be worthwhile to devote some time to manually checking and correcting wrong alignments, not only with the aim of increasing alignment accuracy, but also because checking alignments can be seen as an important analytical phase, useful to identify and categorize problematic points in translation and the reasons why automatic alignment failed.

Some of the methodologies described have been integrated into programs which researchers should be able to use 'out of the box', though even these programs are not devoid of problems. Alignment programs differ along a number or parameters, including the computational environment in which they operate, the type of approach to alignment adopted, the type of input accepted and the type of output produced. Some alignment applications output a file for each pair of documents containing both L1 and L2 segments in separate columns, possibly together with a third column stating the confidence in the alignment expressed as a percentage. Others output an alignment map, that is a list of coordinates which identify paired segments in external files. Still others offer the choice between a number of different output formats, both as regards the representation of the alignment (as bi-text or as alignment map) and the annotation format (e.g. plain or XML annotated text). It should also be noted that the output of the alignment may need to be further processed to make it compatible with the tools used to analyze the parallel corpus, including parallel concordancing software.

ParaConc Aligner is a Windows-based utility packaged with the *ParaConc* stand-alone parallel concordancer (Barlow 2003) which is based on the Gale and Church (1993) algorithm. It takes as input pairs of texts in either plain text or lightly annotated format[8] and, after the texts have been aligned at paragraph level, it attempts to carry out sentence alignment based on either punctuation or markup. While the program attempts to use markup to perform a first automatic alignment, and can exploit hierarchical annotation to apply alignment recursively to parts, paragraphs and sentences, results are not always consistent. Better results are obtained using texts pre-aligned at the paragraph level, that is, when both texts in a pair contain the same number of end-of-line characters. The user interface (Figure 6.2) allows the user to edit the alignment by splitting and merging segments, or by inserting empty units. The resulting alignment map is saved as a separate file as part of a 'workspace' (Barlow 2003, 2008). When a 'workspace' is opened, both the parallel corpora and the alignment map are retrieved.

Another Windows-based program is *Alinea* (Kraif 2001, Kraif and Chen 2004), which uses a mix of different methods and can carry out the alignment in three steps. First, it extracts anchor points relying on chains of identical words such

[8] The current version (March 2011) of the program is not XML compliant, but it can handle some types of markup, such as SGML and HTML tags, to some extent (Barlow 2008:73-77).

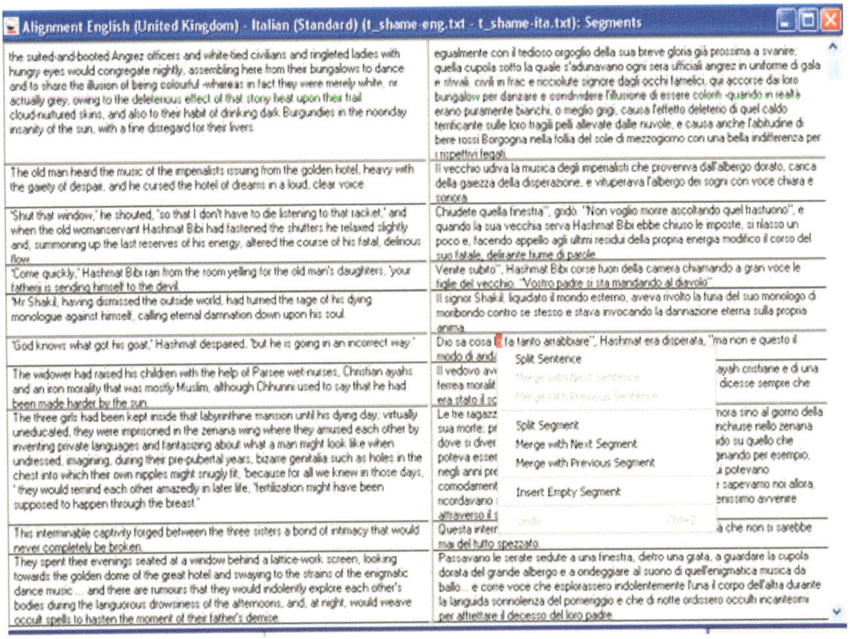

Figure 6.2. ParaConc Aligner

as numbers and proper names, and optionally, cognate words. Then it proceeds to compute alignment pairs using a combination of approaches to automatic alignment such as Gale and Church (1993) and Simard *at al.* (1992), and extracts a sequence of correspondences between sentences (1-1, 1-0, etc.). Finally, the system can extract word-to-word correspondences (see §6.5), though in order to perform this step a large number of parallel texts is required to compute reliable statistics. Figure 6.3 shows the interface used to set the various parameters concerning the three steps, while Figure 6.4 shows the interface which can be used for manually editing the output as well as for searching and browsing parallel concordances.

Alinea can use both plain and XML annotated text files (in XCES format) as input and it can output aligned files in plain text, XCES format and HTML, as well as KWIC concordances in plain text. Though the program does not rely on language-specific knowledge, its performance can be improved by using optional parameters such as 'stop lists' for function words and false friends, which are provided for some language pairs. *Alinea* is freely distributed for research purposes, and it is claimed that the program can obtain more than 90% precision and recall on a corpus of literary texts (Kraif and Chen 2004). Both *ParaConc Aligner* and *Alinea* will be used in the Tasks section of this chapter.

The *Translation Corpus Align* (*TCA*) is a custom-built application which was created to align the *English Norwegian Parallel Corpus* (Hofland and Johansson 1998). It was based on anchor words from a bilingual dictionary, proper names, numbers and words that are similar in texts pairs. A new version of the program,

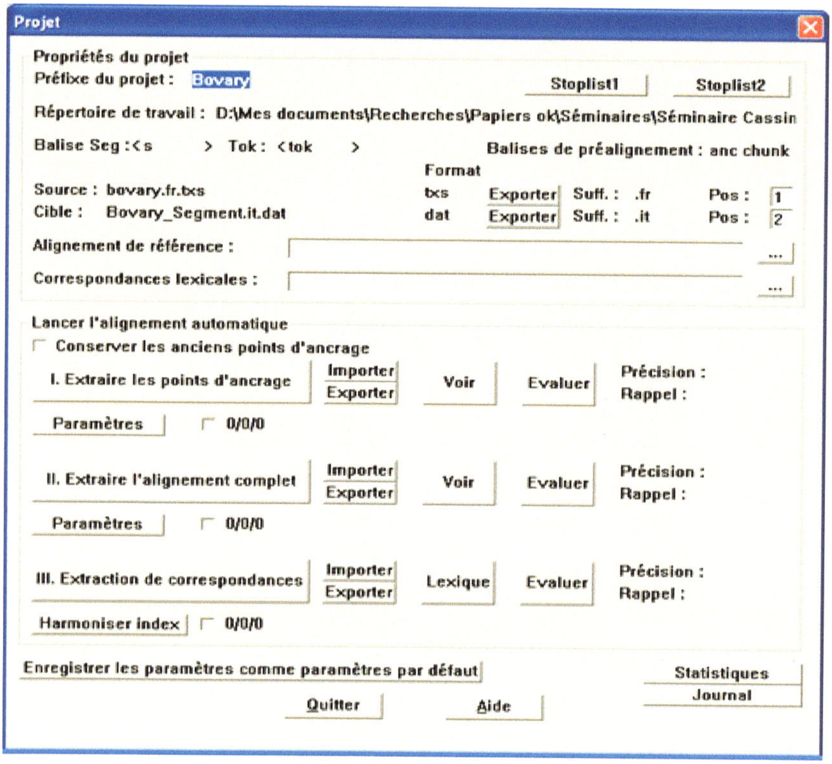

Figure 6.3. Alinea *project settings*

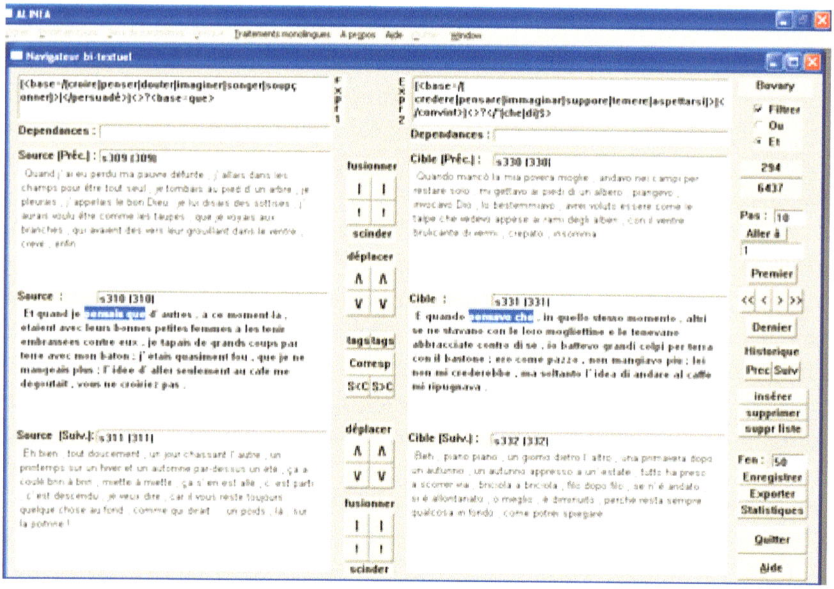

Figure 6.4. Alinea *user interface*

TCA2[9], is being developed in order to provide a user-friendly interface, which is planned to be available online, for building searchable collections of parallel texts also for other language pairs. The new version of the *Translation Corpus Align* will not be based solely on 'content', that is on 'anchor words', but also on statistical measures such as sentence length (Gale and Church 1993) and 'dynamic time warping', a word matching algorithm which measures similarity between words on the basis of their positions in a text pair (Fung and McKeown 1994). The program is planned to support XML. It uses as input text pairs encoded according to TEI/CES guidelines, and contains an integrated module for interactive control of the output. It is foreseen that the program will be able to save the output of the alignment in different formats, i.e. in XML, in a plain text format suitable for use with programs such as *ParaConc*, in HTML or in the 'vertical' format used by the *CWB*. The interface of a prototype version of *TCA2* is shown in Figure 6.5.

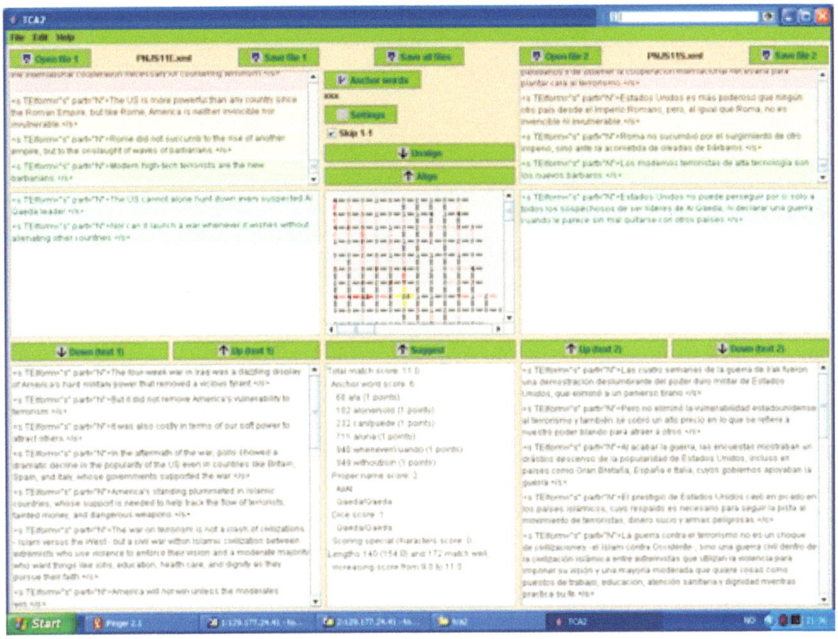

Figure 6.5. TCA2 *graphical interface*

Finally, the *Interactive Sentence Alignment* (ISA, see Figure 6.6) is an online Web-based alignment interface (Tiedemann 2006) which includes alignment visualization and editing tools for manual editing of parallel texts previously aligned using a combination of techniques and tools. It first performs automatic alignment using the length-based Gale and Church (1993) approach to sentence alignment, with the addition of a 'cognate recognition' algorithm. The online interface is then used to correct and improve the quality of the alignment by

[9] http://gandalf.aksis.uib.no/tca2. Accessed on 15 December 2010.

manually splitting and merging existing segments. The *ISA* interface, which takes as input parallel XML documents and is based on the *Uplug* system, has been used to manually improve the alignment of the *Swedish-Turkish Parallel Corpus* (Megyesi and Dahlqvist 2007, Megyesi *et al.* 2008).

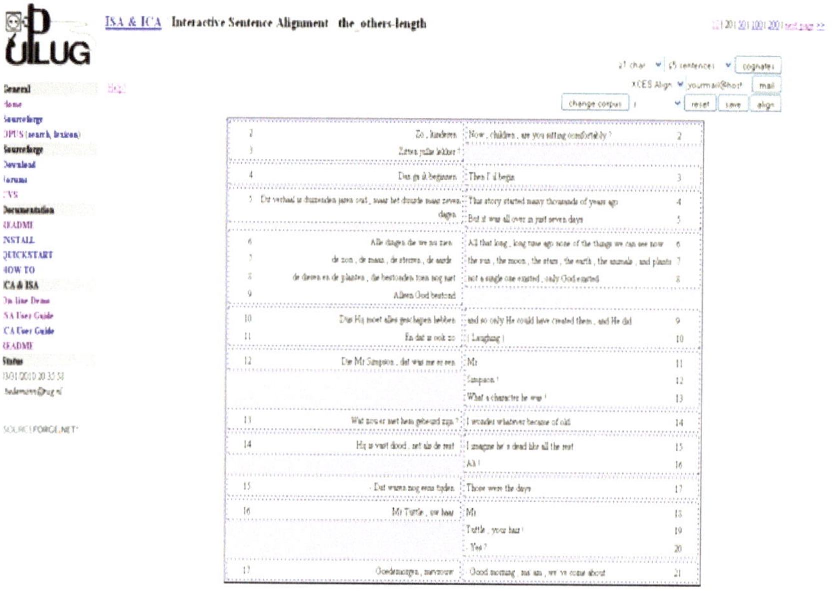

Figure 6.6. ISA *online demo interface*

To sum up, alignment programs can be based on length (using character or sentence length, distance between words, or frequency information), content (using anchor points such as formally similar words, a bilingual lexicon, or words which show similar patterns of behaviour across languages), or a combination of these. Length-based methods are language independent, while content-based methods tend to be specific to language pairs. Algorithms for automatic alignment were developed by researchers from the natural language processing community usually working in a Unix environment, but are being integrated in end user applications working in a Windows or system independent environment. None of these programs can guarantee a perfect alignment, so that manual intervention is required.

6.3 Case study: the OPUS corpus

This section provides details about the alignment of the *OPUS* corpus[10], which is an open source collection of several multilingual parallel corpora, including the

[10] http://www.let.rug.nl/~tiedeman/OPUS/. Accessed on 15 February 2011.

Europarl corpus, a corpus of film subtitles, several corpora of localized software documentation, and the *Emea* corpus of documents related to medical products in the 22 official languages of the European Union. *OPUS* is constantly growing as more openly distributed corpora are added to the collection, converted into XCES format and made available through an online query interface.

The *OPUS* project provides not only a publicly available parallel corpus, but also a collection of open source tools, since all the software applications used to create the *OPUS* corpus are integrated into the *Uplug* open source collection of NLP tools. *Uplug* is structured as a modular system which includes, among others, a series of Unix scripts used to convert the corpora collected from the Web into XML format, applications for tokenization, sentence-splitting, sentence and word alignment, indexing, and Web search interfaces, many of which have been discussed in Chapter 5, and two interfaces for interactive alignment of sentences and words, *ISA* (described in the previous section) and *ICA* (*Interactive Clue Alignment*). All the applications included in *Uplug* are either available in the open domain or they were specifically created within the project and integrated within the workflow.

The application used to align the corpora at sentence level was an aligner based on the Gale and Church (1993) algorithm and *hunalign* (Varga *et al.* 2005). The output of the alignment is saved as a set of XML files in XCES format, which include 'cesAna' files, alignment maps pointing to correspondences between sentences in file pairs. The fragment below is taken from the alignment map for a text pair, the two files given as values of the attributes <fromDoc> and <toDoc> respectively, of the <linkGrp> root element which contains the English and Italian transcriptions of a session from the European Parliament proceedings, respectively.

```
<?xml version=”1.0” encoding=”utf-8”?>
<!DOCTYPE cesAlign PUBLIC “-//CES//DTD XML cesAlign//EN” “”>
<cesAlign version=”1.0”>
<linkGrp targType=”s” fromDoc=”xml/en/ep-00-01-17.xml.gz”
toDoc=”xml/it/ep-00-01-17.xml.gz”>
<link xtargets=”1;1”/>
<link xtargets=”2;2”/>
<link xtargets=”3;3 4”/>
<link xtargets=”4;5”/>
<link xtargets=”5;6”/>
<link xtargets=”6;7”/>
<!--other link elements here-->
</cesAlign>
```

Each <link> element points to corresponding groupings of sentences, so that every sentence in the English document is linked to one or more sentences in the Italian document, and vice versa. In the example above, the first two sentences in the aligned text pairs have a 1-1 alignment; the third alignment is of the type 1-2, while a 1-1 alignment is resumed in the following three sentences, so that the fourth English sentence is aligned with the fifth Italian sentence, and so on.

The fragment below is taken from the bi-text file generated by the alignment map for the two documents:

```
# xml/en/ep-00-01-17.xml.gz
# xml/it/ep-00-01-17.xml.gz

================================
(src)="1"> Resumption of the session
(trg)="1"> Ripresa della sessione
================================
(src)="2"> I declare resumed the session of the European Parliament adjourned on Friday 17 December 1999 , and I would like once again to wish you a happy new year in the hope that you enjoyed a pleasant festive period .
(trg)="2"> Dichiaro ripresa la sessione del Parlamento europeo , interrotta venerdì 17 dicembre e rinnovo a tutti i miei migliori auguri nella speranza che abbiate trascorso delle buone vacanze .
================================
(src)="3"> Although , as you will have seen , the dreaded 'millennium bug ' failed to materialise , still the people in a number of countries suffered a series of natural disasters that truly were dreadful .
(trg)="3"> Come avrete avuto modo di constatare il grande " baco del millennio " non si è materializzato .
(trg)="4"> Invece , i cittadini di alcuni nostri paesi sono stati colpiti da catastrofi naturali di proporzioni davvero terribili .
================================
(src)="4"> You have requested a debate on this subject in the course of the next few days , during this part-session .
(trg)="5"> Avete chiesto che si tenesse una discussione su tale tema nei prossimi giorni , nel corso della presente tornata .
================================
(src)="5"> In the meantime , I should like to observe a minute ' s silence , as a number of Members have requested , on behalf of all the victims concerned , particularly those of the terrible storms , in the various countries of the European Union .
(trg)="6"> Nel frattempo è mio desiderio , come del resto mi è stato chiesto da alcuni colleghi , osservare un minuto di silenzio in memoria di tutte le vittime delle tempeste che si sono abbattute sui diversi paesi dell ' Unione europea .
================================
(src)="6"> Please rise , then , for this minute ' s silence .
(trg)="7"> Vi invito pertanto ad alzarvi in piedi per osservare appunto un minuto di silenzio .
```

The aligned corpus is then linguistically annotated using other freely available tools, converted into the tabular format used by the *CWB*, and indexed (see Tiedemann 2003a, 2009 for further details). Finally, it is made available for analysis through an online interface, which will be examined in Chapter 7.

The main focus of the *OPUS* project is "to collect parallel documents from various domains and to pre-process them in such a way that they are directly useful for applications such as statistical machine translation and multilingual terminology extraction" (Tiedemann 2009:237). However, the *OPUS* corpus is also possibly the largest collection of parallel corpora freely accessible online to other types of users, such as for example translation researchers, learners and professionals.

As they exist, the *OPUS* parallel corpora are certainly not optimal for descriptive translation research, since no indication is provided about the translation status of the texts and their source language, or about the source language producers, interpreters or translators. Some of this information may however be retrieved from the open source version of the parallel corpora included in the collection, and added to a re-processed version of them (see e.g. Cyrus 2006). As we shall see in Chapter 7, the search interface(s) provided for browsing the corpora do not allow for the manipulation of parallel concordances, nor for the types of data analysis described in Chapter 5. In any case, the *OPUS* project is making available to the research community corpus resources which can be analyzed using different corpus query systems, and provides a model and tools which can be implemented and built on for the creation of parallel corpora designed for translation descriptive and learning/professional purposes.

6.4 Parallel corpora and translation memories

A translation memory, or TM for short, is a database containing paired source text and translation segments, hence it is a type of parallel corpus. What makes TMs different from other types of parallel corpora is the purpose for which they are created and used, and the format in which they are accordingly stored and retrieved. A translation memory is the main asset of a translator's workstation, which is a working environment for professional translators working usually with technical texts (Somers 2003b). A translator's workstation combines a text editor, which can either be an external application or a facility integrated within the system, with a translation memory management system (TMMS), a term base management system (TBMS), and other utilities such as filters for working with various file formats, possibly a Fully Automatic Machine Translation (FAMT) system which can be used to create draft translations, and so on. Translation memories are usually a by-product of the translation process, since they are not provided with a translator's workstation but are created by storing together source and target text segments in the system's 'memory', as new translations are carried out or by aligning sentences from the source and target texts of past translations. In the resulting database each Translation Unit (TU), that is, each aligned text segment pair, is archived together with administrative information, including details about when each unit was created and by whom, in the course of which translation project, etc. When a new source text unit is considered for translation, the system searches the database in order to find identical or similar source text segments in the TM. If an exact or 'fuzzy' match is found, the system retrieves the corresponding target segment, which is proposed as a candidate translation. It is then up to the translator to accept the translation solution proposed by the system as it is, to modify it, or to reject it. The new TU produced by the translator is then stored in the database in order to be considered again for future translations.

Figure 6.7 shows a screenshot of one of the most popular translator's workstations, *SDL Trados Studio* (2009 edition). German translation segments which are found to correspond to English source text segments are displayed along with the text to be translated as candidate translations, together with a number showing the precision of the match as a percentage. Colour coding and other visual aids are used to help translators orient themselves in the rather cluttered display, which includes project management utilities and a term recognition window plugging into a terminological database.

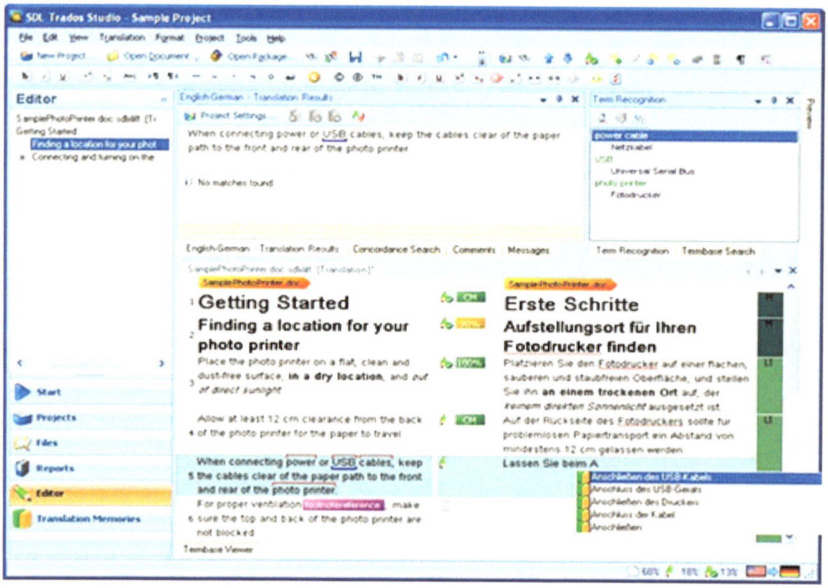

Figure 6.7. SDL Trados Studio 2009 *workstation screenshot*

A translation memory can thus be defined as a bilingual text archive allowing storage of aligned text segments which can be retrieved against various search conditions. It is of course also possible to derive a translation memory from an existing parallel corpus, by aligning text pairs and saving the results of the alignment process in a compatible format. The *Acquis Communautaire* parallel corpus, for instance, is available both in XCES format and as a translation memory in TMX

(Translation Memory eXchange) format. This is an open XML standard developed by the Localization Industry Standards Association (LISA 2005) to allow for the interchange of translation memory data across different tools, translators and translation vendors. Translator's workstations usually also include an alignment utility which first processes input files automatically, often using a mix of length- and anchor-based methods, then allows the user to optimize the output through an alignment editor. Figure 6.8 shows a screenshot of SDL Trados' WinAlign utility, in which adjustments to automatic alignment can be manually made through a graphic editor interface.

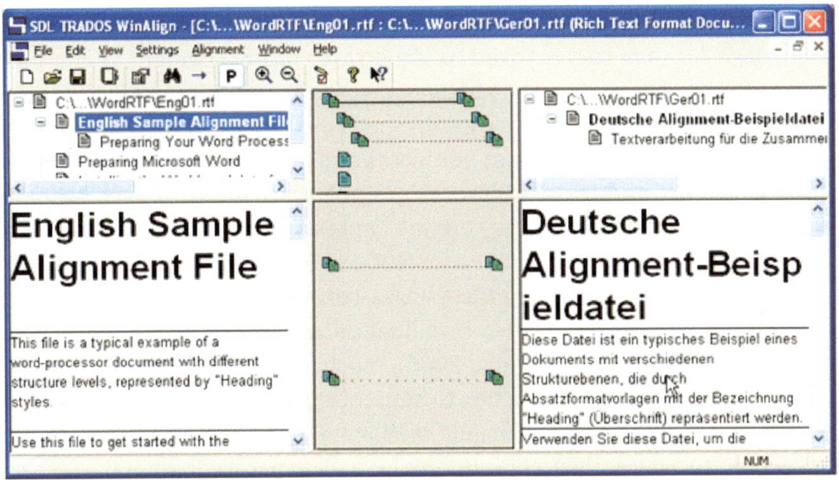

Figure 6.8. SDL Trados Align alignment editor

While many translator's workstations often include a utility for parallel concordancing, there are a number of differences between such tools and stand-alone bilingual concordancers. Bowker and Barlow (2008) describe in some detail what these differences are from the point of view of a translator using them as an aid in the translation process. The main difference is that in translation memories TUs are stored without any relation to the original context, because information about the original sentence order in the text is not preserved. It is thus not possible to expand the length of the texts retrieved as a result of a search beyond a TU. Furthermore, bilingual concordancers allow for more flexible searches: whereas the functionalities of translator's workstations aim at maximum automation, bilingual concordancers provide more control over both what is searched (by allowing for pattern searches) and over how results are displayed (see Chapter 7). However, as the TMX format is being further developed and still new functionalities are added to translator's workstations, it may be that in the future, TMs will not differ from other parallel corpus types, and translator's workstations' concordancing facilities will not differ from those of stand-alone bilingual concordancers.

6.5 Alignment below sentence level

Alignment below sentence level may apply to single words or to groups of words, and can be used to establish bidirectional correspondences between words both in parallel and comparable corpora.

6.5.1 Alignment of comparable corpora

When applied to comparable corpora, alignment means something rather different from what has been discussed so far in relation to parallel corpora. Here the alignment of sentences follows a linear pattern, the first segment of a text in language A in a bi-text is linked to the first (or more) segment(s) of a text in language B. The links established between words or word clusters in the components of a comparable corpus are established solely on the basis of content, and what is aligned are not sentences but words and phrases supposedly equivalent across languages and texts. Sentences are not translations of each other, but are associated in as much as they are the contexts in which linked word/cluster pairs appear.

Links can be the result of processing a corpus through a bilingual lexicon (Peters and Picchi 1998) often in combination with more statistically oriented techniques (Munteanu and Marcu 2006), much in the same way as techniques used in content-based approaches to sentence alignment. Peters *et al.* (2000) describe how an electronic bilingual dictionary and a morphological analyzer can be used to align comparable corpora (as well as parallel corpora) by creating links (based on Mutual Information scores) between groups of collocate words in the two languages whose individual components are translation equivalents, according to an electronic bilingual dictionary. Other studies have been carried out based on the assumption that the translations of words that are collocationally related in one language are also related (Rapp 1995). For example, Kaji and Morimoto (2002:411) describe a methodology to "extract a collection of statistically significant pairs of related words from each language corpus independently of the other language, and then align the pairs of related words translingually with the assistance of a bilingual dictionary. Pekar *et al.* (2006, 2007) propose to improve the accuracy of retrieval of translation equivalents for rare words using distributional similarity between words in different languages.

Envisaged applications of comparable corpus alignment are usually restricted to statistical machine translation and multilingual terminology retrieval. It is also possible, however, to think of an exploitation of such techniques for translation studies research, depending on the availability of bilingual comparable corpora, bilingual lexicons, and general-purpose programs implementing the statistical algorithms described in the literature. Bilingual concordancing, based on the word alignment techniques described, of comparable corpora, both general and and specialized, could undoubtedly prove to be a useful resource for translation scholars, learners and educators alike.

6.5.2 *Word alignment*

The word is the lowest unit of alignment one finds in parallel corpora. However, with the knowledge that translations hardly consist of the linear one-by-one replacement of individual words from a text in one language into another text in a different language, one may wonder whether alignment at word level is even possible, and if so if it would have useful applications in descriptive translation studies. Kraif (2002) suggests that at the level of the word we should distinguish between lexical correspondence and alignment. The first is "a relation of denotational (conceptual, extra-linguistic) equivalence between two lexical units in the context of two segments that are translation units" (*ibid.*:284), whereas a 'maximal resolution alignment' is "the matching of the smallest possible segments in accordance with the principle of translational compositionality" (*ibid.*:285). So, for example, while the words 'peas' in English and 'pois' in French are lexical equivalents, in the context of 'green peas' and 'petit pois' in an English-French parallel corpus they are not maximally aligned since 'green peas' and 'petit pois' cannot be decomposed. As in sentence alignment, word alignment models are either length- or content-based. Form-based models are based on cognateness, that is, formal resemblance between word pairs which share the same first characters (see §2.2) and association measures at phrase ('cluster') level (see Chapter 5). Length-based approaches compute the mutual information score "in two texts divided in N segments, for two words W1 and W2 occurring in each text in N1 and N2 segments respectively, and co-occurring in N12 segments" (*ibid.*:279).

Research on the extraction of lexical equivalents has been largely based on probabilistic models which make it possible to extract lexical correspondences by comparing the distribution of lexical items in a parallel corpus, and "[w]ord alignment usually includes links between so-called multi-word units (MWUs) in cases where lexical items cannot be split into separated words with appropriate translations in another language" (Tiedemann 2004). A discussion of approaches, methodologies and techniques for word alignment is beyond the scope of this volume. Word alignment is more properly at the centre of debate in statistical and corpus-based machine translation and in multilingual terminology. For the purpose of descriptive studies, whether from a contrastive or translational point of view, automatic means of retrieving parallel concordances in which the alignment is based on 'word' rather than 'sentence' may provide an interesting 'entry point' into parallel texts. The selection and retrieval of aligned sentence pairs based on word alignment may at times result in faulty output, but may also serve to focus the attention on target text words rather than just source text words. The next chapter will examine the techniques for accessing and exploring the *Europarl* multilingual parallel corpus, using the search interface of the word alignment database created by Jörg Tiedemann and available through the *OPUS* corpus project website.

The parallel corpora available at the *OPUS* project website were aligned at word level using "a probabilistic alignment framework for the combination of statistical and linguistic resources" (Tiedemann 2003b:3), which implements a statistical model in five steps of increasing complexity using the GIZA++ package (Och and Ney 2003) and a combination of 'clues', such as pre-set correspondences derived from bilingual dictionaries, and clues derived from training data through association measures (*ibid.*:12-19). The *Uplug* suite of tools also contains the *Interactive Clue Aligner (ICA)* application, which provides an interface for fine-tuning alignment at word level.

6.6 Tasks

6.6.1 Aligning a text pair

In this task you will use the *ParaConc Aligner* to align one text pair from a 'bilingual parallel corpus' consisting of just one text for each language. The English version of the document, *The right of the deaf child to grow up bilingual*, was used in the Tasks section of Chapter 4 to create a single-text corpus, annotated in XML following the TEI guidelines. In this task a plain text version of the same document will be aligned with the Italian translation, but the reader can opt for one of the other language versions available at the author's website, at http://www.francoisgrosjean.ch/.

1. Go to: http://www.francoisgrosjean.ch/the_right_en.html and download the English and Italian versions of the document, then convert them from PDF to text only format following the guidelines of task 4.6.3. Edit the files to delete mid-sentence hard returns and empty lines, then save them in your working folder as *deaf_child_en.txt* and *deaf_child_it.txt*. Copies of the files, both in PDF files and text only format, are available on the DVD.

2. Open the two text only files in a text editor (or in one of the XML editors available on the DVD), and display them side by side. Each paragraph should be displayed on a single line, with line numbers visible. You will notice that the Italian translation is longer than the English source text (37 lines as opposed to 30), since it also contains a preface which acknowledges the translator. The English text however contains a paragraph which is absent from the translation, that is the last item in the reference section. Insert a new paragraph (marked with a dot '.') where a paragraph is missing in the translation or in the source text. Both texts should eventually contain 38 lines each. Save your files in a working folder. Copies of the two texts aligned at paragraph level are available on the DVD.

3. Align the text pair at sentence level using the *ParaConc* Demo version contained on the DVD. The following list of actions will guide you through all the steps:

- Open the program and from the *File* menu select *Load corpus files*.
- In the dialog box, select *English (United Kingdom)* and *Italian (Standard)* as languages for the two files, respectively.
- Click on *Add*, then select and load the text files, for both languages.
- Click on *Format* (for both files). In the dialog box, select *New line delimiter* as the format for *Paragraphs* and *Automatic recognition* as the format for *Sentences*. Leave default setting for *Headings* (this is not relevant, since the files do not contain a header). Click on *Options* for *Sentences* and tick the *Smart Abbreviation Detect* checkbox, leaving default *Sentence delimiters* (*.!?*), then click on *OK*.
- Set the *Align format* option to *Not aligned*, then click on OK.
- From the *File menu* select *Save Workspace* and save your work and your alignment settings in your working folder (e.g. as *deaf_child.pws*).
- From the *File menu* select *View corpus alignment*, then select your files and click on *Alignment*. Look at the results. The corpus should be aligned sentence by sentence, but the program may have misinterpreted some punctuation marks, for instance assigning to some of them the status of 'sentence'. You can correct the alignment by right-clicking on the spot where you would like to split or join sentences and selecting the appropriate option from the pop-up menu. Save your Workspace before leaving the program if you make any changes to the alignment.

You will be able to use the aligned file pair in *ParaConc* in the Tasks section of Chapter 7. To quickly see the results of the alignment select *Search...* from the *Search* menu and perform a query for the word *child*.

6.6.2 A parallel corpus of literary texts

In this task you will use *Alinea* to align a corpus containing two English texts and their Italian translations. Alternatively, you can use two parallel texts of your choice in a different language pair (e.g. choosing from the sample texts included in the program package). The first text pair is the short story *Four Meetings* by Henry James (available in plain text as well as in other formats from the Project Gutenberg website), and its Italian translation *Quattro incontri* by Laura Sanna (published in 1995 on the website of the Sun Moon Lake publishing house). The second text pair is the novel *Alice in Wonderland* by Lewis Carroll (also available from the Project Gutenberg website), and an Italian translation available from the Liber Liber project website.

1. Download the English and Italian texts from
   - http://www.gutenberg.org/
   - http://www.sunmoonlake.net/oldsml/incontri.html
   - http://www.liberliber.it/

and edit them as needed, then save them as plain text in UTF-8 format in your working folder. Copies of a clean and edited version of the files in text only format are available on the DVD.

2. Download and install the *Alinea* program and its utilities on your computer (a copy of the program is available on the DVD) and use it to align the parallel corpus. The following list of actions will guide you through all the steps involved in the alignment of the first text pair:

- Open the program and from the *Aligner* menu select *Aligner directement*.
- In the dialog box, click on the three dots … and select the file containing the Italian translation of the short story by Henry James (less than 1,000 words) as the *Source*, and the file containing the source English text (which is about 70 words longer) as the *Cible* (the relative status of the texts must be inverted since the package does not include a parameter file for the English into Italian translation direction). Click on *Paramètres* and select the file *param.it.en.dat* from the *Param* folder in the *Alinea* main directory.
- Click on *Aligner* and wait until the files are processed and the *Navigateur bi-textuel* window opens up.
- The navigator shows three alignment units. The one in the middle is the active one, meaning that it is the one to which editing commands refer. The 'direct alignment' mode does not allow the user to manually split or join alignment units. For this, a text pair has to be aligned as a 'project'. However, the automatic procedure should have produced a pretty accurate alignment for this text pair, as you will be able to see by navigating through the text.
- The navigational buttons on the right of the screen < << > >> allow the user to proceed back and forth one alignment unit at a time < > or at a fixed interval << >> (the default value is set at 10). You can also go to the first (*Premier*) or last (*Dernier*) alignment unit, or to a specific alignment unit by typing a number in the text box and clicking on *Aller à*.
- Click on *Exporter* to save the aligned file pair. Choose a name for the files (e.g. *4meetings*) and select a working directory (*Répertoire*) for your alignment project, then click on *Save*. In the dialog box select *TXT* as *Format* and *UTF-8* as *Codage*, then click on *OK*. Three files are saved: one file, e.g. *4meetings.txt*, which contains a bi-text of interspersed translated and original aligned segments, and two other files, e.g. *4meetings.1.txt* and

4meetings.2.txt, which contain the aligned versions of the two texts (i.e. the two files contain the same number of lines). You will use the aligned text pair for the activities in Chapter 7.
- Click on *Quitter* to end the alignment procedure.

3. The second text pair is rather longer than the first (over 27,000 words for English and over 22,000 words for Italian) and quite 'noisy'. In order to obtain a good alignment you need to interactively edit the results of the two-step automatic alignment procedure, first fine-tuning the alignment of anchor points, then correcting the results of the length-based alignment performed on the manually improved results of the first alignment. The following list of actions will guide you through all the steps involved in the alignment of the second pair of parallel texts:

- Open the program and from the *Aligner* menu select *Nouveau Project*.
- Type a name for the project (e.g. *Alice*) in the text box at the top of the dialog box, and select a working directory (*Répertoire*) for your alignment project. Add the file with the Italian translation of the novel by Lewis Carroll as *Source*, and the original English text as *Cible*.
- Set text format (*TXT*), *Codage* (*UTF-8*), *Langue source* (*it*) and *Langue cible* (*en*) values. Select the files *stoplist.it.txt* and *stoplist.en.txt* from the *Param* folder in the *Alinea* main directory as stoplists for the two languages, respectively (these are very frequent words which are ignored when computing content-based alignment in the first step). For *Paramètres* select the file *param.it.en.dat* in the same directory. Then click on *Créer le project*.
- After the two files are loaded into the system, a dialog box allows the user to interact with alignment procedures and edit the alignment. Summary instructions are given below for basic processing, and the user is referred to the online Help page (Kraif 2002-2006) for more details about the different settings and procedures.
- Click on *I. Extraire le points d'ancrage*, then on *Voir* to revise the first alignment run. The form-based automatic alignment should have extracted 267 anchors. Use navigational buttons to scroll down the alignment and identify misalignments. First check every tenth set of anchor point candidates, editing the alignment by using the buttons *insérer* and *supprimer* to add new anchor points or to delete wrong ones. After a first cursory editing, click on *Quitter* and save the corrections. You can also save changes at any time while revising the alignment by clicking on *Enregistrer*.
- To obtain better results, you can re-run the content-based automatic alignment, to find new anchor points within the bi-textual subdivisions already established. Tick the *Conserver les anciens*

points d'ancrage checkbox, click on *I. Extraire le points d'ancrage* and then on *Voir* to revise the alignment.

- Click on *II. Extraire l'alignement complet* for the second step of the process, that is, the length-based automatic alignment built on top of the anchor points inserted in step one. Then click on *Voir* to edit the results.
- Use the >> button to move forward through the parallel text pair, checking alignment results at every ten sentences. Use the ‹ and › buttons to scroll back and forth to problematic translation units. Use the | button to merge (*fusionner*), and the ! button to split (*scinder*) two consecutive units in one or the other language. Only units consisting of more than one segment (boundaries between segments are shown by the ¤ symbol) can be split.[11] Use the ∧ button and the ∨ button to include the first or last segment of a unit in the previous of following unit (*déplacer*). Empty units (1-0 and 0-1 alignments) can be also created in this way. The aim is not to obtain the shortest possible alignment units, but to segment the text pair into meaningful alignment units, and to allow for a minimum context when viewing parallel concordances. In the case of very short segments, a 2-2 alignment may be preferable to two 1-1 alignments.
- Estimate the accuracy of automatic alignment for this text pair: do you think it is above or below the 90% accuracy rate claimed by Kraif and Chen (2004) for literary texts? When you have finished editing the alignment, click on *Exporter* to save the results as two aligned text files.
- Save the alignment as text only in UTF-8 encoding format. The aligned text pair will be used in the Tasks section of Chapter 7.

6.6.3 Corpus creation checklist

The aim of this task is to help you focus on the main aspects involved in the construction of multilingual corpora. This checklist will help you to reconsider some of the issues outlined in the corpus building project sketched in the Tasks section of Chapter 3, and specify details concerning aspects dealt with in this and other chapters. Go through the different points and write notes concerning each aspect. If possible discuss project details with a fellow student or researcher.

1. Project objectives and general description

[11] Editing concerns the alignment map, not the actual texts, so that units consisting of only one segment cannot be split.

Revise the project description to include a bilingual or multilingual component, if not already present in the corpus designed in the Tasks section of Chapter 3. Revise the objectives of the project accordingly, including specifications about future users of the resources to be created.

2. Corpus design and creation
Provide specifications concerning corpus type, for instance about whether the corpus should be comparable and/or parallel, the languages involved, the type and source of the texts to be included (e.g. electronic vs. printed sources), the type of text producers (e.g. trainee vs. professional translators), and so on. Consider all the different issues involved in corpus construction, such as matters concerning copyright and text acquisition (e.g. digitization and format conversion).

3. Corpus annotation and management
List the aspects which are involved in the compilation of your corpus, including the type of documentary information to be recorded for each text, annotation formats, and the various tools which may be used for the annotation, alignment and indexing of corpus data. Take into consideration the analysis tools which will be used to analyze the data (see Chapter 7 for details on parallel concordancing software).

4. Resources
Try to come up with an approximate estimate of the resources needed for the implementation of the whole project, or for part of it. Consider factors such as time and costs involved in hardware and software acquisition and management, and the time and computational expertise needed to include texts into the corpus and process them in order to obtain a suitable resource for the envisioned uses. Then "...double your estimate".

6.7 Further reading and software

Various papers on technical aspects related to tools and resources for the creation of multilingual corpora can be found in the proceedings of conferences such as *LREC* (Language Resources and Evaluation), *COLING* (Conference on Computational Linguistics) and in the *ACL* (Association of Computational Linguistics) Anthology.[12] Comprehensive collections of papers on often technical aspects of parallel corpora and on alignment issues are the volumes edited by Véronis (2000), Botley *et al.* (2000) and Borin (2002), while Tiedemann 2003a provides an exhaustive description of theoretical issues as well as practical applications. For an introduction to translator's workstations and translation memories see

---

[12] A Digital Archive of Research Papers in Computational Linguistics, at http://aclweb.org/anthology-new/. Accessed on 20 March 2011.

Austermühl (2001) and Somers (2003b). For a survey of translator's workstations up to 2006, see Lagoudaki (2006).

Introductions to alignment at word level are found in Tiedemann 2003a and in Kraif (2002). The websites of the Portuguese-English parallel corpus (*COMPARA*), of the *English Norwegian Parallel Corpus* (*ENPC*) and of the *OPUS* multilingual parallel corpus contain exhaustive documentation of the various tools and methods used to create and align the respective parallel corpus collections.

Software for parallel corpus creation

Alinea, Windows application for interactive sentence alignment, language independent but includes optional parameters for specific language pairs, freeware, at http://w3.u-grenoble3.fr/kraif/.

CTK (*Champollion Tool Kit*), a suite of Unix tools for lexicon-based sentence alignment, available for the language pairs English-Arabic and English-Chinese, open source software, at http://champollion.sourceforge.net/.

GMA (*Geometric Mapping and Alignment*), a suite of Unix tools for sentence alignment, content- based (stoplists are provided for English, French, and Malay and a bilingual lexicon for English-Malay), open source software, at http:nlp.cs.nyu.edu/GMA/.

InterText, an editor for aligned parallel texts which builds on the *TCA2* and *hunalign* automatic aligners (developed by Pavel Vondřička, still in progress as this book goes to print, at http://wanthalf.saga.cz/intertext).

NATools, a workbench for parallel corpora processing which includes a sentence aligner and a Probabilistic Translation Dictionary extractor, a word aligner and a set of other tools, Unix environment, open source software, at http://sourceforge.net/projects/natools/.

ParaConc with *Aligner*, Windows application, language independent, commercial software, at http://www.athel.com/para.html.

Vanilla aligner, Unix scripts for automatic sentence alignment, freeware, at http://nl.ijs.si/telri/Vanilla/.

Giza++, a statistical machine translation toolkit for word alignment, freeware, at http://code.google.com/p/giza-pp/.

hunalign, sentence aligner, source files freely available for various software platforms, at http://mokk.bme.hu/resources/hunalign.

Uplug, a suite of tools for pre-processing parallel corpora. Contains a tokenizer, a sentence-splitter, XML-tools, a sentence aligner, a word aligner, a corpus indexer (using the *CWB*), and Web search interfaces. Open source, at http://stp.lingfil.uu.se/~joerg/uplug/.

7. Using multilingual corpora

This chapter discusses tools and techniques for the analysis of multilingual corpora, with a focus on parallel corpora.

7.1 Comparable and parallel corpora

Multilingual comparable corpora play an important role in descriptive studies of translation, as they represent the backdrop against which features of source and target texts in parallel corpora can be assessed (see §2.2.3 and §3.1). For instance, the *European Comparable and Parallel Corpora* (*ECPC*) corpus suite (Calzada Pérez and Luz 2006) is planned to contain two parallel corpora - one of speeches given in English at the European Parliament together with their translations into Spanish and another of speech pairs in the opposite translation direction - and two monolingual (sub)corpora in the two languages. The monolingual English (sub)corpus, consisting of speeches given at the British House of Commons and at The Irish Dáil, will be used in conjunction with both the subcorpus containing original English EU Parliament speeches, and with the subcorpus containing EU Parliament speeches translated from Spanish into English. The monolingual Spanish (sub)corpus, consisting of speeches given at the *Congreso de los Diputados*, can be used in conjunction with both the subcorpus containing original Spanish EU Parliament speeches, and with the subcorpus containing EU Parliament speeches translated from English into Spanish. The two monolingual (sub)corpora together form a comparable corpus.

Monolingual subcorpora of both comparable and parallel corpora can be analyzed separately using the techniques and methods illustrated in Chapter 5. Word count statistics can be carried out independently for each language, for instance to measure and compare the overall length and lexical density of a subcorpus of original texts vis-à-vis the corpus of their translations. These types of analysis may help to provide an answer to questions such as whether translations are longer and whether their lexical density is lower than that of source texts, which can in turn be interpreted as indicators of universal tendencies, norms or strategies of translation (see Chapter 2). When comparing statistics for subcorpora in a parallel corpus, however, it is important to remember that source and target texts are not directly commensurable, and that statistical data such as type/token ratio and other measures need to be compared with standard measures from reference corpora for each language.

Similar or equivalent features across languages in both comparable and parallel corpora may also be investigated by looking at concordances in each subcorpus independently (e.g. Kenny 2000). In comparable corpora, the links between similar features in different languages can be those explicitly established through word alignment automated routines (see Chapter 6), or be posited by the researcher or translator on the basis of correspondences found in a parallel corpus, in a bilingual dictionary, or derived from his or her bilingual competence and intuition (Tognini-Bonelli 2002. Comparable corpora can be either created from scratch or derived from existing monolingual corpora in different languages, but for ease and consistency of analysis they need to be converted to a common encoding format (see Chapter 4) and analyzed using a uniform interface (Sharoff 2006c). To date, no tools or resources seem to be available for the computer-assisted analysis of 'aligned' comparable corpora, i.e. for the retrieval and display of bi- or multi-lingual texts and contexts through automatically linked words in comparable subcorpora.

The links between equivalent segments in a parallel corpus is instead provided by sentence or word alignment, which allows the researcher to query one subcorpus and retrieve and display the results of a search together with their aligned segments in the other subcorpus. The main tool for searching and displaying data from parallel corpora is parallel concordancing software, and some of the programs available for searching and viewing parallel concordances are surveyed in §7.2.

7.2 Display and analysis of parallel corpora

Research based on aligned parallel corpora is crucially dependent on parallel concordancers and on the search and display features they are equipped with. Much in the same way as with software for the analysis of monolingual corpora (see Chapter 5), a distinction can be made between software applications based on a client-server architecture, which act as an interface between the user and a corpus stored on a remote server, and stand-alone applications which access a corpus stored on a local machine. Some research projects have created their custom applications which work in conjunction with annotated and indexed parallel corpora residing on a server. These include the *Translation Corpus Explorer*, *DISPARA* and the *OPUS multilingual search interface*, which are used to generate parallel concordances from, respectively, the *ENPC*, *COMPARA* and the *OPUS* collection of multilingual corpora. Other studies using parallel corpora have relied on stand-alone commercial software products such as *WordSmith Tools* (e.g. Rodrigues Júnior 2005), *MultiConcord* (e.g. Kenny 2000, Pearson 2003, Winters 2009), and *ParaConc* (e.g. Hansen and Teich 2001, Calzada Pérez and Luz 2006).

These applications require input files with different types of alignment and annotation formats. Applications using a client server architecture perform a query on indexed aligned data, and are thus very efficient in working with large annotated corpora. Stand-alone applications, on the other hand, do not require indexing (but they do require aligned input in one format or another), and seem better suited to working with small, plain text, sentence-aligned parallel corpora. These applications also differ in the way they display the results of a search and in the degree to which they allow the user to manipulate them.

The *Translation Corpus Explorer (TCE)*, the application created for the display of bilingual concordances for the *ENPC* (Ebeling 1998), provides an example of 'horizontal' display. Figure 7.1 shows a page of results for the word 'time' using the online version of the program, *WebTCE*[1], which allows access to a few small bilingual corpora in English, Norwegian and German. The *TCE* takes as input parallel texts aligned with the *Translation Corpus Aligner* (*TCA*, see Chapter 6), and produces as default output intercalated source and target segments, each beginning at the start of a new line. Figure 7.1 presents a screenshot of the output of a search for the word 'time' in the subcorpus of English non-translated texts of the *ENPC*, showing the contexts in which the search word occurs, together with their aligned translations.

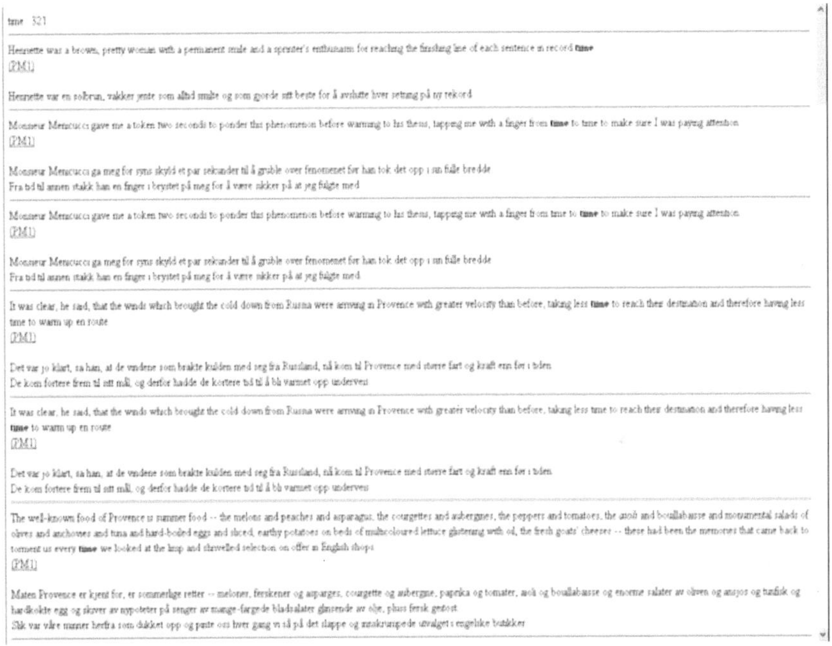

Figure 7.1. Concordance for 'time' in the ENPC *non-fiction subcorpus*

The *TCE* allows one to search in selected subcorpora (on the basis of language and translation status attributes), and to search within direct speech, since these features have been marked up in the corpus.

The DISPARA interface (Santos 2002), developed alongside the Portuguese-English parallel corpus *COMPARA*, is a "system for DIStributing PARAllel corpora on the Web", and provides an interface to the corpus which has been previously aligned, annotated and indexed using the *IMS Corpus Workbench* (*CWB*) (see Chapter 5). In contrast to the *TCE*, the *DISPARA* interface displays the results of a search as juxtaposed vertical segments. Figure 7.2 shows a screenshot with the results of a search for the expression 'set off' in the English non-translated subcorpus, together with the corresponding Portuguese translations.

[1] http://khnt.hd.uib.no/webtce.htm. Accessed on 25 March 2011.

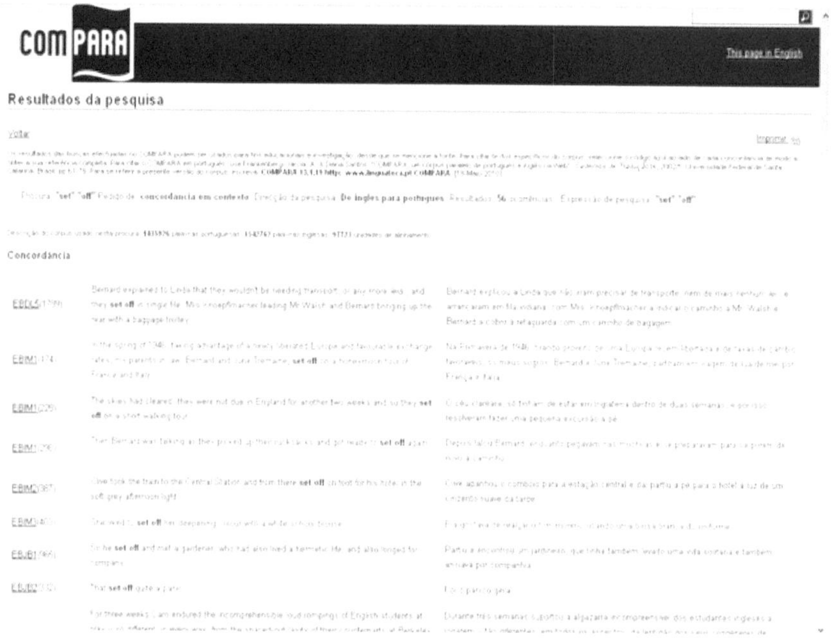

Figure 7.2. Results of a search for 'set off' in the COMPARA *corpus*

The user can search the corpus using the CQP query language, which allows very fast, flexible and powerful searches in linguistically annotated corpora. Documentary information can be used to filter results, by restricting a search to only one language and/or direction of translation (see task 2.5.2), to texts belonging to a specific linguistic variety (e.g. Continental Portuguese vs. Brazilian Portuguese), to texts by specific authors or translators, or to specific segments which have been marked up during corpus compilation, including translator's notes, foreign words, emphatic expressions and proper names. The system can also produce a list of such segments and of misalignments, so that it is possible to systematically classify footnotes, as well as cases of sentence omission, addition, merging and splitting (Frankenberg-Garcia 2009b). Research using *COMPARA* has been carried out also on the use of italics (Saldanha 2005) and on colour words using semantic annotation (Santos *et al.* 2008).

Like *COMPARA*, the *OPUS* search interface is based on the *CWB*. As pointed out in Chapter 6, since the *OPUS* collection of parallel corpora was envisaged for use in statistical machine translation and terminology retrieval rather than for linguistics or translation descriptive purposes, it does not allow for the discrimination between translated and non-translated texts. In contrast to *COMPARA/DISPARA*, however, the *OPUS* query interface presents the user with the option to view the results of a search in one of three different display formats: vertical (similar to the one used for *COMPARA*), in which alignment units are arranged side by side; horizontal (similar to the *TCE*), in which concordance lines are displayed as alternated sentences/segments in different languages; and KWIC horizontal display, with alternated concordance lines centred around the search expression. Figure 7.3 is a screenshot of a KWIC display of the results of a search for the lemma SET followed by the word 'off' in the *Europarl* corpus, for the language combination English-Italian, using the *OPUS multilingual search interface*. This interface will be used for a practical activity in the Tasks section of this chapter.

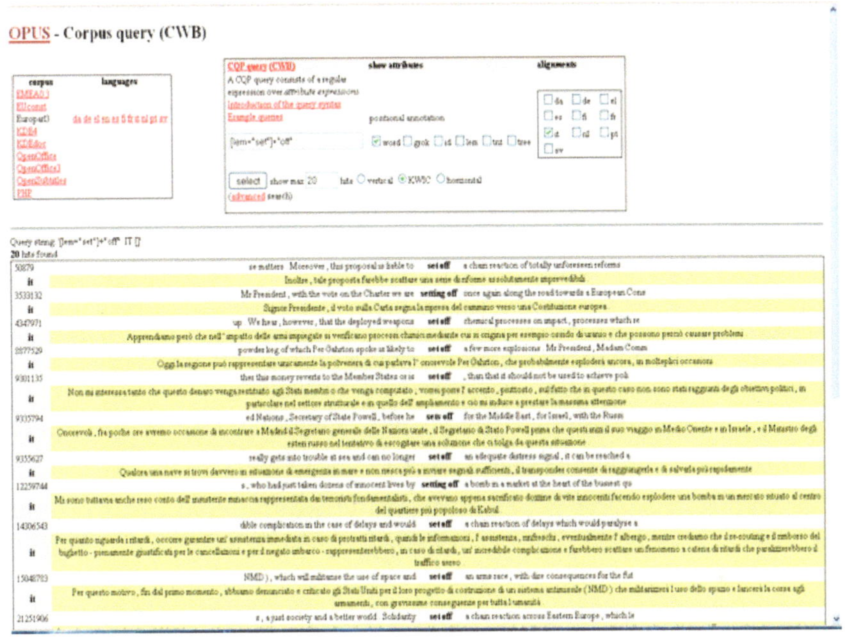

Figure 7.3. Results of a search for '[lem="set"]+"off"' in the Europarl *corpus using the* OPUS *multilingual search interface*

Different display formats are useful for focusing on different aspects of bi-textual correspondences. For instance, the horizontal display of interspersed source and target sentences may favour the observation of linguistic features occurring in sentence initial position in both source texts and their translations (Johansson 2004), while the KWIC display may favour the observation of source language patterns and their translations (see §7.3 below). One limitation of the online interfaces just introduced is that they do not allow for the manipulation of results, which cannot be sorted, randomized or classified. However, some of the resources and methods used for the creation of corpora such as *COMPARA* and *OPUS* could be integrated with other approaches. For example, the *Europarl* parallel corpus is currently being used as a test bed for a parallel concordancing utility based on the *CWB* to be included in the *Sketch Engine* system (Kilgarriff, 23/06/09, email communication).

Different stand-alone applications use as input parallel corpora with different alignment formats. Input files can be the output of the alignment of parallel texts carried out using a utility bundled with the concordancing software, e.g. *WordSmith Tools*'s *Viewer and Aligner* or *ParaConc*'s *Aligner*, or they can be created by a different alignment application and made available in the format accepted by the concordancing software. *WordSmith Tools*'s *Concord* monolingual concordancer can take as input a corpus of bi-texts with source and target alignment units alternating within the same files and display the results of a search in a format which resembles that of parallel concordances. This is done by increasing the context of a KWIC concordance as much as needed to include in the results the target (or source) segments preceding (or following) the segments in which the results of a search occur. Figure 7.4 shows the results of a search for "commanded" in the *Rushdie English-Italian parallel corpus* (Zanettin 2001b), with the display set at 2 lines of context.

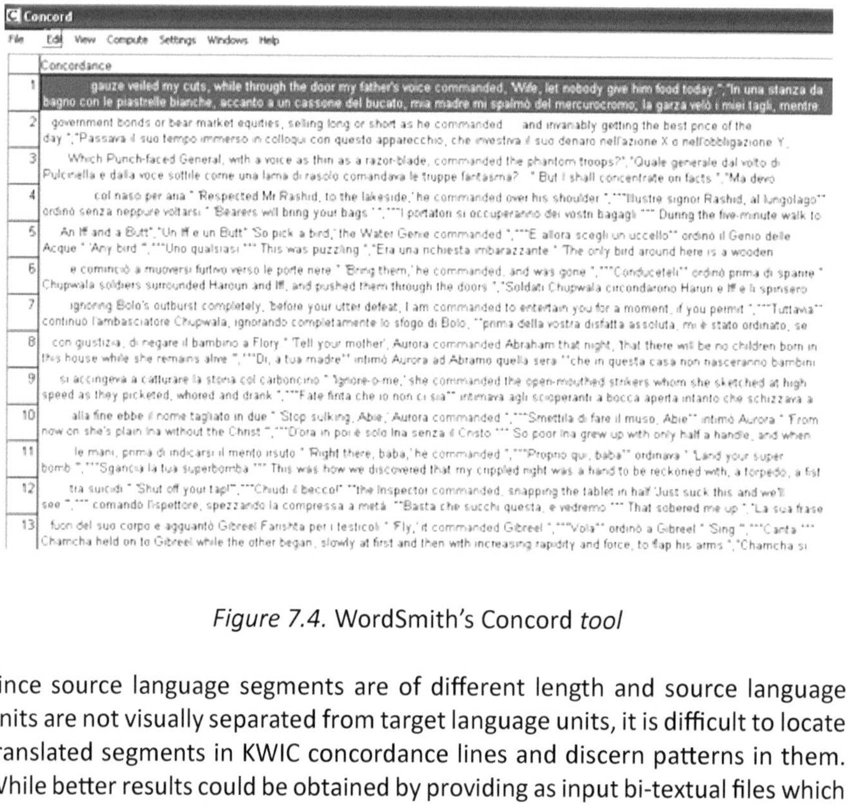

Figure 7.4. WordSmith's Concord *tool*

Since source language segments are of different length and source language units are not visually separated from target language units, it is difficult to locate translated segments in KWIC concordance lines and discern patterns in them. While better results could be obtained by providing as input bi-textual files which contain segments of regular length, it is clear that *WordSmith Tools*, not being designed to be a parallel concordancer, presents some shortcomings.

One of the first parallel concordancers was *MultiConcord* (Woolls 1995, King and Woolls 1996, Woolls 2000). It was conceived of as a tool for using parallel corpora as a source of material for Computer Assisted Language Learning (CALL) activities. *MultiConcord* takes as input text pairs pre-aligned at paragraph level, and performs sentence level alignment on the fly (using the Gale and Church 1993 algorithm, see Chapter 6). Figure 7.5 shows the results of a search for the expression 'set off' in a parallel English-French corpus. Sentences in English are displayed in the left column, vertically aligned with their respective translations. The upper part of the screen contains a box with settings for display and test creating functions. In this case, search results are presented as a C-test on the French sentences, which learners can complete using the source English sentences as clues.

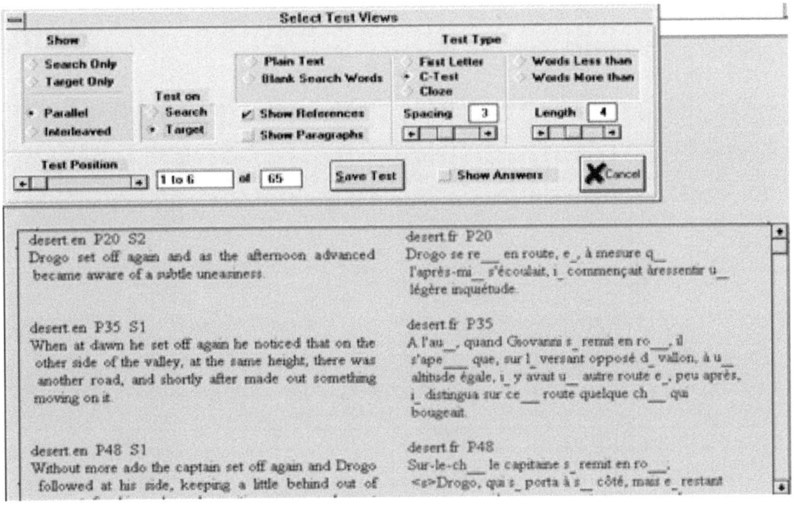

Figure 7.5. MultiConcord, *parallel concordance of "set off" in an English-French corpus*

ParaConc (Barlow 2000, 2002, 2008) is a fully-fledged multilingual parallel concordancer more specifically created for research in contrastive and translation studies. *ParaConc* is based on the monolingual concordancer *MonoConc Pro* (Barlow 2004), and presents all the advantages (and shortcomings) of a robust stand-alone concordancer (see Chapter 5). The program takes as input two (three, or four) text files, which must be either pre-aligned at sentence level or aligned using the *ParaConc Align* utility (see Chapter 6). Better results are obtained using a pre-aligned parallel corpus, in which each file contains the same number of lines, each representing an alignment unit. The output of a search is displayed in two horizontal windows, the upper window containing by default a KWIC concordance of the search expression in the source subcorpus and the lower window containing the aligned target segments in the same order (Figure 7.6).

ParaConc can generate separate wordlists and collocations for each subcorpus (up to 4 languages), and produce parallel concordances from searches carried out in each language. Concordances can be sorted and classified, and the program also allows the user to carry out a search in a subcorpus in language A, and then sort the results according to patterns in language B. Figure 7.6 shows the results of a search for the word 'Alice' in *Alice in Wonderland*, arranged according to the sorting order for the same word in the Italian translation. The concordance lines in the bottom half of the lower window are those whose aligned segments do not contain the word 'Alice'.

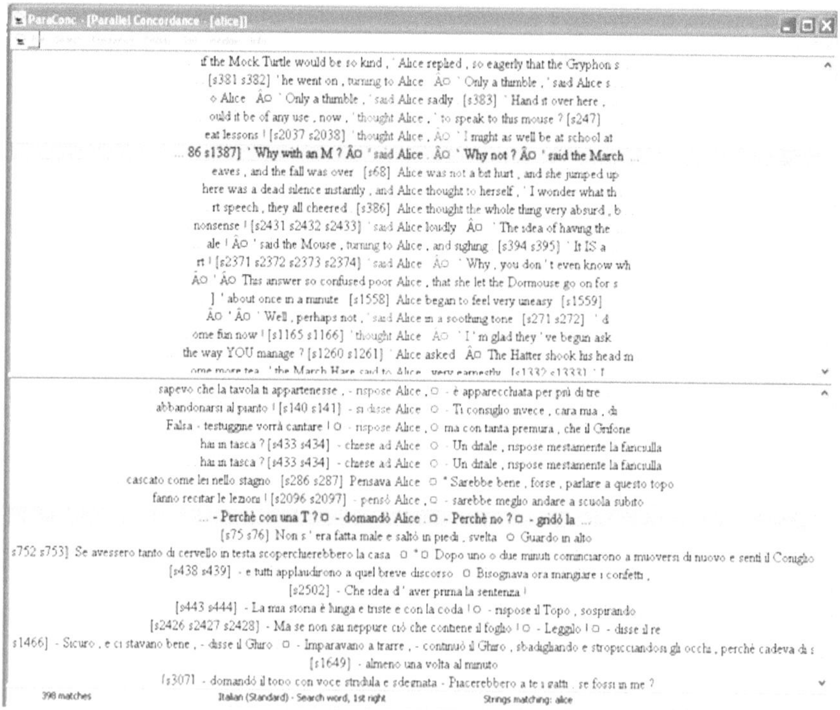

Figure 7.6. ParaConc, *parallel concordance for 'Alice' in an English-Italian corpus*

The horizontal display and the separation of results on the basis of language allows a better visualization of linguistic patterns in KWIC concordances, which both the interspersed horizontal view and the vertical view tend to impede. The link between segment pairs in different languages is not provided by spatial proximity, with segment pairs displayed in adjacent columns or lines, but by sorting order and highlighting. Source text segments and their translations are arranged in the same sorting order, and concordance lines are highlighted in pairs. When the results in one language are re-sorted or otherwise manipulated, much as they can be using a monolingual concordancer, aligned units in the other language are re-ordered accordingly.

ParaConc is also equipped with a function, called 'hot words', which produces translation candidates automatically. By right-clicking on the lower window the user can call up the 'hot words' dialogue box, that is, a list of words from the target results ranked according to frequency information, which are proposed as translation candidates for the expression searched in the source window. Words ranked higher are those whose observed frequency in the results deviates most from the expected frequency. 'Hot words' may include not only actual translations of the search word, but also translations of search words' collocates, and collocates of search words' translations. Hot words can be selected and used as search words in target results, and concordance lines sorted accordingly (Figure 7.7).

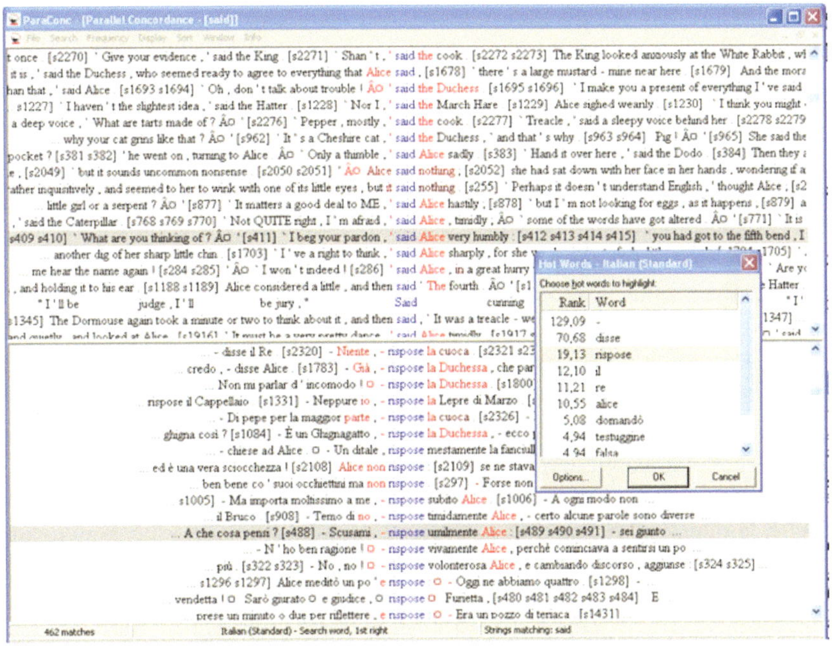

Figure 7.7. ParaConc's *'hot words' function*

While this automated feature has been found to be highly useful as an indicator of translation equivalents in parallel corpora (Prinsloo and de Schryver 2005, Moropa 2009), it should be remembered that much of what can be found in a corpus depends on how the query is formulated. As Michel Barlow (2003:30) points out, it is important to interpret the results with caution, since the system only works with "(assumed) equivalence at the sentence or segment level" and can be used

> to help determine word or phrase equivalents, but there is no guarantee that an English word highlighted in the KWIC display will be translated in the equivalent French sentence. The program is simply indicating the sentence or text segment that is equivalent on the basis of alignment to the English sentence that contains the keyword (*ibid.*)

The software for the analysis of parallel concordances depends on the format in which corpora are aligned. Stand-alone programs such as *ParaConc* do not always process satisfactorily text pairs which have not been previously aligned at sentence level. Web interfaces such as the *TCE*, *DISPARA* and the *OPUS* interface, which produce parallel concordances from annotated, aligned and indexed corpora, can carry out rather complex searches based on linguistic and documentary annotation, but are currently less flexible in terms of how they can sort and display the results.

Section 7.3 illustrates some types of analysis which can be carried out on a plain text, pre-aligned parallel corpus using *ParaConc*. This will be followed by another case study, based on the *Europarl* corpus accessed through the *OPUS* word alignment search interface.

7.3 Case study: The Rushdie English-Italian parallel corpus

The *Rushdie English-Italian Parallel Corpus* contains five novels and a short story by Salman Rushdie together with their Italian translations (Zanettin 2001b). Altogether the corpus is about 1.5 million words, with translations being slightly longer than the respective source texts. The first four novels (*Midnight's Children*, *Shame*, *Haroun and the Sea of Stories* and *The Satanic Verses*) were translated by Ettore Capriolo, while the short story "Chekov and Zulu" and the novel *The Moor's Last Sigh* were translated by Vincenzo Mantovani. Both are well-known and respected Italian literary translators.

As seen in Chapter 6, English and Italian conventions for reporting direct speech in fictional writing differ as regards punctuation, and this may result in 'alignment fuzziness'. The two languages also differ in the types of structure they can use to introduce or immediately follow direct speech. In the *Rushdie corpus*, direct speech is usually introduced in English by a verb of saying, often post-modified by an adverb, for example "she said dryly" or "he said ironically", but at other times it is followed by a verb indicating a facial expression or a movement of the body, for example "she pouted" or "she shrugged". Most instances of the first type of construction can be easily retrieved by *ParaConc* by using the search expression 'said *ly' (where the asterisk is a wildcard character which stands for any number of characters), a query which retrieves the concordance lines shown in the upper window of the program in Figure 7.8.

Concordance lines are sorted according to the target language (in the lower window), rather than according to the results of the search in the source texts. This allows variation in translation patterns to be more easily discerned in the Rushdie Italian subcorpus and to be grouped into five categories. The largest category (40% of all instances) includes the formally equivalent Italian structure, in which the verb *disse* (or *diceva*, a different form of past tense for the verb *dire*, 'to say') is followed by a word ending in *-mente*, this being the standard suffix for adverbs in Italian. Sometimes the same English adverb is translated by a different one in Italian (e.g. 'mildly' is translated as either *dolcemente*, *pacatamente* or *gentilmente*). This pattern is used to render unconventional or creative uses in the source text in an equally creative way (e.g. 'gummily' translated as *gengivamente*). In 25% of the cases the adverb following 'said' is translated as *con* (with) followed by an abstract noun (e.g. 'fiercely' translated as *con ferocia*, *con*

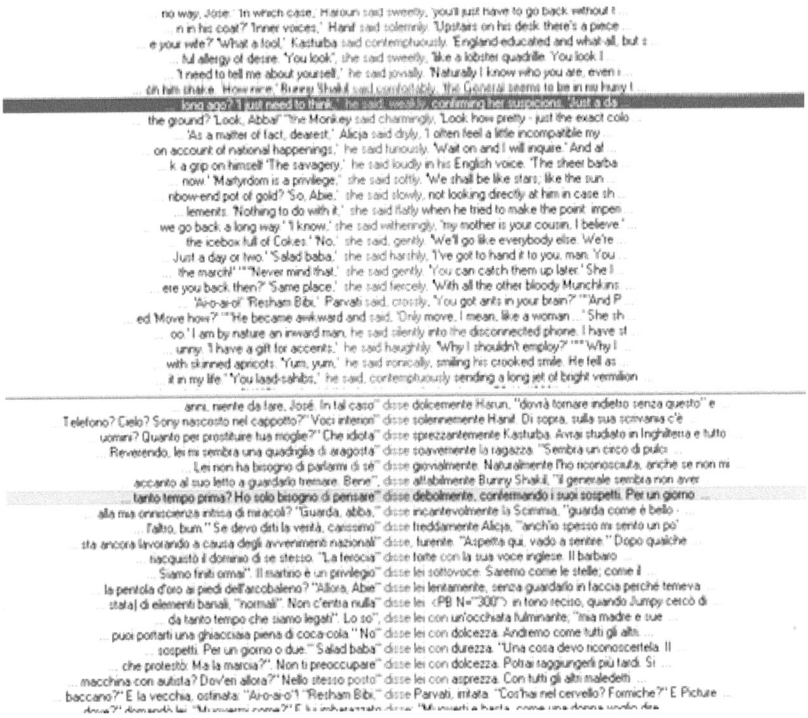

*Figure 7.8. 'Said *ly', sorted according to target language patterns*

asprezza or *con ardore*, 'meekly' translated as *con umiltà*, 'firmly' translated as *con fermezza*). The remaining third is almost equally distributed between three different types of linguistic patterns: 15% are instances of prepositional phrases which include a noun referring to tone of voice (*tono, voce*) or attitude (*aria*) post-modified by an adjective or a prepositional phrase (e.g. 'approvingly' translated as *in tono d'approvazione*, 'coquettishly' as *in tono civettuolo*, 'innocently' as *con aria innocente*, 'contemptuously' as *con aria sprezzante*). 10% are instances of adjectives referring to the attitude or expression of the speaker rather than to the way the reported speech is conveyed, for instance 'she said moodily' translated as *disse imbronciata*, meaning that the character wore a sulky expression when she uttered the words, 'grimly' as *truce* (grim), 'flatly' as *risoluta* ('firm, resolute'). The remaining occurrences are translated with different phrasal constructions. For example, 'I said helplessly' is translated as *dissi, nella mia impotenza*, 'he said indistinctly through his untoothed gums' is translated as *farfugliò con le sue sdentate gengive*, and 'said quickly' is translated as *si affrettò a dire*.

Different Italian patterns are used to translate the same English expression, as can be seen by sorting search results according to source rather than to target language (Figure 7.9). For example the expression 's/he said flatly' is translated as *disse recisamente, disse categoricamente, disse in tono reciso, disse con voce neutrale, disse risoluta*.

*Figure 7.9. 'Said *ly', sorted according to source language patterns*

Even more interesting are those cases where direct speech is not introduced by a 'verb of saying' but rather accompanied by a verb which refers to a physical action accompanying what is being said. For example:

- 'But now it is Miss World competition,' pouted Nadia.
- 'Wonderful,' Naseem pouted. 'So now I must find a new doctor.'
- 'One more high-rise, one less piece of old Bombay,' she shrugged.

This is not an uncommon structure in English fiction. A search for "he/she shrugged" in a 10- million-word subcorpus of imaginative, written texts in the *BNC* produced 669 occurrences of the two forms combined. Of these about 15% were cases in which shrug/pout appeared in a similar structure, for example "'here's no answer to that,' he shrugged" (from *White Darkness*, by David McIntee, 1985) and "'If you can't stand the heat...' he shrugged" (from *Bay of Rainbows*, by James Dana, 1993).

In the *Rushdie corpus*, instances of these structures were translated with *disse* followed by either an adjective or a phrase, following the pattern used to translate 'said' followed by adverb in English.

- "Ma ora si tratta di concorrere all'elezione di Miss Mondo" *disse* Nadia *facendo il broncio*.
- "Magnifico!" *disse* Naseem *imbronciata*. "Così ora dovrò trovarmi un nuovo medico."

- "Un grattacielo in più, un pezzo della vecchia Bombay in meno" *disse con una scrollata di spalle.*

Other expressions used to translate 'shrugged' include *disse alzando le spalle, disse scrollando le spalle*, and so on. There are, however, four cases in the corpus in which the verb 'to shrug', which can be translated into Italian literally as *alzare le spalle, fare spallucce, scrollare le spalle* is translated without including an explicit verb of 'saying' but rather using a structure which seems modelled on the English one. These are shown in Table 7.1.

'Well, anyhow,' the voluptuous 'Mary the Copt' shrugged, 'name or no name, we want you to start acting like him.'	"Be', comunque" la voluttuosa "Maria la Copta" *alzò le spalle*, "nome o non nome, vogliamo che tu cominci a comportarti come lui."
'Why not, after all, he shrugged.	"Perché no, in fondo" *alzò le spalle*.
'Well, in that case,' Panikkar shrugged, making as if to leave.	"Be', in tal caso." Panikir *alzò le spalle*, e fece per andarsene.
'God knows what you women are,' he shrugged.	"Dio sa che razza di donne siete", e *si strinse nelle spalle*.

Table 7.1. Translations of 'shrugged' in the Rushdie *corpus*

The examples may strike an Italian reader as somewhat odd, and leave him or her wondering whether they may be considered instances of 'translationese' (see Chapter 2). In order to find out whether a phrase such as *si strinse nelle spalle, alzò le spalle, scrollò le spalle* is used in a similar way in texts originally produced in Italian, a number of searches were carried out in an *ad hoc* corpus of about 1 million words from 17 contemporary Italian novels (Zanettin 2001b). Only examples with forms of the verb *dire* followed by nominal phrases such as *alzata di spalle* were found, except for two cases in which no verbs of saying were found. In these two examples (respectively from *Il visconte dimezzato* by Italo Calvino, and *Magia Rossa* by Gianfranco Manfredi), however, the expressions *si strinse nelle spalle* and *alzò le spalle* precede rather than follow direct speech:

- *Si strinse nelle spalle*: - Ammazzare adesso non mi conviene e non mi serve
- Lei *alzò le spalle*, senza guardarlo: "Chissà? Può darsi invece che cominci davvero a rendersi conto che non può continuare così..."

Similar searches were carried out using advanced search functions on the digital book archive *Google Books* (see Chapter 3). The results of these searches, which produced a few hundred hits, were scanned and random pages looked at, which seemed largely to confirm the results from the Italian fictional reference corpus.

Most examples were of the *disse con un'alzata di spalle* type, though a few 'deviant' examples were also found (e.g. *alzò le spalle* preceding direct speech). No examples of the type 'direct speech followed by *alzò le spalle*' were found, except two dubious ones in translated fiction.[2]

A second example concerns translators' stylistic preferences when translating expressions denoting indeterminacy (Zanettin 2001b). The attenuators "a kind of", "a sort of" and "something of a" occurred in the corpus a total of 142 times altogether, with 82, 51 and 9 occurrences, respectively. These expressions occur in the works translated by Ettore Capriolo more than twice as often than in the works translated by Vincenzo Mantovani (103 as opposed to 39 occurrences). As the translations by Capriolo are about 80% of the whole corpus these figures are averaged on a 100% basis. The three English expressions were translated in most cases either with *una specie di* or with *una sorta di*, by both translators. Both translators in a minority of cases also used other expressions, Capriolo on average more frequently than Mantovani with 20% and 5% of the cases, respectively.

The distribution of the two most recurring Italian expressions does not correlate with the distribution of the English expressions, that is to say that, for instance, 'a sort of' is not consistently, or even preferably, translated with *una sorta di*, its cognate Italian expression. Rather, Capriolo seems to prefer *una sorta di* (by which he translates 'a kind of' 39 out of 82 times), while Mantovani seems to prefer *una specie di* (the only expression he uses to translate 'a sort of'). Both translators use their preferred expression in about two thirds of the cases, as can be seen from Table 7.2.

	Capriolo	%	Mantovani	%
una sorta di	72	69.9 %	4	10.2 %
una specie di	10	9.7 %	30	76.9 %
other	21	20.3 %	5	12.8 %
Total	103	100 %	39	100 %

Table 7.2. Translations of 'a sort of', by translator

Parallel corpora can also be used to investigate how specific words, discourse functions or semantic properties of lexical units are translated into another language. For instance, the *Rushdie corpus* could be used to investigate whether already researched English semantic prosodies are adhered to or flouted by Rushdie, and how they are translated into Italian. One of Sinclair's favourite examples of semantic prosody is the expression 'border on' which, he observes, when not referring to a geographical border, typically occurs "with an object

[2] Since access to the content of the two works in Google Books was restricted by copyright arrangements to the 'snipped view', it was not possible to visualize larger contexts in order to see whether the two examples, from a Russian and an American translated novel, respectively, were of this type.

that has as its head an abstract expression" (Sinclair 2003:70-71). This is either "an abstract noun without any article ... [or] ... the definite article followed by a word that is normally regarded as an adjective" (*ibid.*). The whole expression, argues Sinclair, "serves to define an area that is on the limit of what is acceptable in ordinary life" (*ibid.*).

In the *Rushdie corpus* there are 5 instances of forms of 'border on' which do not refer to a geographical border and which occur in the typical structure described by Sinclair:

1. for this father she bears a reverence *bordering on idolatry* (Shame)
2. a condition so unusual in our overcrowded country as to *border on abnormality* (Midnight's Children)
3. the greenies and peacemarchers and world-changers with whom she instinctively felt at home treated her with deep suspicion, *bordering on resentment* (Satanic Verses)
4. dedicated himself with a will *bordering on obsession* (Satanic Verses)
5. events had begun to *border on the farcical* (Satanic Verses)

The unit of meaning constructed around the phrase *border on* (as used by Salman Rushdie) was translated into Italian (by Ettore Capriolo) in 4 cases out of 5 following a structure similar to that described by Sinclair for English, i.e. with a verb followed by a preposition, followed by a definite article, followed by an abstract noun. In one case 'border on' was translated with the expression *al limite di* followed by a determinate article, followed by an abstract noun: *al limite dell'ostilità*, literally 'on the limit /at the edge of resentment'.

The verbs used in the first type of structure were *sconfinare in,* which was used twice (*sconfinare nell'ossessione/nell'anormalità*, lit. 'to cross the border of, to trespass into obsession/abnormality'), *confinare con* (*confina con l'idolatria*, lit. 'borders on idolatry') and *sfiorare* (*sfiorare il farsesco*, lit. 'to skim over, to brush against the farcical'). This is interesting to note that *confinare con* and *sconfinare in* literally mean quite different things. In the Italian data, it would seem that the 'area of what is acceptable in ordinary life' is sometimes trespassed into and at other times only brushed against.

In order to ascertain whether the different Italian translations are just stylistic variations with similar connotations, or convey different nuances from the source text, the verbs and expressions used in the translation where compared to their typical patterns of use in a very large corpus of Italian, the *itWaC* corpus. This is a 1.5-billion-word corpus of Italian created using the *BootCaT* procedure described in Chapter 3, annotated and indexed, and pre-loaded in the *Sketch Engine* corpus query system. *Word Sketches* (see Chapter 5) of the verbs *sconfinare, confinare* and *sfiorare* provided useful data, which were compared with the semantic profile of 'border on'. A *Word Sketch* of *sconfinare* seems to support a description of a semantic prosody very similar to that described by Sinclair for 'border on'. *Sconfinare* is in fact often used in a figurative sense, that is, without referring to a geographical border. It is often followed by the preposition 'in' combined with a definite article followed by an abstract noun, as in the examples from the *Rushdie corpus* (e.g. sconfinare nel *surreale*, nella *fantasia*, nella *paranoia*, nell'*arbitrio*, nella *follia*). *Confinare*, on the other hand, seems to take as an object almost exclusively physical entities (land, estate, gardens), with the notable exception of *pazzia* (folly, madness). Typical collocates of *sfiorare* in object position are words such as *tragedia*, *ridicolo* and *grottesco*, all abstract nouns related to the semantic area of comedy.

To sum up, two of the three Italian verbs used to translate 'border on' (*sconfinare in* and *sfiorare*) show a semantic profile similar to that described by Sinclair for 'border on'. The third Italian verb (*confinare con*), whose literal meaning is closer 'to border on' than that of the other verbs, seems to be rarely used in figurative expressions. It is hard to say whether its use in the translated sentence classifies as a legitimate stylistic variation or as an instance of interference, but the point of this example is to illustrate a methodology by which a parallel corpus can be used to compare different translations of source language features, which in turn can be evaluated against the backdrop provided by a monolingual reference corpus in the target language.

7.4 Case study: the OPUS Word alignment database

The *OPUS Word Alignment Database* (Tiedemann 2009) contains three parallel corpora, *Europarl3*[3], the *OpenSubtitles* corpus and the *European Constitution* corpus aligned at word level. The database can be queried by searching for a word in one language and retrieving its 'equivalents' in one or more other languages, the result of automatic word alignment, ranked according to frequency. Since in the *OPUS* corpus there is no way of separating translations from non-translations, nor of knowing the source language for a given translation (see Chapter 6), the methodology illustrated here can be considered an exercise in contrastive linguistics, providing some insight into how meanings in different languages map onto each other.

Figure 7.10 shows a screenshot of a search for the word 'eye' in English in the *OPUS Word Alignment Database*, with most frequent alignment results for five languages (German, Hungarian, Italian, Russian and Spanish).

In the list of Italian words at the centre of the screen, the five words are the top five 'bilingual collocates' of 'eye', that is to say, the five words (or expressions) which the word alignment algorithm has found to have a maximal resolution alignment with the word 'eye'. The literal back-translations of the Italian words are, respectively, 'eye', 'eyes', 'attention', 'sight' and 'view'. The database provides access to parallel concordances, that is, by clicking on the frequency number next to a word (or multiword expression, e.g. *occhi davanti* in Figure 7.11) in the list of Italian 'equivalents' a window is generated containing concordance lines for that word (or multiword expression), while a click on a word in Italian (or any other language) generates a list of English alignments for that word. Figure 7.11

[3] That is, version 3 or the *Europarl* multilingual aligned parallel corpus.

shows a window with parallel concordances for *occhio* in the *Europarl3* corpus, generated by clicking on the number 552 next to that word.

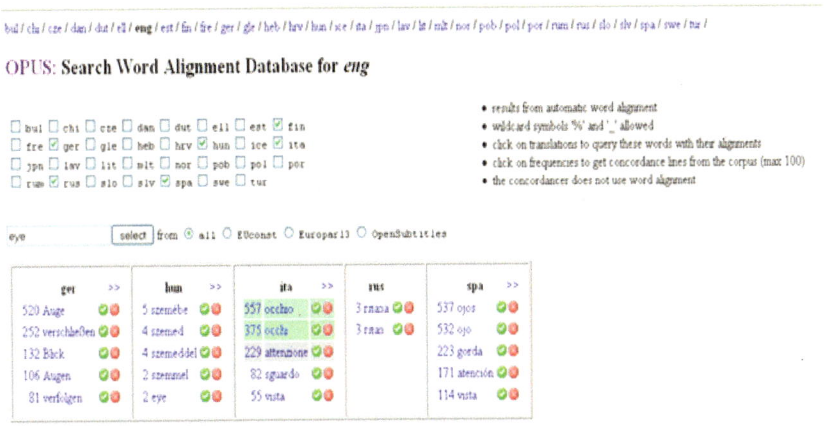

Figure 7.10. Screenshot of search for 'eye' in the OPUS Word Alignment Database

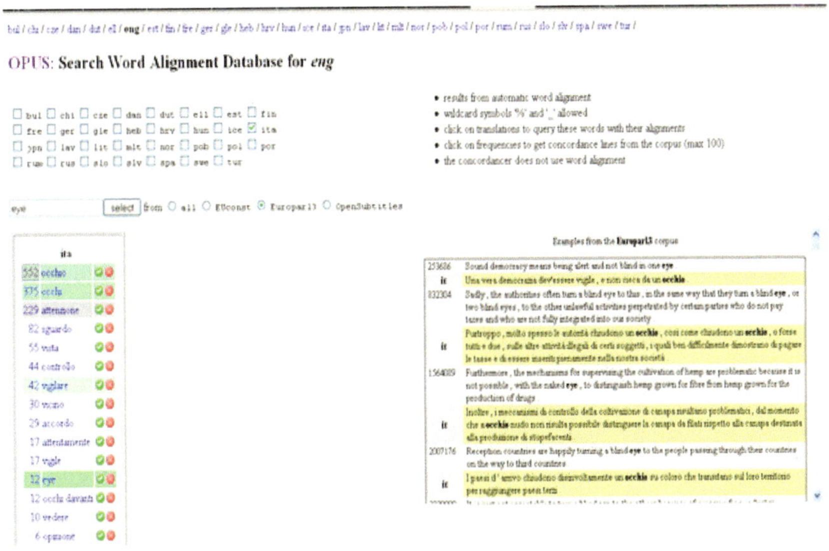

Figure 7.11. Word alignment and parallel concordances in the Europarl *corpus*

The parallel concordance generated does not include all occurrences of *occhio*, but only those which are found to hold between the two words in the English-Italian alignment direction. Thus, the parallel concordance will not contain those segments in which *occhio* is aligned with 'an eye', nor those in which it is aligned with 'eyes'. Moreover, while in order to improve accuracy the system only extracts word pairs with an alignment frequency higher than five (Tiedemann 2008), some misalignments are still also present. Misalignments at word level may nonetheless point to correct alignments at sentence level, as in the examples shown in Table 7.3, where the system wrongly computed the words *vista* and *attenzione* as the most likely lexical correspondents of 'eye' in the English sentence.

Our objective , particularly bearing in mind enlargement , must be to involve the candidate countries in this process , and with an **eye** to the elections to Parliament in 2004 to ensure that equal representation of men and women can be achieved .	I nostri obiettivi devono essere , proprio in **vista** dell' allargamento , il coinvolgimento nel processo dei paesi candidati e , guardando alle elezioni legislative del 2004 , l' impegno a raggiungere una rappresentanza equilibrata di donne e uomini .
We do not , as I shall go on to say , agree about everything , but the fact that we agree about so much means that there is always a distorting focus on the minority of issues where we do not see **eye** to eye .	Non siamo , come continuerò a ripetere , d ' accordo su tutto , ma concentrare sempre l ' **attenzione** su quella minoranza di questioni che non valutiamo allo stesso modo significa assumere un atteggiamento mistificatorio .

Table 7.3. Incorrect word alignments

The parallel concordances generated for a word alignment are displayed in a vertical arrangement, and cannot be sorted or further manipulated. Regardless of these limitations, the search interface based on the word alignment database allows the researcher to navigate the corpus using as search words a set of words and expressions which are related by being frequently aligned to the same word in a parallel corpus, though in this case not always linked through direct translation. By switching between groups of 'translational collocates' in the two languages it may be possible to carry out a tentative investigation of the extent to which the profile of a word in one language is matched by that of one or more 'equivalent' words in another language.

It may be interesting, for example, to see whether the words 'eye' and *occhio* present similar collocational patterns and semantic associations. According to Sinclair (2003:167-172) the singular form 'eye' has a different meaning from that of the plural form 'eyes'. While the plural word form collocates with words of colour, body parts and general verbs of seeing, the singular form predominantly appears in fixed idiomatic phrases ('turn a blind eye', 'with the naked eye', etc). Thus, the word 'eye' does not usually refer to the organ of sight, but appears in expressions which concern monitoring, critical examination and various points of view.

An analysis of the concordances for 'eye' in the *Europarl* corpus shows that, apart from quite a high number of occurrences of the proverbial expression 'an eye for an eye and a tooth for a tooth' and its Italian literal corresponding expression *occhio per occhio, dente per dente*, almost all instances of 'eye' occur in expressions such as to 'turn a blind eye to' and 'keep an eye on', respectively aligned to *chiudere un occhio* and *tenere d'occhio*. Other frequent translations of 'eye' include the words *occhi, attenzione, sguardo, vista* and *controllo*, which are next examined in turn.

The vast majority of alignments for *occhi* is for the expression *chiudere gli occhi*, aligned with instances of 'turn a blind eye', with some cases accounting for expressions such as *irritazione degli occhi* and *guardare negli occhi*, which correspond to the English constructions 'eye irritation' and 'look in the eye'. *Attenzione* appears in expressions like *seguire con attenzione* ('to keep a [watchful] eye on'), *fare, prestare attenzione* ('to keep an eye on'), or *attirare l'attenzione di qualcuno* ('to catch someone's eye'). The word *sguardo* is aligned to English expressions such as 'cast an eye' (*gettare uno sguardo*), 'turn a blind eye' (*volgere, distogliere lo sguardo*) and 'watchful eye' (vigile sguardo), and the word *vista* to expressions such as 'to keep a close eye on' (*non perdere di vista*) and 'with an eye to' (*in vista di*). Other frequent alignments include words like *controllo* ('control'), *vigilare* ('watch over') and *vicino* ('close', as in *seguire da vicino*, 'keep a close eye on'). Altogether, these 'translation collocates' (i.e. collocates of the translations of the word 'eye') seem to confirm the description of the word 'eye' elaborated by Sinclair.

A slightly different picture is presented by the Italian word most frequently aligned to 'eye' in the database i.e. *occhio*. A search for the word *occhio* in the Italian-English alignment direction retrieves the following alignments: 'eye', 'eyes', 'blind eye', 'an eye', 'favourably', 'eye on', 'watching', 'a', 'welcome' and 'view'. 'Eye' accounts for about 80% of all occurrences (552 out of 677) and an examination of parallel concordances shows that the Italian word appears indeed in contexts similar to those in which 'eye' appears in English also when aligned with different words or expressions.

However, while in English the words 'eye' and 'eyes' occur in rather different contexts, with the plural form mostly indicating the organ of sight, the plural form *occhi* is used in Italian in contexts which are similar to those in which the singular form *occhio* appears, that is, expressions referring to monitoring and critical examination. In fact, expressions such as 'turn a blind eye' are aligned with both *chiudere un occhio* and *chiudere gli occhi*. On the other hand, the Italian *occhio* is only very rarely aligned with the word 'eyes' (44 occurrences). This non-reciprocal picture is of course not in any way attributable to translation. Rather, *OPUS Word Alignment* interface to the *Europarl* corpus allows the user to observe similar structures in two (or more) subcorpora which are comparable as well as parallel. They are comparable in that they contain the entire production, consisting of both original texts and texts translated from many languages, of a very specialized corpus of transcribed speeches, and they are parallel in that all text pairs are aligned at sentence and word level.

Regardless of how word alignment was achieved, searches using a word alignment database may be used in conjunction with 'regular' searches in a sentence aligned parallel corpus. The integration of searches in a word alignment database into parallel concordancing, which automatically select candidates for bilingual equivalence, may help the researcher focus his or her attention on frequent patterns of correspondence, much as the *Hot Word* function does in *ParaConc* (see previous section).

7.5 Multilingual corpora in translator training and practice

Corpora and corpus tools, including the 'Web as corpus' (see Chapter 3), have come to flank more traditional reference works such as dictionaries and encyclopaedias as practical aids during the process of translation. Large and general as well as small and specialized corpora, monolingual and bilingual, comparable and parallel, are being used in translator training and by professional translators (see § 7.7 for further references on how corpus resources can be integrated in the curriculum of trainee translators). This section briefly considers (bilingual) comparable and parallel corpora which, like different types of dictionaries, may provide information about different aspects or problems of translation and may be used to answer different types of questions. However, while dictionaries focus on the word as a unit of analysis, corpora offer information on language use also above the word level, and provide important information on collocation, terminology and phraseology.

Comparable corpora which can be used by translation trainees and professionals include large as well as smaller specialized corpora. Large 'globally' comparable monolingual corpora such as the Leeds collection of Internet corpora or the 'WaC' series of large Internet corpora pre-loaded in the *Sketch Engine* can be consulted through a common interface and used as global reference for cross-linguistic comparison. For instance, Gatto (2009:140-145) describes how the English (*ukWaC*) and Italian (*itWaC*) corpora preloaded in the *Sketch Engine* can provide contrastive information about the collocational patterns of the vocabulary used in tourist literature. A comparison between two English equivalents of the Italian word *paesaggio*, i.e. 'landscape' and 'scenery', shows that the Italian word covers phraseological patterns which in English are associated with either one of the English words. The *Word Sketch* function provides summary views of the most frequent phraseological patterns, which for *paesaggio* are in fact *paesaggio agricolo/urbano*, corresponding to 'agricultural/urban landscape', and *paesaggio mozzafiato/spettacolare/da favola/da cartolina*, corresponding to 'breathtaking/spectacular/stunning/magnificent scenery'. Also, a comparison between the two corpora highlights that whereas in English the Adj+N construction ('stunning scenery') is preferred, Italian often resorts to a N+da+N construction (e.g. *paesaggio da favola*).

Specialized DIY monolingual or comparable bilingual disposable small Web corpora can be easily compiled using tools such as *BootCaT*, and analyzed using stand-alone software such as *WordSmith Tools* or *AntConc*, or by subscribing to a service like the *Sketch Engine* (see Chapter 3). For instance, Zanettin (2002b) reported on how, using a monolingual concordancer, students found evidence of contrastive phraseology in a DIY comparable English-Italian corpus on construction and engineering which was (manually) created to help them translate a text on earthquakes from a scientific magazine. They discovered, for instance, that while in Italian both *gli edifici* and *i muri crollano*, in English buildings 'collapse' while walls 'fall'. By searching the two subcorpora for prima-facie translation equivalents such as the adjectives *strutturale* and 'structural', students were able to retrieve and establish a correspondence between *cedimenti strutturali gravi* and 'heavy structural damage'. Similarly, Gatto (2010) illustrates the compilation and analysis of a comparable corpus of medical texts in English and Italian in the context of a classroom activity with a group of post-graduate trainee translators. This time the comparable corpus was created using the version of *BootCaT* integrated in the *Sketch Engine* and analyzed through its online interface. In this case the students found, for instance, that whereas in English the verb 'diagnose' is normally used in the pattern "'patients + (BE) diagnosed with N', where N was almost invariably a disease ..., in Italian it is the disease ... that is diagnosed (diagnosticato), the basic pattern being 'essere/venire diagnosticato', preceded by an indirect object referring to people or preceded/followed by the subject (the disease)" (Gatto 2010:73-74). A typical example is "ogni anno il diabete viene diagnosticato a 600.000 persone", literally "every year diabetes is diagnosed to 600,000 people".

While a comparable corpus may be likened to two 'monolingual dictionaries' providing evidence of standard usage, parallel corpora may be seen as more akin to bilingual dictionaries. However, whereas bilingual dictionaries are inventories of pre-established translation equivalents which are proposed as translation candidates, parallel corpora may offer information not only regarding linguistic regularities in source and target texts but also a repertoire of strategies deployed by past translators. In selecting a translation equivalent from a general bilingual dictionary a translator has to assess the appropriateness of the candidate to the new context by starting from a definition and a few usage examples. A parallel corpus will show the translation strategies past translators have most frequently resorted to when confronted with problems similar to the ones that have prompted a search in a parallel corpus (Pearson 2003).

Parallel corpora can not only offer information about equivalence but also about non-equivalence, i.e., cases where there is no direct equivalent for words, terms or phrases across languages, thus providing evidence of how translators have dealt with this problem. For example, Zanettin (2001b) found that in the *Rushdie corpus* the word 'edges' in expressions such as 'around the edges' and 'at the edges' was never translated literally, thus not resulting in a 'maximum resolution alignment' (see Chapter 6). Table 7.4 contains all instances of 'edges' occurring in such patterns:

biting the skin around the edges of a nail	mordicchiandosi la pelle attorno all'unghia
around the edges of Gibreel Farishta's head	intorno alla testa di Gibreel Farishta
around the edges of the circus-ring	intorno alla pista da circo
and there was a fluidity, an indistinctiness, at the edges of them	vicinissime a loro c'erano una fluidità e un'indeterminatezza
the horses grew fuzzy at the edges	i cavalli diventavano sempre più sfocati
blurred at the edges, my father	con la mente annebbiata, mio padre
looking somewhat ragged at the edges	con l'aria di un uomo distrutto
Mrs Qureishi, too, was beginning to fray at the edges	anche Mrs Qureishi si stava consumando

Table 7.4. Translations for 'around/at the edges' in the Rushdie *corpus*

In all these cases, the two professional translators have consistently chosen to resort to 'zero-equivalence', a translation equivalence which would hardly be reported in any bilingual dictionary.

In 1996 Teubert predicted that computerized corpora would supplant traditional reference sources, and wrote that "bilingual dictionaries as we know them will ... be replaced by bilingual and multilingual databases" (*ibid.*:249-250). While this has not yet happened, and dictionaries might not eventually fall completely out of favour, corpora and concordancing tools will continue to provide translators with examples of how language features such as words, terms and collocates have been previously translated (parallel corpora) and of standard language production onto which to map candidate translations (comparable corpora).

7.6 Tasks

7.6.1 Searching a parallel corpus of literary texts

This task is meant to give you some guidance in exploring the small parallel corpus of literary texts created in the Tasks section of Chapter 6.

1. Analyze the parallel corpus you created and aligned using *Alinea* in task 6.6.2. The following list of actions will guide you through the basic steps involved in parallel concordancing using the *ParaConc* Demo version contained on the DVD. For further details on *ParaConc*'s functions, see Barlow (2003, 2008).

- Open *ParaConc* and from the *File* menu select *Load Corpus File(s)*.
- In the dialog box, select *English (United Kingdom)* and *Italian (Standard)* as languages.
- Click on *Add*, for both languages, and add the 2 file pairs created and saved in task 6.6.2. Copies of the files are also available on the DVD.
- Click on *Format*, for both languages. In the dialog boxes select *Automatic recognition* as the format for *Sentences*. Click on *OK*.
- After the parallel corpus has been loaded, select *Save Workspace* from the *File menu* and save your corpus settings (e.g. as *lit_corpus.pws*).
- Select *Search ...* from the *Search* menu and type *child** in the *Text search* window. Then click on *OK*.
- In the upper part of the screen a KWIC concordance for all words beginning with the string *child* is shown. Each monolingual subcorpus can be analyzed independently, as you would do with a monolingual concordancer. Each subcorpus becomes 'active' when you click on the respective window. From the *Frequency* menu select the appropriate submenu to compute wordlists and collocational data. You can change font type and context options (characters, words, lines, sentences, or segments) from the *Display* menu, and order results according to word patterns from the *Sort* menu.
- The lower window contains the segments in the Italian texts which are aligned with those in English containing all the words beginning with the string 'child'. Since the parallel corpus is aligned at sentence rather than word level, in the target concordance window aligned segments are displayed in 'horizontal' rather than KWIC display.
- Right click in the lower window and select *Hot Words*. In the pop-up window select *bambina*. Right click again on the lower window and select *KWIC/Highlight* from the pop up menu. The word *bambina* will be highlighted in the target window and the segments which contain it will be arranged in KWIC format. Use the *Sort* menu to change sorting options with reference to the KWIC concordance in the target window. Aligned source segments will change order accordingly. How are the words 'child' and 'children' translated, other than as *bambino/a/i/e*?
- Search in the target results. Right click on the lower window (the results from the Italian subcorpus), and from the pop up menu select *Search Query*. Using the *Text Search Query* dialog box search for other possible Italian equivalents of the English word(s), typing *fanciull** ('maiden*') and then *ragazz** ('girl*'). Can you detect any difference in how the words are used? Are the different Italian words

used to translate the same English word in different translations?

- Select *Advanced Search* from the *Search ...* menu. In the dialog box, select *English* from the *Language* menu and *Regular Expression* as *Search syntax*. Leave default values for all other settings and type *\ba\W\w+\Wof\b* as search pattern. This will select all strings beginning with the word 'a', followed by any word, followed by the word 'of'.[4] Click on *OK*.
- Sort results in both languages. To order results according to the English subcorpus, click on the upper window to activate it, then from the *Sort* menu select *Search term, No second sort*. To order results according to the Italian subcorpus, right click on the lower window and use the *Hot Words* and *KWIC/Highlight* functions, then sort results to highlight possible patterns.
- Select *Parallel Search* from the *Search ...* menu. In the dialog box, click on *Pattern...* for both languages. For English, use the same search pattern as above (*\ba\W\w+\Wof\b*). For Italian use the regular expression *\buna?\W\w+\Wdi\b*, which will select all strings beginning with the word *un* or *una* ('a/an'), followed by any word, followed by the word *di* ('of'). Click on *OK*. In the results you should see only those occurrences of the English phrase which appear in segments aligned with translated segments containing the analogous Italian structure. Sort results in both languages. Can you display results in a sort of 'word level' alignment? Are there any 'spurious' results? Can you see any repeated patterns in the two languages, respectively, and in how they are translated?
- Repeat the *Parallel Search*, but this time tick the *Not* checkbox next to the search *Pattern...* for Italian. Your query will return only those occurrences of the English phrase appearing in segments which are aligned with Italian segments which do not contain the analogous Italian structure. Sort and classify results in both languages. What are the main differences between these results and those including only parallel concordances containing the 'same' structure in the two languages?
- Repeat the *Parallel Search*, but this time select the Italian subcorpus as 'source' and the English one as 'target'. Type the regular expression *bambin? | ragazz? | fanciull?* as a search pattern for Italian, and *child** as the one for English. In the results, you will see all occurrences of the three lemmas, which are frequently used to translate the lemma CHILD, when they are used to translate different English words or expressions. Sort and classify results in both languages to find frequently occurring patterns.

[4] See Barlow (2003, 2008) for further details on the search syntax.

7.6.2 Exploring the Europarl multilingual corpus

For this task you will use the *OPUS multilingual search interface* to look at how the meaning of an English word with a very specific semantic profile, 'budge' (Sinclair 2003, see task 5.4.4) is expressed in other languages.

1. Go to: http://urd.let.rug.nl/tiedeman/OPUS/ and click on *OPUS multilingual search interface.*

2. Click on *Europarl3* to select the *Europarl* parallel corpus, version 3, then click on *en* to select English as subcorpus in which to carry out your queries. In the following screen, tick the checkbox(es) for the language(s) for which you would like to see parallel concordances.

3. The corpus is indexed with the *CWB*, so the query language is the same used for searching the *COMPARA* corpus in task 2.5.2 (CQP, Corpus Query Language). Type *[lem="budge"]* in the search box, set the *show max* value at 50, select *KWIC* as display format, and click on the *Select* button. The system should retrieve 28 concordances containing forms of the lemma BUDGE, together with their aligned segments in the other language(s). Do these results confirm your previous analysis of 'budge' using data from the *OANC* in task 5.4.6?

4. How is the word 'budge' rendered in (an)other language(s)? Can you see any recurring patterns and fixed collocations, or infer any 'parallel' semantic prosodies? Switch among *KWIC*, *vertical* and *horizontal* display formats to better identify regularities in different languages. Switch between (or among) 'source' corpora to see English segments aligned to the words or expressions most frequently aligned with 'budge', using these words or expressions to query the subcorpora in (an)other language(s).

7.7 Further reading

Articles describing techniques and methodologies for the analysis of multilingual corpora are contained in various collected volumes, e.g. Botley *et al.* (2000), Altenberg and Granger (2002), Anderman and Rogers (2008) and Xiao (2010). On techniques for the analysis of parallel corpora using *ParaConc* see Barlow (2003, 2008).

On the use of multilingual corpora in translator training and professional settings see various contributions in the volumes edited by Bernardini and Zanettin (2000), Zanettin *et al.* (2003), Yuste Rodrigo (2008) and Beeby *et al.* (2009). Tengku Mahadi *et al.* (2010) provides an introduction to corpora in translation, focusing on their use in translator training.

8. Conclusions

Information and communication technologies have considerably affected the way texts, including translated texts, are produced, disseminated and consumed and the way language services providers, including translators, carry out their work. Similarly, they have been instrumental in developing the corpus-based approach (Laviosa 1998a), which makes it possible for "decentralized, multilocal investigations to proceed thanks to virtually instantaneous access to shared primary materials" (Tymoczko 1998:652). Moreover, translation corpora "lend themselves to joint intellectual endeavours unimpeded by time or space, facilitated by intercommunication across the globe" (*ibid.*).

As Tymoczko points out, the development of corpora and corpus-based methods "represents a long-term investment for the field of Translation Studies" (*ibid.*:658). Progress relies on the accumulation of research findings and data and on the cross-validation of results, as well as on the refinement of theoretical and practical tools for corpus construction and investigation. In this respect, corpus-based translation studies are still at an early stage of development, and have not yet risen to fully meet the promises foreshadowed by the new methodologies. Corpus-based translation studies is a collective enterprise and while advancements always depend on the questions that are being asked, the answers also depend on the availability of corpus data and on the computational tools and techniques which are used. As a way of concluding, I briefly discuss what seems a promising way forward as concerns these two aspects.

The creation of corpus resources depends first of all on the acquisition of the texts to be included in a corpus. Early research mainly relied on the digitization of printed material, and the dissemination of data has often been hampered by copyright restrictions. Corpus projects are now increasingly including texts already available in electronic format, the main form in which textual information is created and circulated. While the great bulk of this textual material is composed of ephemeral genres such as e-mail messages, blogs and Web pages, pre-Internet production formats such as newspapers, journals and books are also increasingly migrating into electronic form. Many publishers of newspapers, magazines, journals, and books are now producing electronic versions of copyright protected material. Services such as *Google Books* are digitizing both in- and out-of-print books and making them available online. *Google Books* allows readers to view the full text of publications in the public domain and two or three lines of text of books covered by copyright. As the practice of permitting access to short extracts of copyright protected materials gains ground, it is likely that their inclusion in corpora will become more accepted or tolerated (see §3.2).

A second aspect related to the advancement of corpus-based translation studies concerns corpus tools and techniques. Different priorities and research purposes dictate the choice of which software tools to adopt for the construction of corpus resources in different projects, thus making it difficult to predict which users' needs will orient future developments of corpus software. However, it seems likely that, while stand-alone software will probably still continue to play an important role, descriptive as well as applied research will be more and more affected by the challenges brought about by the Web as a platform for distributing and sharing corpus resources and tools.

Some services already integrate different tools in a common interface. One such service is the *Sketch Engine* (Kilgarriff 2010b), a (commercial) Web-based environment for working with corpora which allows even non-technical users to build a corpus through a corpus compilation pipeline created by integrating a variety of open-source programs, combined with custom-built corpus analysis applications such as the one behind the *Word Sketch* function (see §5.2.4). Another example of corpus compilation pipeline is the *Corpógrafo*[1] (Maia and Sarmento 2006, Sarmento *et al.* 2004, 2006), which is described as "an on-line suite of tools for the creation and analysis of personal corpora and the creation of terminological databases" (Maia and Sarmento 2006:55). The *Corpógrafo*, which is more geared towards terminology compilation and translator training than descriptive translation studies, also includes an alignment utility, though the project is more focused on the compilation and analysis of special domain comparable corpora rather than parallel corpora.

These 'linguistic Web services' provide a common interface and a series of procedures which guide the user through the stages of corpus acquisition, and analysis by interlocking existing tools and creating specific applications which fill the gaps in the workflow in order to satisfy the requirements of the project. Within the emerging paradigm of Service Oriented Architecture (SOA), language technology is increasingly being made available through distributed architectures such as Web services. In a distributed architecture, multiple autonomous Web services interact with each other in order to allow communication and data exchange between applications, and research is underway to extend such services to linguistic processing pipelines through the combination of more than one component that may be located on different sites. In this way linguistic Web services can be combined into a composite Web service, and well-established practices can be organized into workflows and support the exchange of data (see e.g. Ogrodniczuk and Przepiórkowski 2010). This type of computational model also allows for dynamic, on demand, *ad hoc* corpus selection. For example, it is planned that the *TEC* toolkit software architecture will be converted from a client-server model into "a peer-to-peer architecture through the definition of a protocol which will allow servers to specify services they are able to provide and clients to select and query corpora built and maintained by geographically dispersed research groups, thus enhancing the potential for collaboration and increasing availability of data to the research community" (Calzada Pérez and Luz 2006:57). The new computational paradigm also allows for corpus building to become a collective research effort through what is known as 'crowdsourcing', whereby different tasks are outsourced to a community of users through

[1] http://www.linguateca.pt/Corpografo. Accessed on 30 March 2011.

an open call, and discrete work is distributed to different individuals and across a range of projects.

Corpus-based research in translation studies is thriving and embracing new directions (see Kruger *et al.* 2011, in press, and the Research Models in Translation Studies II conference held in Manchester on April/May 2011). Open-source and crowdsourcing are two developmental models which undoubtedly favour Tymoczko's (1998) vision of a globally growing repository of translation-driven corpora accessible over the Internet for the Translation Studies research community.

References

Ahmad, Khurshid (2008) 'Being in Text and Text in Being: Notes on Representative Texts', in Gunilla Anderman and Margaret Rogers (eds) *Incorporating Corpora: The Linguist and the Translator*, Clevedon, Buffalo & Toronto: Multilingual Matters, 60-94.

------, Paul Holmes-Higgin and Syed Sibte Raza Abidi (1994) 'A Description of Texts in a Corpus: "Virtual" and "Real" Corpora', in Willy Martin, Willem Mejis, Margaret Moerland, Elsemiek ten Pas, Piet van Sterkenburg and Piek Vossen (eds) *EURALEX 1994 Proceedings*, Amsterdam: Vrije Universiteit, 390-402.

Aijmer, Karin (2008) 'Translating Discourse Particles: A Case of Complex Translation', in Gunilla Anderman and Margaret Rogers (eds) *Incorporating Corpora: The Linguist and the Translator*, Clevedon, Buffalo & Toronto: Multilingual Matters, 95-116.

Altenberg, Bengt and Sylviane Granger (2002) 'Recent Trends in Cross-Linguistic Lexical Studies', in Bengt Altenberg and Sylviane Granger (eds) *Lexis in Contrast. Corpus-based Approach*, Amsterdam & Philadelphia: John Benjamins, 3-48.

Alves, Fabio, Adriana Pagano, Stella Neumann, Erich Steiner and Sivia Hansen-Schirra (2010) 'Translation units and grammatical shifts: Towards an integration of product- and process-based translation research', in Erik Angelone and Gregory Shreve (eds) *Translation and Cognition: Recent Developments*, Amsterdam & Philadelphia: John Benjamins, 109-142.

Anderman, Gunilla and Margaret Rogers (eds) (2008) *Incorporating Corpora: The Linguist and the Translator*, Clevedon, Buffalo & Toronto: Multilingual Matters.

Anderson, Jean, David Beavan and Christian Kay (2007) 'SCOTS: Scottish Corpus of Texts and Speech', in Joan C. Beal, Karen P. Corrigan and Hermann L. Moisl (eds) *Creating and Digitizing Language Corpora: Volume 1: Synchronic Databases*, Basingstoke: Palgrave Macmillan, 17-34.

Aston, Guy (2000) 'I corpora come risorsa per la traduzione e per l'apprendimento', in Silvia Bernardini and Federico Zanettin (eds) *I corpora nella didattica della traduzione*, Bologna: CLUEB, 21-29.

------ (2001) 'Text Categories and Corpus Users: A Response to David Lee', *Language Learning & Technology* 5(3): 72-76.

------ (2009) 'Foreword', in Allison Beeby, Patricia Rodríguez Inés and Pilar Sánchez-Gijón (eds) *Corpus Use and Translating: Corpus Use for Learning to Translate and Learning Corpus Use to Translate*, Amsterdam & Philadelphia: John Benjamins, xi-x.

------ and Lou Burnard (1998) *The BNC Handbook*, Edinburgh: Edinburgh University Press.

Atkins, Sue, Jeremy Clear and Nicholas Ostler (1992) 'Corpus Design Criteria', *Literary and Linguistic Computing* 7(1): 1-16.

Austermühl, Frank (2001) *Electronic Tools for Tranlators*, Manchester: St Jerome.

Baker, Mona (1993) 'Corpus Linguistics and Translation Studies: Implications and Applications', in Mona Baker, Gill Francis and Elena Tognini-Bonelli (eds) *Text and Technology: In Honour of John Sinclair*, Amsterdam & Philadelphia: John Benjamins, 233-250.

------ (1995) 'Corpora in Translation Studies: An Overview and Some Suggestions for Future Research', *Target* 7(2): 223-43.

------ (1996) 'Corpus-based Translation Studies – the Challenges that Lie ahead', in Harold Somers (ed.) *Terminology, LSP & Translation*, Philadelphia & Amsterdam: John Benjamins, 175-86.
------ (2000) 'Towards a Methodology for Investigating the Style of a Literary Translator', *Target* 12(2): 241-66.
------ (2004) 'A Corpus-based View of Similarity and Difference in Translation', *International Journal of Corpus Linguistics* 9(2): 167-93.
------ (2007) 'Patterns of Idiomaticity in Translated vs. Non-Translated Text', *Belgian Journal of Linguistics* 21: 11-21.
Barlow, Michael (2000) 'Parallel Texts in Language Teaching', in Simon P. Botley, Tony McEnery and Andrew Wilson (eds) *Multilingual Corpora in Teaching and Research*, Amsterdam: Rodopi, 106-15.
------ (2002) 'ParaConc: Concordance Software for Multilingual Parallel Corpora', in Elia Yuste Rodrigo (ed.) *Language Resources for Translation Work and Research*, Proceedings of the Third International Conference on Language Resources and Evaluation, Las Palmas, Spain (LREC 2002), Paris: ELRA, 20-24. Available at http://www.mt-archive.info/LREC-2002-Barlow.pdf [Accessed on 31 March 2011].
------ (2003) *ParaConc: A Concordancer for Parallel Texts*, Houston, TX: Athelstan Available at http://www.athel.com/paraconc.pdf [Accessed on 25 March 2011].
------ (2004) *MonoConc Pro*, version 2.2, Houston, TX: Athelstan.
------ (2008) ParaConc *and Parallel Corpora in Contrastive and Translation Studies*, Houston, TX: Athelstan.
Barnbrook, Geoff (1996) *Language and Computers*, Edinburgh: Edinburgh University Press.
Baroni, Marco and Silvia Bernardini (2003) 'A Preliminary Analysis of Collocational Differences in Monolingual Comparable Corpora', in Dawn Archer, Paul Rayson, Andrew Wilson and Tony McEnery (eds) *Proceedings of the Corpus Linguistics 2003 Conference, UCREL Technical Papers 16:* 82-91.
------ (2004) 'BootCaT: Bootstrapping Corpora and Terms from the Web', in *Proceedings of the Fifth International Conference on Language Resources and Evaluation, Lisbon, Portugal (LREC 2004),* Paris: ELRA, 1313-16. Available at https://nats-www.informatik.uni-hamburg.de/intern/proceedings/2004/LREC/pdf/509.pdf [Accessed on 30 March 2011].
------ (eds) (2006a) *Wacky! Working Papers on the Web as Corpus*, Bologna: GEDIT.
------ (2006b) 'A New Approach to the Study of Translationese: Machine-learning the Difference between Original and Translated Text', *Literary and Linguist Computing* 21(3): 259-74.
------, Adriano Ferraresi and Eros Zanchetta (2009) 'The WaCky Wide Web: A Collection of Very Large Linguistically Processed Web-crawled Corpora', *Journal of Language Resources and Evaluation* 43(3): 209-26.
------, Federica Comastri, Lorenzo Piccioni, Alessandra Volpi, Guy Aston and Marco Mazzoleni (2004) 'Introducing "La Repubblica" Corpus: A Large, Annotated, TEI(XML)-Compliant Corpus of Newspaper Italian', in *Proceedings of the Fourth International Conference on Language Resources and Evaluation Lisbon, Portugal (LREC 2004)*, Paris: ELRA, 1771-74. Available at https://nats-www.informatik.uni-hamburg.de/intern/proceedings/2004/LREC/pdf/247.pdf [Accessed on 30 March 2011].

Becher, Viktor (2010a) 'Towards a More Rigorous Treatment of the Explicitation Hypothesis in Translation Studies', *trans-kom* 3(1): 1-25. Available at http://www.trans-kom.eu/bd03nr01/trans-kom_03_01_01_Becher_Explicitation.20100531.pdf [Accessed on 11 January 2011].
------ (2010b) 'Abandoning the Notion of "Translation-inherent" Explicitation: Against a Dogma of Translation Studies', *Across Languages and Cultures* 11(1): 1-28.
Beeby, Allison, Patricia Rodríguez Inés and Pilar Sánchez-Gijón (eds) (2009) *Corpus Use and Translating: Corpus Use for Learning to Translate and Learning Corpus Use to Translate*, Amsterdam & Philadelphia: John Benjamins.
Bergh, Gunnar (2005) 'Min(d)ing English Language Data on the Web: What Can Google Tell us?', *ICAME JOURNAL* 29: 25-46.
Berla, Erica (1994) 'Italy Takes to Foreign Fiction', *European Bookseller*, January/February: 62-63.
Bernardini, Silvia (2003) 'Bidirectional Corpora and Translation: The CEXI Corpus', in Susan Conrad (ed.) *TESOL Quarterly Special Issue on Corpus Linguistics in TESOL*, 528-37.
------ (2005) 'Reviving Old Ideas: Parallel and Comparable Analysis in Translation Studies – with an Example from Translation Stylistics', in Karin Aijmer and Cecilia Alvstad (eds) *New Tendencies in Translation Studies*, Göteborg: University of Göteborg, 5-18.
------ and Adriano Ferraresi (forthcoming) 'Old Needs, New Solutions. Comparable Corpora for Language Professionals', in Serge Sharoff, Reinhard Rapp, Pierre Zweigenbaum and Pascale Fung (eds) *BUCC: Building and Using Comparable Corpora*, New York & Heidelberg: Springer.
------ and Federico Zanettin (eds) (2000) *I corpora nella didattica della traduzione. Corpus Use and Learning to Translate*, Bologna: CLUEB.
------ and Federico Zanettin (2004) 'When is a Universal not a Universal? Some Limits of Current Corpus-based Methodologies for the Investigation of Translation Universals', in Anna Mauranen and Pekka Kujamäki (eds) *Translation Universals: Do they exist?*', Amsterdam & Philadelphia: John Benjamins, 51-62.
------, Marco Baroni and Stefan Evert (2006) 'A WaCky Introduction', in Marco Baroni and Silvia Bernardini (eds) *Wacky! Working Papers on the Web as Corpus*, Bologna: GEDIT, 9-40.
Biber, Douglas, Susan Conrad and Rendi Reppen (1998) *Corpus Linguistics: Investigating Language Structure and Use*, Cambridge: Cambridge University Press.
Blum-Kulka, Shoshana (1986) 'Shifts of Cohesion and Coherence in Translation', in Juliane House and Shoshana Blum-Kulka (eds) *Interlingual and Intercultural Communication. Discourse and Cognition in Translation and Second Language Acquisition*, Tübingen: Narr, 17-35.
Borin, Lars (ed.) (2002) *Parallel Corpora, Parallel Worlds*, Amsterdam: Rodopi.
Borras, John (2003) 'OASIS. Recent Technical Developments, XML and Related Technologies', in *Workshop on Challenges, Perspectives and Standardization Issues in E-Government (Geneva, 5-6 June 2003)*. Available at http://www.itu.int/itudoc/itu-t/workshop/e-gov/ [Accessed on 08 October 2009].
Bosseaux, Charlotte (2001) 'A Study of the Translator's Voice and Style in the French Translations of Virginia Woolf's The Waves', *CTIS Occasional Papers* 1: 55-75.
------ (2004) 'Point of View in Translation: a Corpus-based Study of French Translations of

Virginia Woolf's To The Lighthouse', *Across Languages and Cultures* 5(1): 107-23.
------ (2006) 'Who's Afraid of Virginia's you: a Corpus-based Study of the French Translations of The Waves', *Meta* 51(3): 559-610. Available at http://id.erudit.org/iderudit/013565ar [Accessed on 31 March 2011].
------ (2007) *How Does it Feel? Point of View in Translation. The Case of Virginia Woolf into French*, Amsterdam & New York: Rodopi.
Botley, Simon Philip, Tony McEnery and Andrew Wilson (eds) *Multilingual Corpora in Teaching and Research*, Amsterdam & Atlanta, GA: Rodopi.
Bowker, Lynne (1998) 'Using Specialized Monolingual Native-Language Corpora as a Translation Resource: A Pilot Study', in Sara Laviosa (ed.) *L'Approche Basée sur le corpus/The Corpus-Based Approach*, *Meta* 43(4): 631-51. Available at http://id.erudit.org/iderudit/002134ar [Accessed on 31 March 2011].
------ (2002a) *Computer-aided Translation Technology: A Practical Introduction*, Ottawa: University of Ottawa Press.
------ (2002b) 'Working Together: A Collaborative Approach to DIY Corpora', in Elia Yuste Rodrigo (ed.) *Language Resources for Translation Work and Research*, Proceedings of the Third International Conference on Language Resources and Evaluation, Las Palmas, Spain (LREC 2002), Paris: ELRA, 29-36. Available at http://www.ifi.unizh.ch/cl/yuste/postworkshop/repository/lbowker.pdf [Accessed on 31 March 2011].
------ and Michael Barlow (2008) 'A Comparative Evaluation of Bilingual Concordancers and Translation Memory Systems', in Elia Yuste Rodrigo (ed.) *Topics in Language Resources for Translation and Localisation*, Amsterdam & Philadelphia: John Benjamins, 1-22.
------ and Peter Bennison (2003) 'Student Translation Archive and Student Translation Tracking System. Design, Development and Application', in Federico Zanettin, Silvia Bernardini and Dominic Stewart (eds) *Corpora in Translator Education*, Manchester: St. Jerome Publishing, 103-17.
------ and Jennifer Pearson (2002) *Working with Specialized Language: A Practical Guide to Using Corpora*, London & New York: Routledge.
Brown, Peter F., Jennifer C. Lai and Robert L. Mercer (1991) 'Aligning Sentences in Parallel Corpora', in *Proceedings of the 29th Annual Meeting of the Association for Computational Linguistics, 18-21 June 1991, University of California, Berkeley, California, USA*, Stroudsburg, PA: ACL, 169-76. Available at http://portal.acm.org/ft_gateway.cfm?id=981366&type=pdf&CFID=24136484&CFTOKEN=69308561 [Accessed on 31 March 2011].
Burnard, Lou (2005) 'Metadata for Corpus Work', in Martin Wynne (ed.) *Developing Linguistic Corpora: A Guide to Good Practice*, Oxford: Oxbow Books, 30-46. Available at http://www.ahds.ac.uk/creating/guides/linguistic-corpora/chapter3.htm [Accessed on 31 March 2011].
------ (ed.) (1995) *Users Reference Guide for the British National Corpus*, Oxford UK: Oxford University Computing Services.
------ and Michael Sperberg-McQueen (2006) *TEI Lite: Encoding for Interchange: An Introduction to the TEI — Revised for TEI P5 Release*. Available at http://www.tei-c.org/release/doc/tei-p5-exemplars/html/teilite.doc.html [Accessed on 30 March 2011].
Calzada Pérez, María and Saturnino Luz (2006) 'ECPC – Technology as a Tool to Study

the (Linguistic) Functioning of National and Trans-National European Parliament', *International Journal Of Technology, Knowledge And Society* 2(5): 53-61.

Castagnoli, Sara, Dragoş Ciobanu, Natalie Kübler, Kerstin Kunz and Alexandra Volanschi (forthcoming) 'Designing a Learner Translator Corpus for Training Purposes', in Natalie Kübler (ed.) *Practical Approaches of Theorical Models for Language Corpora and Language-related Teaching*, Bern: Peter Lang.

Cencini, Marco (2002) 'On the Importance of an Encoding Standard for Corpus-based Interpreting Studies. Extending the TEI Scheme', in *CULT2K, inTRAlinea*. Available at http://www.intralinea.it/specials/cult2k/ita_more.php?id=107_0_42_0_C [Accessed on 31 March 2011].

------ and Guy Aston (2002) 'Resurrecting the Corp(us¦se): Towards an Encoding Standard for Interpreting Data', in Giuliana Garzone and Maurizio Viezzi (eds) *Interpreting in the 21st Century. Challenges and Opportunities*, Amsterdam & Philadelphia: John Benjamins, 47-62.

Chesterman, Andrew (2004) 'Beyond the Particular', in Anna Mauranen and Pekka Kujamäki (eds) *Translation Universals. Do they exist?*, Amsterdam & Philadelphia: John Benjamins, 33-49.

------ (2007) 'What is a Unique Item?', in Yves Gambier, Miriam Shlesinger and Radegundis Stolze (eds) *Doubts and Directions in Translation Studies: Selected Contributions from the EST Congress, Lisbon 2004*, Amsterdam & Philadelphia: John Benjamins, 3-13.

Corpas Pastor, Gloria (2008) *Investigar con corpus en traducción: los retos de un nuevo paradigma*, Bern: Peter Lang.

------ and Miriam Seghiri (2007) 'Specialized Corpora for Translators: A Quantitative Method to Determine Representativeness', *Translation Journal* 11(3). Available at http://translationjournal.net/journal//41corpus.htm [Accessed on 31 March 2011].

------, Ruslan Mitkov, Naveed Afzal and Lisette Garcia Moya (2008) 'Translation Universals: Do they Exist? A Corpus-based and NLP Approach to Convergence', in Pierre Zweigenbaum, Éric Gaussier and Pascale Fung (eds) *Proceedings of the Workshop on Building and Using Parallel Corpora, Marrakech, Morocco (LREC 2008)*, Paris: ELRA, 1-6.

Čulo, Oliver, Silvia Hansen-Schirra, Stella Neumann and Karin Maksymski (forthcoming) 'Querying the CroCo Corpus for Translation Shifts. Beyond Corpus Construction: Exploitation and Maintenance of Parallel Corpora', in Silvia Hansen-Schirra, Stella Neumann and Oliver Čulo (eds) *Beyond Corpus Construction: Exploitation and Maintenance of Parallel Corpora. Special Issue of the International Journal of Corpus Linguistics*.

Cyrus, Lea (2006) 'Building a Resource for Studying Translation Shifts', in *Proceedings of the Fifth International Conference on Linguistic Resources and Evaluation, Genoa, Italy (LREC 2006)*, Paris: ELRA, 1240-45. Available at http://www.mt-archive.info/LREC-2006-Cyrus.pdf [Accessed on 15 March 2011].

Danielsson, Pernilla and Daniel Ridings (1997) *Practical Presentation of a "Vanilla" Aligner*. Available at http://nl.ijs.si/telri/Vanilla/doc/ljubljana/ [Accessed on 31 March 2011].

Davies, Mark (2009a) 'The 385+ Million Word Corpus of Contemporary American English (1990-2008+): Design, Architecture, and Linguistic Insights', *International Journal of Corpus Linguistics* 14(2): 159-90.

------ (2009b) 'Composition of the Corpus', *The Corpus of Contemporary American English*. Available at http://www.americancorpus.org/ [Accessed on 31 March 2011].

Dayrell, Carmen (2007) 'A Quantitative Approach to Compare Collocational Patterns in Translated and Non-translated Texts', *International Journal of Corpus Linguistics* 12(3): 375-414.

de Beaugrande, Robert (1994) 'Function and Form in Language Theory and Research: The Tide is Turning', *Functions of Language* 1(2): 163-200.

------ (1997) 'On History and Historicity in Modern Linguistics. Formalism versus Functionalism Revisited', *Functions of Language* 4(2): 169-213.

------ (1998) 'Language and Society: The Real and the Ideal in Linguistics, Sociolinguistics, and Corpus Linguistics', *Journal of Sociolinguistics* 3(1): 128-39.

Denoyer, Ludovic and Patrick Gallinari (2006) 'The Wikipedia XML Corpus', *SIGIR Forum* 40(1): 64-69.

Dickinson, Markus and Detmar Meurers (eds) (2002) *Corpora and Corpus Annotation Tools on the WWW*. Available at http://www.ling.ohio-state.edu/~dickinso/corpus.html [Accessed on 31 March 2011].

Dyrberg, Gunhild and Joan Tournay (1990) 'Définition des équivalents de traduction de termes économiques et juridiques sur la base de textes parallèles', *Cahiers de lexicologie* 56/57: 261-74.

Ebeling, Jarle (1998) 'The Translation Corpus Explorer: A Browser for Parallel Texts', in Stig Johansson and Signe Oksefjell (eds) *Corpora and Crosslinguistic Research: Theory, Method, and Case Studies*, Amsterdam: Rodopi, 101-12.

Erjavec, Tomaž (2010) 'MULTEXT-East Version 4: Multilingual Morphosyntactic Specifications, Lexicons and Corpora', in *Proceedings of the Seventh International Conference on Linguistic Resources and Evaluation Conference, Valletta, Malta (LREC 2010)*, Paris: ELRA, 2544-2547. Available at http://nl.ijs.si/ME/V4/doc/bib/mte-lrec2010.pdf [Accessed on 21 January 2011].

Eskola, Sari (2004) 'Untypical Frequencies in Translated Language: A Corpus-based Study on a Literary Corpus of Translated and Non-translated Finnish', in Anna Mauranen and Pekka Kujamäki (eds) (2004) *Translation Universals. Do they exist?*, Amsterdam & Philadelphia: John Benjamins, 83–99.

Even-Zohar, Itamar (1979) 'Polysystem Theory', *Poetics Today* 1(1-2): 287–310.

Evert, Stefan (2005) *The CQP Query Language Tutorial (CWB version 2.2.b90)*. Available at http://www.ims.uni-stuttgart.de/projekte/CorpusWorkbench/CQPTutorial/html/cqp-tutorial.html [Accessed on 31 March 2011].

Ferraresi, Adriano (2009) 'Identifying Collocations in Specialised Corpora: A Preliminary Investigation Combining Frequency and Semantic Information', Paper Presented at the *Aston Postgraduate Conference on Corpus Linguistics,* 23 may 2009, Aston University, Birmingham, UK.

------, Silvia Bernardini, Giovanni Picci and Marco Baroni (2010) 'Web Corpora for Bilingual Lexicography. A Pilot Study of English/French Collocation Extraction and Translation', in Richard Xiao (eds) *Using Corpora in Contrastive and Translation Studies*, Newcastle upon Tyne: Cambridge Scholars Publishing, 337-59.

Firth, John Rupert (1957) *Papers in Linguistics 1934-1951*, London: Oxford University Press.

Fissaha Adafre, Sisay and Maarten de Rijke (2006) 'Finding Similar Sentences across

Multiple Languages inWikipedia', in *EACL 2006 - Proceedings of the Workshop on NEW TEXT Wikis and Blogs and Other Dynamic Text Sources, April, 4, 2006 Trento, Italy,* Association for Computational Linguistics. Available at http://acl.ldc.upenn.edu/W/W06/W06-2810.pdf [Accessed on 22 January 2011].

Fletcher, William H. (2004) 'Facilitating the Compilation and Dissemination of Ad-hoc Web Corpora', in Guy Aston, Silvia Bernardini and Dominic Stewart (eds) *Corpora and Language Learners*, Amsterdam & Philadelphia: John Benjamins, 271-300.

Francis, Gill (2011) *Colouring Meaning. Collocation and Connotation in Figurative Language*, Amsterdam & Philadelphia: John Benjamins.

Frankenberg-Garcia, Ana (2005) 'A Corpus-based Study of Loan Words in Original and Translated Texts', in Pernilla Danielsson and Martijn Wagenmakers (eds) *Proceedings from the Corpus Linguistics Conference Series (PCLC)* 1(1). Available at http://anafrankenberg.synthasite.com/resources/FG2005ACorpus-BasedStudyOfLoanWords.pdf [Accessed on 25 March 2011].

------ (2006) 'Using a Parallel Corpus in Translation Practice and Research', in *Actas da Contrapor 2006, 1ª Conferência de Tradução Portuguesa, Faculdadede Ciências e Tecnologia* (Universidade Nova de Lisboa, 11-12 September 2006), 142-48. Available at http://www.linguateca.pt/documentos/Frankenberg-GarciaContrapor2006.pdf [Accessed on 31 March 2011].

------ (2009a) 'Are Translations Longer than Source Texts? A Corpus-based Study of Explicitation', in Allison Beeby, Patricia Rodríguez and Pilar Sánchez-Gijón (eds) *Corpus Use and Translating*, Amsterdam & Philadelphia: John Benjamins, 47-58.

------ (2009b) 'Compiling and Using a Parallel Corpus for Research in Translation', *International Journal of Translation* (21)1: 57-71.

------ and Diana Santos (2003) 'Introducing COMPARA, the Portuguese-English Parallel Translation Corpus', in Federico Zanettin, Silvia Bernardini and Dominic Stewart (eds) *Corpora in Translation Education*, Manchester: St. Jerome Publishing, 71-87.

------, Diana Santos and Rosário Silva (2008) *Construção do COMPARA*. Available at http://www.linguateca.pt/COMPARA/construcao_compara.php [Accessed on 31 March 2011].

Frawley, William (2000[1984]) 'Prolegomenon to a Theory of Translation', in Lawrence Venuti (ed.) *The Translation Studies Reader*, London: Routledge, 250-63.

Fung, Pascale and Kathleen McKeown (1994) 'Aligning Noisy Parallel Corpora across Language Groups: Word Pair Feature Matching by Dynamic Time Warping', in *Proceedings of AMTA 94, Columbia, Maryland: Oct. 1994*, 81-88, Available at http://xxx.lanl.gov/abs/cmp-lg/9409011 [Accessed on 31 March 2011].

Fung, Pascale, Pierre Zweigenbaum and Reinhard Rapp (eds) (2009) *BUCC 2009. Proceedings of the Second 2ndWorkshop on Building and Using Comparable Corpora: from Parallel to Non-parallel Corpora*, ACL (The Association for Computational Linguistics). Available at http://www.fb06.uni-mainz.de/lk/bucc2010/documents/Proceedings-BUCC-2009.pdf [Accessed on 28 February 2011].

Gale, William A. and Kenneth W. Church (1993) 'A Program for Aligning Sentences in Bilingual Corpora', *Computational Linguistics* 19(1): 75-102.

Garside, Roger (1987) 'The CLAWS Word-tagging System', in Roger Garside, Geoffrey Leech and Geoffrey Sampson (eds) *The Computational Analysis of English: A Corpus-based Approach*, London: Longman, 30-41.

------ (1996) 'The Robust Tagging of Unrestricted Text: the BNC Experience', in Jenny

Thomas and Michael H. Short (eds) *Using Corpora for Language Research: Studies in Honour of Geoffrey Leech,* London: Longman, 167-80.
------ and Nick Smith (1997) 'A Hybrid Grammatical Tagger: CLAWS4', in Roger Garside, Geoffrey Leech and Anthony McEnery (eds) *Corpus Annotation: Linguistic Information from Computer Text Corpora*, London: Longman, 102-21.
Gamallo Otero, Pablo and Isaac González López (2010) 'Wikipedia as Multilingual Source of Comparable Corpora', in Reinhard Rapp, Pierre Zweigenbaum and Serge Sharoff (eds) *BUCC 2010. Proceedings of the Third Workshop on Building and Using Comparable Corpora: Applications of Parallel and Comparable Corpora in Natural Language Engineering and the Humanities*, Paris: ELRA, 21-25.
Gaspari, Federico and Silvia Bernardini (2010) 'Comparing Non-native and Translated Language: Monolingual Comparable Corpora with a Twist', in Richard Xiao (ed.) *Using Corpora in Contrastive and Translation Studies*, Newcastle upon Tyne: Cambridge Scholars Publishing, 215-34.
Gatto, Maristella (2009) *From 'Body' to 'Web'. An Introduction to the Web as Corpus*, Bari: Laterza – University Press Online. Available at http://www.universitypressonline.it [Accessed on 31 March 2011].
------ (2010) 'From Language to Culture and Beyond: Building and Exploring Comparable Web Corpora', in Reinhard Rapp, Pierre Zweigenbaum and Serge Sharoff (eds) *BUCC 2010. Proceedings of the Third Workshop on Building and Using Comparable Corpora: Applications of Parallel and Comparable Corpora in Natural Language Engineering and the Humanities*, Paris: ELRA, 72-78. Available at http://www.fb06.uni-mainz.de/lk/bucc2010/documents/Proceedings-BUCC-2010.pdf [Accessed 28 February 2011].
Gellerstam, Martin (1986) 'Translationese in Swedish Novels Translated from English', in Lars Wollin and Hans Lindquist (eds) *Translation Studies in Scandinavia*, Lund: CWK Gleerup, 88-95.
------ (2005) 'Fingerprints in Translation', in Gunilla Anderman and Margaret Rogers (eds) *In and Out of English: For Better, For Worse?*, Clavedon: Multilingual Matters, 201-13.
Goeuriot, Lorraine, Emmanuel Morin and Béatrice Daille (2009) 'Compilation of Specialized Comparable Corpora in French and Japanese', in *Proceedings of the 2nd Workshop on Building and Using Comparable Corpora, ACL-IJCNLP 2009,* Suntec, Singapore, 6 August 2009, 46–54.
Göpferich, Susanne (2010) 'Data Documentation and Data Accessibility in Translation Process Research', *The Translator* 16: 1, 93-124.
Granger, Sylviane (1996) 'From CA to CIA and back: An Integrated Approach to Computerized Bilingual and Learner corpora', in Karin Aijmer, Bengt Altenberg and Matts Johansson (eds) *Languages in Contrast. Text-based Cross-linguistic Studies*, Lund: Lund University Press, 37-51.
------ (1998) *Learner English on Computer*, London & New York: Longman.
------ (1999) 'Use of Tenses by Advanced EFL Learners: Evidence from an Error-tagged Computer Corpus', in Hilde Hasselgard and Signe Oksefjell (eds) *Out of Corpora-Studies in Honour of Stig Johansson*, Amsterdam & Atlanta: Rodopi,191-202.
------, Jacques Lerot and Stephanie Petch-Tyson (eds) (2003) *Corpus-based Approaches to Contrastive Linguistics and Translation Studies*, Amsterdam & New York: Rodopi.

Graubart Champe, Gertrud (2000) 'Translationese', in Oliva Classe (ed.) *Encyclopedia of Literary Translation into English*, London & New York: Routledge, 1421-22.

Greaves, Chris (2009) *ConcGram*, version 1.0, Amsterdam & Philadelphia: John Benjamins.

Grefenstette, Gregory and Julien Nioche (2000) 'Estimation of English and Non-English language Use on the WWW', in *Proceedings of the RIAO (Recherche d'Informations Assistee par Ordinateur)*, Paris, 237-246.

Hale, Terry (1996) 'Redressing the Balance', *European Bookseller*, June/July: 27-29.

Hansen, Silvia and Elke Teich (2001) 'Multi-layer Analysis of Translation Corpora: Methodological Issues and Practical Implications', in *Proceedings of EUROLAN 2001 Workshop on Multi-layer Corpus-based Analysis, Iasi, Romania, July*, 44-55.

Hansen-Schirra, Silvia, Stella Neumann and Mihaela Vela (2006) 'Multi-dimensional Annotation and Alignment in an English-German Translation Corpus', in *Proceedings of the Workshop on Multi-dimensional Markup in Natural Language Processing (NLPXML-2006), EACL,* Trento, Italy, April 2006, 35-42.

Hansen-Schirra, Silvia, Stella Neumann and Erich Steiner (2007) 'Cohesive Explicitness and Explicitation in an English-German Translation Corpus', in *Information Structuring Resources in Contrast, Languages in Contrast* 7(2): 241-65.

Harris, Brian (1988) 'Bi-text, a New Concept in Translation Theory', *Language Monthly* 54: 8-11.

Hartmann, Reinhard Rudolf Karl (1980) *Contrastive Textology. Comparative Discourse Analysis in Applied Linguistics*, Heidelberg: Julius Groos Verlag.

Heiss, Christine and Marcello Soffritti (2008) 'Forlixt 1 – The Forlì Corpus of Screen Translation: Exploring Macrostructures', in Delia Chiaro, Christine Heiss and Chiara Bucaria (eds) *Between Text and Image. Updating Research in Screen Translation*, Amsterdam & Philadelphia: John Benjamins, 51-62.

Hermans, Theo (1996) 'The Translator's Voice in Translated Narrative', *Target* 8(1): 23-48.

------ (2010) 'The Translator as Evaluator' in Mona Baker, Maeve Olohan and María Calzada Pérez (eds) *Text and Context: Essays on Translation & Interpreting in Honour of Ian Mason*, Manchester: St Jerome, 63-76.

Hoey, Michael (2005) *Lexical priming: a new theory of words and language*, London & New York: Routledge

Hofland, Knut and Stig Johansson (1998) 'The Translation Corpus Aligner: A Program for Automatic Alignment of Parallel Texts', in Stig Johansson and Signe Oksefjell (eds) *Corpora and Crosslinguistic Research: Theory, Method, and Case Studies*, Amsterdam: Rodopi, 87-100.

Holmes, James S. (1972/1988) 'The Name and Nature of Translation Studies', in James S. Holmes, *Translated! Papers on Literary Translation and Translation Studies*, Amsterdam: Rodopi, 67–80.

House, Juliane (2008) 'Beyond Intervention: Universals in Translation?', in Juliane House (ed.) *Beyond Intervention: Universals in Translation Processes, trans-kom* 1(1): 6-19. Available at http://www.trans-kom.eu/bd01nr01/trans-kom_01_01_02_House_Beyond_Intervention.20080707.pdf [Accessed on 30 March 2011].

Hubbard, Philip (2005) *Google as a Tool for Academic Writing*, Stanford University. Available at http://www.stanford.edu/~efs/google/index.htm [Accessed on 31 March 2011].

Hüning, Matthias (2001-2002) *WebCONC. Konkordanzen aus dem Web*. Available at http://www.niederlandistik.fu-berlin.de/cgi-bin/web-conc.cgi? [Accessed on 30 March 2011].

Hunston, Susan (2002) *Corpora in Applied Linguistics*, Cambridge: Cambridge University Press.

Ide, Nancy and Greg Priest-Dorman (2000) *Corpus Encoding Standard - Document CES 1. Title Page. Version 1.5. Last Modified 20 March 2000.* Available at http://www.cs.vassar.edu/CES/ [Accessed on 31 March 2011].

Ide, Nancy and Keith Suderman (2006) 'The American National Corpus First Release', in *Proceedings of the Fifth Language Resources and Evaluation Conference*, Genoa, Italy (LREC 2006), Paris: ELRA, 1681-84. Available at https://nats-www.informatik.uni-hamburg.de/intern/proceedings/2004/LREC/518.pdf [Accessed on 30 March 2011].

Jääskeläinen, Riitta (2010) 'Think-aloud protocol', in Yves Gambier and Luc van Doorslaer (eds) *Handbook of Translation Studies*, Amsterdam & Philadelphia: John Benjamins, 371–73.

Jantunen, Jarmo Harri (2001) 'Synonymity and Lexical Simplification in Translations: A Corpus-based Approach', *Across Languages and Cultures* 2(1): 97–112.

------ (2004) 'Untypical Patterns in Translation. Issues of Corpus Methodology and Synonymity', in Anna Mauranen and Pekka Kujamäki (eds) (2004) *Translation Universals. Do they exist?*, Amsterdam & Philadelphia: John Benjamins, 101-26.

Janus, Daniel and Adam Przepiórkowski (2007) 'Poliqarp: An Open Source Corpus Indexer and Search Engine with Syntactic Extensions', in *Proceedings of the ACL 2007 Demo Session, Prague, Czech Republic.* Available at http://www.aclweb.org/anthology/P/P07/P07-2.pdf [Accessed on 30 March 2011].

Jiménez-Crespo, Miguel A. (2010) 'The Intersection of Localization and Translation: A Corpus Study of Spanish Original and Localized Web Forms', *Translation and Interpreting Studies* 5(2): 186-207.

Johansson, Stig (1998) 'On the Role of Corpora in Cross-linguistic Research', in Stig Johansson and Signe Oksefjell (eds) *Corpora and Cross-linguistic Research: Theory, Method, and Case Studies*, Amsterdam & Atlanta, GA: Rodopi, 3-24.

------ (2003) 'Reflections on Corpora and their Uses in Cross-linguistic Research', in Federico Zanettin, Silvia Bernardini and Dominic Stewart (eds) *Corpora in Translator Education*, Manchester: St. Jerome, 135-48.

------ (2004) 'Why Change the Subject? On Changes in Subject Selection in Translation from English into Norwegian', *Target* 16(1): 29-52.

------ (2007) *Seeing through Multilingual Corpora: On the Use of Corpora in Contrastive Studies*, Amsterdam: John Benjamins.

------ and Knut Hofland (1994) 'Towards an English-Norwegian Parallel Corpus', in Udo Fries, Gunnel Tottie and Peter Schneider (eds) *Creating and Using English Language Corpora*, Amsterdam & Atlanta, GA: Rodopi, 25-37.

------ and Signe Oksefjell (eds) (1998) *Corpora and Cross Linguistic Research. Theory, Method and Case Studies*, Amsterdam & Atlanta, GA: Rodopi.

------, Jarle Ebeling and Signe Oksefjell (1999-2002) *English-Norwegian Parallel Corpus: Manual*. Available at http://www.hf.uio.no/ilos/tjenester/kunnskap/sprak/omc/enpc/ENPCmanual.html [Accessed on 30 March 2011].

------, Geoffrey Leech and Helen Goodluck (1978) *Manual of Information to Accompany the Lancaster-Oslo/Bergen corpus of British English, for Use with Digital*

Computers, Department of English, University of Oslo. Available at http://khnt.hit.uib.no/icame/manuals/lob/index.htm [Accessed on 31 March 2011].

Kaji, Hirojuki and Yasutsugu Morimoto (2002) 'Unsupervised Word Sense Disambiguation Using Bilingual Comparable Corpora', in *COLING 2002: The 19th International Conference on Computational Linguistics*, ACL, 411-17. Available at http://www.aclweb.org/anthology/C/C02/C02-1058.pdf [Accessed on 31 March 2011].

Kanter, Ido, Haggai Kfir, Brenda Malkiel and Miriam Shlesinger (2006) 'Identifying Universals of Text Translation', *Journal of Quantitative Linguistics* 13(1): 35-43.

Kemppanen, Hannu (2004) 'Keywords and Ideology in Translated History Texts: A Corpus-based Analysis', *Across Languages and Cultures* 5(1): 89-107.

Kennedy, Graeme (1998) *An Introduction to Corpus Linguistics*, London: Addison Wesley Longman.

Kenny, Dorothy (1997) '(Ab)normal Translations: A German-English Parallel Corpus for Investigating Normalization in Translation', in Barbara Lewandowska-Tomaszczyk and Patrick James Melia (eds) *PALC '97. Practical Applications in Language Corpora*, Łódz: Łódz University Press, 387-92.

Kenny, Dorothy (1998) 'Creatures of Habit? What Translators Usually Do with Words', in Sara Laviosa (ed.) *L'Approche Basée sur le corpus/The Corpus-Based Approach, Meta* 43(4): 515-23. Available at http://id.erudit.org/iderudit/003302ar [Accessed on 31 March 2011].

------ (2000) *Lexis and Creativity in Translation: A Corpus-based Study*, Manchester: St. Jerome Publishing.

Kilgarriff, Adam (2010a) 'Comparable Corpora Within and Across Languages, Word Frequency Lists and the KELLY Project', in Reinhard Rapp, Pierre Zweigenbaum and Serge Sharoff (eds) *BUCC 2010. Proceedings of the Third Workshop on Building and Using Comparable Corpora: Applications of Parallel and Comparable Corpora in Natural Language Engineering and the Humanities*, Paris: ELRA , 1-5.

------ (2010b) 'Corpora by Web Services' in *Workshop on Web Services and Processing Pipelines in HLT: Tool Evaluation, LR Production and Validation (LREC 2010)*, 45-51. Available at http://www.lrec-conf.org/proceedings/lrec2010/workshops/W3.pdf [Accessed on 30 March 2011].

------ (forthcoming) 'BootCatting Comparable Corpora', in Serge Sharoff, Reinhard Rapp, Pierre Zweigenbaum and Pascale Fung (eds) *BUCC: Building and Using Comparable Corpora*, New York & Heidelberg: Springer.

------ and Gregory Grefenstette (2003) 'Introduction to the Special Issue on the Web as Corpus', *Computational Linguistics* 29(3): 1-15.

------, Pavel Rychly, Pavel Smrz and David Tugwell (2004) 'The Sketch Engine', in *Proceedings of the Eleventh EURALEX International Congress, Lorient, France*. Available at ftp://ftp.itri.bton.ac.uk/reports/ITRI-04-08.ps [Accessed on 30 March 2011].

King, Philip (2003) 'Parallel Concordancing and its Applications', in Sylviane Granger, Jacques Lerot and Stephanie Petch-Tyson (eds) *Corpus-based Approaches to Contrastive Linguistics and Translation Studies*, Amsterdam & New York: Rodopi, 157-68.

------ and David Woolls (1996) 'Creating and Using a Multilingual Parallel Concordancer', in Barbara Lewandowska-Tomaszczyk and Marcel Thelen (eds) *Translation and Meaning, Part 4. Proceedings of the Łódź Session of the 1995 Maastricht-Łódź Duo*

Colloquium on "Translation and Meaning", 22-24 September 1995, Maastricht: Maastricht School of International Communication, 459-66.

Klaudy, Kinga and Krisztina Károly (2005) 'Implicitation in Translation: Empirical evidence for Operational Asymmetry in Translation', *Across Languages and Cultures* 6(1): 13-28.

Koehn, Philipp (2005) 'Europarl: A Parallel Corpus for Statistical Machine Translation,' *MT Summit 2005*. Available at http://www.iccs.inf.ed.ac.uk/~pkoehn/publications/europarl-mtsummit05.pdf [Accessed on 31 March 2011].

Konšalová, Petra (2007) 'Explicitation as a Universal in Syntactic De/Condensation', *Across Languages and Cultures* 8(1): 17-32.

Kraif, Olivier (2001) *Constitution et exploitation de bi-textes pour l'Aide à la traduction*, Doctoral Dissertation, Université de Nice Sophia Antipolis. Available at http://www.u-grenoble3.fr/kraif [Accessed on 22 February 2011].

------ (2002) 'Translation Alignment and Lexical Correspondence', in Bengt Altenberg and Sylviane Granger (eds) *Lexis in contrast. Corpus-based Approach*, Amsterdam & Philadelphia: John Benjamins, 271-90.

------ (2002-2006) *ALINEA – Aide*. Available at http://w3.u-grenoble3.fr/kraif/files/Aide/Aide.htm [Accessed on 15 March 2011].

------ and Boxing Chen (2004) 'Combining Clues for Lexical Level Aligning Using the Null Hypothesis Approach', in *Proceedings of Coling 2004, Geneva, August 2004*, 1261-64.

Kruger, Alet, Kim Wallmach and Jeremy Munday (eds) (2011) *Corpus-based Translation Studies. Research and Applications*, London & New York: Continuum.

Kučera, Henry and W. Nelson Francis (1967) *Computational Analysis of Present-day American English*, Providence: Brown University Press.

Laffling, John (1992) 'On Constructing a Transfer Dictionary for Man and Machine', *Target* 4(1): 17-31.

Lagoudaki, Elina (2006) *Translation Memory Systems: Enlightening Users' Perspectives*. Available at http://www3.imperial.ac.uk/portal/pls/portallive/docs/1/7307707.PDF [Accessed on 31 March 2011].

Laviosa, Sara (1997) 'How Comparable Can 'Comparable Corpora' Be?', *Target* 9(2): 289-319.

------ (1998a) 'The Corpus-based Approach: A New Paradigm in Translation Studies', in Sara Laviosa (ed.) *L'Approche Basée sur le corpus/The Corpus-Based Approach, Meta* 43(4): 474-79. Available at http://id.erudit.org/iderudit/003424ar [Accessed on 31 March 2011].

------ (1998b) 'Core Patterns of Lexical Use in a Comparable Corpus of English Narrative Prose', in Sara Laviosa (ed.) *L'Approche Basée sur le corpus/The Corpus-Based Approach, Meta* 43(4): 557-70. Available at http://id.erudit.org/iderudit/003425ar [Accessed on 31 March 2011].

------ (1998c) 'The English Comparable Corpus: A Resource and a Methodology', in Lynne Bowker, Michael Cronin, Dorothy Kenny and Jennifer Pearson (eds) *Unity in Diversity? Current Trends in Translation Studies*, Manchester: St. Jerome, 101-12.

------ (2002) *Corpus-based Translation Studies: Theory, Findings, Applications*, Amsterdam: Rodopi.

------ (2008) 'Corpus Studies of Translation Universals: A Critical Appraisal', in Aurelia

Martelli and Virginia Pulcini (eds) *Investigating English with Corpora. Studies in Honour of Maria Teresa Prat*, Monza: Polimetrica, 223-38.
Laviosa-Braithwaite, Sara (1996) *The English Comparable Corpus (ECC): A Resource and a Methodology for the Empirical Study of Translation*, Doctoral Dissertation, University of Manchester.
Lawson, Ann (2001) 'Collecting, Aligning and Analysing Parallel Corpora', in Mohsen Ghadessy, Alex Henry and Robert L. Roseberry (eds) *Small Corpus Studies and ELT. Theory and Practice*, Amsterdam & Philadelphia: John Benjamins, 279-309.
Lee, David Y. W. (2001) 'Genres, Registers, Text Types, Domains, and Styles: Clarifying the Concepts and Navigating a Path Through the BNC Jungle', *Language Learning & Technology* 5(3): 37-72.
------ (2010) *Software, Tools, Frequency Lists, etc.* Available at http://www.uow.edu.au/~dlee/software.htm [Accessed on 30 March 2010].
Leech, Geoffrey (2005) 'Adding Linguistic Annotation' in Martin Wynne (ed.) *Developing Linguistic Corpora: a Guide to Good Practice*, Oxford: Oxbow Books: 17-29. Available at http://www.ahds.ac.uk/creating/guides/linguistic-corpora/chapter2.htm [Accessed on 10 February 2011].
------ (2007) 'New Resources, or Just Better Old Ones? The Holy Grail of Representativness', in Marianne Hundt, Nadja Nesselhauf and Carolin Biewer (eds) *Corpus Linguistics and the Web*, Amsterdam & New York: Rodopi, 133-49.
------ and Steven Fligelstone (1992) 'Computers and Corpus Analysis', in Christopher Butler (ed.) *Computers and Written Texts*, Oxford & Cambridge: Blackwell, 115-40.
------, Roger Garside and Michael Bryant (1994) 'CLAWS4: The Tagging of the British National Corpus', in *Proceedings of the 15th International Conference on Computational Linguistics (COLING 94), Kyoto, Japan*, Stroudsburg, PA: ACL, 622-28. Available at http://acl.ldc.upenn.edu/C/C94/C94-1103.pdf [Accessed on 31 March 2011].
LISA (The Localization Industry Standard Association) (2005) *Translation Memory eXchange (TMX)*. Available at http://www.lisa.org/Translation-Memory-e.34.0.html [Accessed on 22 February 2011].
Liu, Zequan (2004) 'A Corpus-based Study of Reporting Verbs in Fictions: A Translational Perspective', *US-China Foreign Language* 2(8): 48-54.
Lottman, Herbert R. (2000) 'Italy Top Market for Translations', *Publishers Weekly*, 1/10/2000: 19.
Louw, Bill (1993) 'Irony in the Text or Insincerity in the Writer? The Diagnostic Potential of Semantic Prosodies', in Mona Baker, Gill Francis and Elena Tognini-Bonelli (eds) *Text and Technology: In Honour of John Sinclair*, Amsterdam: John Benjamins, 157-76.
Luz, Saturnino (2000) 'A Software Toolkit for Sharing and Accessing Corpora Over the Internet', in Maria Gavrilidou, George Carayannis, Stella Markantonatou, Stelios Piperidis and Gregory Stainhauer (eds) *Proceedings of the Second International Conference on Language Resources and Evaluation, Athens, Greece (LREC 2000)*, Paris: ELRA, 1749-54.
------ (2011) 'Web-based Corpus Software', in Alet Kruger, Kim Wallmach and Jeremy Munday (eds) *Corpus-based Translation Studies. Research and Applications*, London & New York: Continuum, 124-149.
------ and Mona Baker (2000) 'TEC: A Toolkit and API for Distributed Corpus Processing', Paper Presented at the Workshop on *Web-Based Language Documentation*

and Description, 12-15 December, Philadelphia, USA. Available at http://www.ldc.upenn.edu/exploration/expl2000/papers/luz/ [Accessed on 31 March 2011].

Ma, Xiaoyi (2000) *Hong Kong Hansards Parallel Text,* Philadelphia: Linguistic Data Consortium.

------ (2006) 'Champollion: A Robust Parallel Text Sentence Aligner', in *Proceedings of the Fifth International Conference on Language Resources and Evaluation, Genoa, Italy (LREC 2006),* Paris: ELRA, 489-92. Available at http://papers.ldc.upenn.edu/LREC2006/Champollion.pdf [Accessed on 31 March 2011].

Maia, Belinda (1997) 'Do-It-Yourself Corpora ... with a Little Bit of Help from your Friends!', in Barbara Lewandowska-Tomaszczyk and Patrick James Metia (eds) *PALC '97. PracticalApplications in Language Corpora*, Łódź: Łódź University Press, 403-10.

------ (1998) 'Word Order and the First Person Singular in Portuguese and English', in Sara Laviosa (ed.) *L'approche basée sur le corpus/The Corpus-Based Approach, Meta* 43(4): 589-601. Available at http://id.erudit.org/iderudit/003539ar [Accessed on 31 March 2011].

------ and Luís Sarmento (2006) 'Corpógrafo – Applications', in *Third International Workshop on Language Resources for Translation Work Research & Training (LR4Trans-III)*, 55-58. Available at http://www.linguateca.pt/documentos/CorpografoApplicationsMaiaSarmentoLR4III.pdf [Accessed on 30 March 2011].

Malmkjær, Kirsten (2008) 'Norms and Nature in Translation Studies', in Gunilla Anderman and Margaret Rogers (eds) *Incorporating Corpora: The Linguist and the Translator*, Clevedon, Buffalo & Toronto: Multilingual Matters, 49-59.

Martin, Joel, Howard Johnson, Benoit Farley and Anna Maclachlan (2003) 'Aligning and Using an English-Inuktitut Parallel Corpus', in *HLT-NAACL 2003 Workshop: Building and Using Parallel Texts Data Driven Machine Translation and Beyond , Edmonton, May-June 2003*, 115-118. Available at http://www.inuktitutcomputing.ca/NunavutHansard/AUEIPC-HLT2003.pdf [Accessed on 31 March 2011].

Mauranen, Anna (2000) 'Strange Strings in Translated Language. A Study on Corpora', in Maeve Olohan (ed.) *Intercultural Faultlines*, Manchester: St Jerome Publishing, 119-41.

------ (2008) 'Universal Tendencies in Translation', in Gunilla Anderman and Margaret Rogers (eds) *Incorporating Corpora: The Linguist and the Translator*, Clevedon, Buffalo & Toronto: Multilingual Matters, 32-48.

------ and Niina Hynninen (eds) (2010) *English as a Lingua Franca, Helsinki English Studies* 6. Available at http://blogs.helsinki.fi/hes-eng/volumes/volume-6/ [Accessed on 23 February 2011].

------ and Pekka Kujamäki (eds) (2004) *Translation Universals. Do they exist?*, Amsterdam & Philadelphia: John Benjamins.

McEnery, Tony and Andrew Wilson (1996 [second edition 2001]) *Corpus linguistics*, Edinburgh: Edinburgh University Press.

McEnery, Tony and Richard Xiao (2004) *The Lancaster Corpus of Mandarin Chinese (LCMC)*, Lancaster University. Available at http://www.lancs.ac.uk/fass/projects/corpus/LCMC/ [Accessed on 31 March 2011].

------ (2005) 'Character Encoding in Corpus Construction' in Martin Wynne (ed.) *Developing Linguistic Corpora: A Guide to Good Practice*, Oxford: Oxbow Books: 47-58. Available at http://www.ahds.ac.uk/creating/guides/linguistic-corpora/chapter4.

htm [Accessed on 10 February 2011].
McEnery, Tony, Richard Xiao and Yukio Tono (2006) *Corpus-based Language Studies. An Advanced Resource Book*, London & New York: Routledge.
Megyesi, Beata B. and Bengt Dahlqvist (2007) 'The Swedish-Turkish Parallel Corpus and Tools for its Creation', in *Proceedings of NoDaLida 2007. May 24-26 2007, Tartu, Estonia.* Available at http://stp.lingfil.uu.se/%7Ebea/publ/megyesi-dahlqvist-nodalida07.pdf [Accessed on 31 March 2011].
------, Eva Petterson and Joakim Nivre (2008) 'Swedish-Turkish Parallel Treebank', in *Proceedings of Language Resources and Evaluation Conference, Marrakesh, Marocco (LREC 2008),* Paris: ELRA, 470-73. Available at http://stp.lingfil.uu.se/%7Ebea/publ/megyesi-etal-lrec08.pdf [Accessed on 31 March 2011].
Melamed, I. Dan (1999) 'Bitext Maps and Alignment via Pattern Recognition', *Computational Linguistics* 25(1):107-30.
Meyer, Charles F. (2002) *English Corpus Linguistics: An Introduction*, Cambridge: Cambridge University Press.
Mikhailov, Mikhail (2002) 'Two Approaches to Automated Text Aligning of Parallel Texts in Fiction', *Across Languages and Cultures* 2(1): 87-96.
Monti, Cristina, Bendazzoli, Claudio, Sandrelli, Annalisa and Mariachiara Russo (2005) 'Studying Directionality in Simultaneous Interpreting through an Electronic Corpus: EPIC (European Parliament Interpreting Corpus', *Meta* 50(4). Available at http://www.erudit.org/revue/meta/2005/v50/n4/019850ar.pdf [Accessed on 31 March 2011].
Moosad, Praveen (2005) 'Syntax rules of XML', *NET Heaven*. Available at http://www.dotnetheaven.com/UploadFile/prvn_131971/syn03092005001815AM/syn.aspx [Accessed on 31 March 2011].
Moropa, Koliswa (2009) 'Utilizing 'Hot Words' in ParaConc to Verify Lexical Simplification Strategies in English-Xhosa Parallel Texts', *South African Journal of African Languages* 29(2): 227-41.
Munday, Jeremy (1998) 'A Computer-assisted Approach to the Analysis of Translation Shifts', in Sara Laviosa (ed.) *L'approche basée sur le corpus/The Corpus-Based Approach, Meta* 43(4): 542-56. Available at http://id.erudit.org/iderudit/003680ar [Accessed on 31 March 2011].
Munteanu, Dragos Stefan and Daniel Marcu (2006) 'Extracting Parallel Sub-sentential Fragments from Non-parallel Corpora', in *Proceedings of the 21st International Conference on Computational Linguistics and the 44th annual meeting of the Association for Computational Linguistics*, Sydney, Australia: Association for Computational Linguistics, 81-88. Available at https://portal.acm.org/citation.cfm?id=1220175.1220186&coll=portal&dl=ACM&CFID=79342841&CFTOKEN=88027892 [Accessed on 31 March 2011].
Musacchio, Maria Teresa and Giuseppe Palumbo (2010) 'Following Norms, Taking Risks: A Study of the Use of Connectives in a Corpus of Translated Economics Articles in Italian', in Carmen Heine and Jan Engberg (eds), *Reconceptualizing LSP. Online proceedings of the XVII European LSP Symposium 2009, Aarhus, Denmark.* Available at http://www.asb.dk/fileexplorer/fetchfile.aspx?file=19215 [Accessed on 31 March 2011].
Neumann, Stella and Silvia Hansen-Schirra (2005) 'The CroCo Project. Cross-linguistic Corpora for the Investigation of Explicitation in Translation', in Pernilla Danielsson and Martijn Wagenmakers (eds) *Proceedings from the Corpus Linguistics*

Conference Series (PCLC) 1(1). Available at http://www.corpus.bham.ac.uk/pclc/cl-134-pap.pdf [Accessed on 25 March 2011].

Newmark, Peter (1991) *About Translation*, Clevedon: Multilingual Matters.

Oakes, Michael (1998) *Statistics for Corpus Linguistics*, Edinburgh: Edinburgh University Press.

Och, Franz Josef (2006) 'Statistical Machine Translation Live', *Google Research Blog*, April 28, 2006. Available at http://googleresearch.blogspot.com/2006/04/statistical-machine-translation-live.html [Accessed on 28 February 2011].

------ and Hermann Ney (2003) 'Systematic Comparison of Various Statistical Alignment Models', *Computational Linguistics* 29(1): 19-51.

Ogrodniczuk, Maciej and Adam Przepiórkowski (2010) 'Linguistic Processing Chains as Web Services: Initial Linguistic Considerations', in *Workshop on Web Services and Processing Pipelines in HLT: Tool Evaluation, LR Production and Validation (LREC 2010)*, 1-7. Available at http://www.lrec-conf.org/proceedings/lrec2010/workshops/W3.pdf [Accessed on 30 March 2011].

Olohan, Maeve (2004) *Introducing Corpora in Translation Studies*, London & New York: Routledge.

------ and Mona Baker (2000) 'Reporting that in Translated English: Evidence for Subconscious Processes of Explicitation', *Across Languages and Cultures* 1(2): 141-58.

Øverås, Linn (1998) 'In Search of the Third Code: An Investigation of Norms in Literary Translation', in Sara Laviosa (ed.) *L'Approche Basée sur le corpus/The Corpus-Based Approach, Meta* 43(4): 571-88. Available at http://id.erudit.org/iderudit/003775ar [Accessed on 31 March 2011].

Pápai, Vilma (2004) 'Explicitation. A Universal of Translated Text?', in Anna Mauranen and Pekka Kujamäki (eds) *Translation Universals. Do they exist?*, Amsterdam & Philadelphia: John Benjamins, 143-64.

Pearson, Jennifer (2003) 'Using Parallel Texts in the Translator Training Environment', in Federico Zanettin, Silvia Bernardini, and Dominic Stewart (eds) *Corpora in Translation Education*, Manchester: St Jerome, 15–24.

Pekar, Viktor, Ruslan Mitkov, Dimitar Blagoev and Andrea Mulloni (2006) 'Finding Translations for Low-frequency Words in Comparable Corpora', *Machine Translation* 20(4): 247-66.

Peters, Carol and Eugenio Picchi (1998) 'Bilingual Reference Corpora for Translators and Translation Studies', in Lynne Bowker, Michael Cronin, Dorothy Kenny and Jennifer Pearson (eds) *Unity in Diversity? Current Trends in Translation Studies*, Manchester: St Jerome, 91-100.

------ and Lisa Biagini (2000) 'Parallel and Comparable Bilingual Corpora in Language Teaching and Learning', in Simon Botley, Tony McEnery and Andrew Wilson (eds) *Multilingual Corpora in Teaching and Research*, Amsterdam: Rodopi, 73-85.

Prinsloo, Daniël Jacobus and Gilles-Maurice de Schryver (2005) 'Managing Eleven Parallel Corpora and the Extraction of Data in All Official South African Languages', in Walter Daelemans, Theo du Plessis, Cobus Snyman and Lut Teck (eds) *Multilingualism and Electronic Language Management. Proceedings of the 4th International MIDP Colloquium, 22-23 September 2003, Bloemfontein, South Africa*, Pretoria: Van Schaik Publishers, 100–22.

Puurtinen, Tiina (2003) 'Genre-specific Features of Translationese? Linguistic Dif-

ferences between Translated and Non-translated Finnish Children's Literature', *Literary and Linguistic Computing* 18(4): 389-406.
Rambousek, Jiří and Jana Chamonikolosová (2008) 'The Existential There- construction in Czech Translation', in Gunilla Anderman and Margaret Rogers (eds) *Incorporating Corpora: The Linguist and the Translator*, Clevedon, Buffalo & Toronto: Multilingual Matters, 133-52.
Rapp, Reinhard (1995) 'Identifying Word Translations in Non-parallel Texts', in *Proceedings of the 33rd annual meeting on Association for Computational Linguistics*, Morristown, NJ: Association for Computational Linguistics, 320–22.
------ (forthcoming) 'Using Word Associations to Measure Corpus Representativity and Corpus Comparability', in Serge Sharoff, Reinhard Rapp, Pierre Zweigenbaum and Pascale Fung (eds) *BUCC: Building and Using Comparable Corpora*, New York & Heidelberg: Springer.
------, Pierre Zweigenbaum and Serge Sharoff (eds) (2010) *BUCC 2010. Proceedings of the Third Workshop on Building and Using Comparable Corpora: applications of Parallel and Comparable Corpora in Natural Language Engineering and the Humanities*, Paris: ELRA. Available at http://www.fb06.uni-mainz.de/lk/bucc2010/documents/Proceedings-BUCC-2010.pdf [Accessed 28 February 2011].
Ratz, Sebastian (n.d.) 'TEI for Linguistic Corpora', *Text Encoding Initiave, TEI: Customization*. Available at http://www.tei-c.org/release/xml/tei/custom/odd/tei_corpus.odd [Accessed on 31 March 2011].
Rayson, Paul (2009) *Wmatrix: A Web-based Corpus Processing Environment*, Computing Department, Lancaster University. Available at http://ucrel.lancs.ac.uk/wmatrix/ [Accessed on 10 February 2011].
Renouf, Antoinette, Andrew Kehoe and Jay Banerjee (2007) 'WebCorp: An Integrated System for Web Text Search', in Marianne Hundt, Nadja Nesselhauf and Caroline Biewer (eds) *Corpus Linguistics and the Web*, Amsterdam: Rodopi, 47-67.
Resnik, Philip and Noah A. Smith (2003) 'The Web as a Parallel Corpus', *Computational Linguistics* 29(3): 349-80.
Rodrigues Júnior, Adail Sebastião (2005) 'An Exploratory Study of Representation of Gay Characters in a Parallel Corpus of Short Stories: A Systemic-functional Approach', *Cadernos de Tradução* 16(2): 83-104.
Romary, Laurent and Patrice Bonhomme (2000) 'Parallel Alignment of Structured Documents', in Jean Véronis (ed.) *Parallel Text Processing*, Dordrecht: Kluwer, 233-53.
Römer, Ute (2007) 'Learner Language and the Norms in Native Corpora and EFL Teaching Materials: A Case Study of English Conditionals', in Sabine Volk-Birke and Julia Lippert (eds) *Anglistentag 2006 Halle. Proceedings*, Trier: Wissenschaftlicher Verlag Trier, 355-63.
Roukos, Salim, David Graff and Dan Melamed (1995) *Hansard French/English*, Philadelphia: Linguistic Data Consortium.
Russo, Mariachiara, Claudio Bendazzoli and Annalisa Sandrelli (2006) 'Looking for Lexical Patterns in a Trilingual Corpus of Source and Interpreted Speeches: Extended Analysis of EPIC (European Parliament Interpreting Corpus)', *FORUM, International Journal of Interpretation and Translation* 4(1): 221-54.
Rybicki, Jan (2006) 'Burrowing into Translation: Character Idiolects in Henryk Sienkiewicz's Trilogy and its Two English Translations', *Literary and Linguistic Computing* 21(1): 91-103.

Rychlý, Pavel (n.d.) *Manatee*. Available at http://www.textforge.cz/products [Accessed on 31 March 2011].

Saldanha, Gabriela (2004) 'Accounting for the Exception to the Norm: Split Infinitives in Translated English', in *Corpus-Based Translation Studies - Research and Applications, Language Matters: Studies in the Languages of Africa* 35(1): 39-53.

------ (2005) *Style of Translation: An exploration of Stylistic Patterns in the Translations of Margaret Jull Costa and Peter Bush*, Doctoral Dissertation, Dublin City University.

------ (2008) 'Explicitation Revisited: Bringing the Reader into the Picture', in Juliane House (ed.) *Beyond Intervention: Universals in Translation Processes, trans-kom* 1(1): 20-35. Available at http://www.trans-kom.eu/bd01nr01/trans-kom_01_01_03_Saldanha_Explicitation.20080707.pdf [Accessed on 30 March 2011].

------ (2011) 'Style of Translation: The Use of Source Language Words in Translations by Margaret Jull Costa and Peter Bush', in Jeremy Munday, Alet Kruger and Kim Wallmach (eds) *Corpus Based Translation Studies*, London: Continuum, 237-258.

Sánchez-Gijón, Pilar (2009) 'Developing Documentation Skills to Build Do-It-Yourself Corpora in the Specialized Translation Course', in Allison Beeby, Patricia Rodríguez Inés and Pilar Sánchez-Gijón (eds) *Corpus Use and Translating: Corpus Use for Learning to Translate and Learning Corpus Use to Translate*, Amsterdam & Philadelphia: John Benjamins, 109-27.

Sandrelli, Annalisa and Claudio Bendazzoli (2006) 'Tagging a Corpus of Interpreted Speeches: The European Parliament Interpreting Corpus (EPIC)', in *Proceedings of the Fifth International Conference on Language Resources and Evaluation, Genoa, Italy (LREC 2006)*, Paris: ELRA, 647-52. Available at http://hnk.ffzg.hr/bibl/lrec2006/pdf/174_pdf.pdf [Accessed on 30 March 2011].

Santos, Diana (2002) 'DISPARA, a System for Distributing Parallel Corpora on the Web', in Elisabete Ranchhod and Nuno J. Mamede (eds) *Advances in Natural Language Processing, Proceedings f the Third International Conference, PorTAL 2002, Faro, Portugal, June 23-26, 2002*, New York & Heidelberg: Springer, 209-218.

------ (2004) *Translation-based Corpus Studies. Contrasting English and Portuguese Tense and Aspect Systems*, Amsterdam & New York: Rodopi.

------, Rosário Silva and Susana Inácio (2008) 'What's in a Colour? Studying and Contrasting Colours with COMPARA', in *Proceedings of the Sixth International Conference on Language Resources and Evaluation, Marrakesh, Marocco (LREC 2008)*, Paris: ELRA, 255-61. Available at http://www.lrec-conf.org/proceedings/lrec2008/pdf/73_paper.pdf [Accessed on 31 March 2011].

Sarmento, Luís, Belinda Maia and Diana Santos (2004) 'The Corpógrafo – a Web-based Environment for Corpora Research', in *Proceedings of the Fourth International Conference of Language Resources and Evaluation, Lisbon, Portugal (LREC 2004)*, Paris: ELRA, 449-52. Available at https://nats-www.informatik.uni-hamburg.de/intern/proceedings/2004/LREC/pdf/236.pd> [Accessed on 30 March 2011].

Sarmento, Luís, Belinda Maia, Diana Santos, Ana Pinto and Luís Cabral (2006) 'Corpógrafo V3: From Terminological Aid to Semi-automatic Knowledge Engine', in *Proceedings of the Fifth International Conference on Language Resources and Evaluation, Genova, Italy (LREC 2006)*, Paris: ELRA: 1502-05. Available at http://www.linguateca.pt/Diana/download/SarmentoetalLREC2006.pdf [Accessed on 30 March 2011].

Schiavi, Giuliana (1996) 'There is Always a Teller in a Tale', *Target* 8(1): 1-21.

Schiller, Heather (1993) 'Fiction: What Works in Britain', *European Bookseller*, September/October: 24-28.

Shen, Ethan (2010) 'Comparison of Online Machine Translation Tools', *tcworld, June 2010*. Available at http://www.tcworld.info/index.php?id=175 [Accessed on 28 February 2011].

Scott, Mike (1996-2011) *WordSmith Tools*, version 5, Oxford: Oxford University Press.

------ (2010) *Wordsmith Tools, V. 5 – Online Manual*. Available at http://www.lexically.net/downloads/version5/HTML/index.html [Accessed on 31 March 11].

SDL Trados (2007) *WinAlign User Guide*, SDL International. Available at http://www.lspzone.com/en/Images/SDL%20Trados%202007%20WinAlign_en_tcm11-795.pdf [Accessed on 31 March 2011].

Seghiri, Miriam and Gloria Corpas Pastor (2009) 'Virtual corpora as documentation resources: Translating Travel Insurance Documents (English – Spanish)', in Allison Beeby, Patricia Rodríguez Inés and Pilar Sánchez-Gijón (eds) *Corpus Use and Translating: Corpus use for learning to translate and learning corpus use to translate*, Amsterdam & Philadelphia: John Benjamins, 75-107.

Serpollet, Noëlle (2008) 'A study of the mandative subjunctive in French and its translations into English', in Gunilla Anderman and Margaret Rogers (eds) *Incorporating Corpora: The Linguist and the Translator*, Clevedon, Buffalo & Toronto: Multilingual Matters, 187-216.

Setton, Robin (2002) 'A methodology for the analysis of interpretation corpora', in Giuliana Garzone and Maurizio Viezzi (eds) *Interpreting in the 21st Century. Challenges and opportunities*, Amsterdam & Philadelphia: John Benjamins, 29-45.

Schäffner, Christina (1998) 'Parallel texts in translation', in Lynne Bowker, Michael Cronin, Dorothy Kenny and Jennifer Pearson (eds) *Unity in diversity? Current trends in translation studies*, Manchester: St Jerome, 83-90.

Sharoff, Serge (2006a) 'Creating general-purpose corpora using automated search engine queries', in Marco Baroni and Silvia Bernardini (eds) *WaCky! Working papers on the Web as Corpus*, Gedit: Bologna, 63-98.

------ (2006b) 'Open-source corpora: using the net to fish for linguistic data', *International Journal of Corpus Linguistics* 11(4): 435-62.

------ (2006c) 'A Uniform Interface to Large-Scale Linguistic Resources', in *Proceedings of the Fifth International Conference on Language Resources and Evaluation, Genoa, Italy (LREC 2006)*, Paris: ELRA, 539-42. Available at http://www.comp.leeds.ac.uk/ssharoff/publications/lrec2006-cqp.pdf [Accessed on 31 March 2011].

------ (forthcoming) 'Measuring the distance between comparable corpora between languages', in Serge Sharoff, Reinhard Rapp, Pierre Zweigenbaum and Pascale Fung (eds) *BUCC: Building and Using Comparable Corpora*, New York & Heidelberg: Springer.

------, Reinhard Rapp, Pierre Zweigenbaum and Pascale Fung (eds) (forthcoming) *BUCC: Building and Using Comparable Corpora*, New York & Heidelberg: Springer.

Shi, Lei, Cheng Niu, Ming Zhou, and Jianfeng Gao (2006) 'A DOM tree alignment model for mining parallel data from the web', in *Proceedings of the 21st International Conference on Computational Linguistics and the 44th annual meeting of the Association for Computational Linguistics (ACL44)*, Stroudsburg, PA: ACL, 489-96.

Shlesinger, Miriam (1998) 'Corpus-Based Interpreting Studies as an Offshoot of

Corpus-Based Translation Studies', in Sara Laviosa (ed.) *L'Approche Basée sur le corpus/The Corpus-Based Approach, Meta* 43(4): 486-93. Available at http://id.erudit.org/iderudit/004136ar [Accessed on 31 March 11].
------ (2009) 'Towards a definition of Interpretese: An intermodal, corpus-based study', in Gyde Hansen, Andrew Chesterman and Heidrun Gerzymisch-Arbogast (eds) *Efforts and Models in Interpreting and Translation Research*, Amsterdam: John Benjamins, 237-53.
Simard, Michel, George Foster, Pierre Isabelle (1992) 'Using Cognates to Align Sentences in Bilingual Corpora', in *Proceedings of the Fourth International Conference on Theoretical and Methodological Issues in Machine Translation (TMI-92)*, Montréal, Canada.
Simões, Alberto and José João Almeida (2003) 'NATools - A statistical Word Aligner Workbench', *Procesamiento del Lenguaje Natural* 31: 217-26. Available at http://www.sepln.org/revistaSEPLN/revista/31/31-Pag217.pdf [Accessed on 31 March 2011].
Simon, Kiril and Petya Osenova (2004) *BulTreeBank Corpus of Bulgarian. Content, Segmentation, Tokenization, BulTreeBank Technical Report BTB-TR02*. Available at http://www.bultreebank.org/TechRep/BTB-TR02.pdf [Accessed on 31 March 2011].
Sinclair, John (ed.) (1987) *Looking Up: An Account of the COBUILD Project in Lexical Computing*, London: HarperCollins.
------ (1991) *Corpus, Concordance, Collocation*, Oxford: Oxford University Press.
------ (1996) 'Reference Corpora', in *EAGLES Preliminary recommendations on Corpus Typology*. Available at http://www.ilc.cnr.it/EAGLES96/corpustyp/node18.html [Accessed on 31 March 2011].
------ (2003) *Reading Concordances: An Introduction*, Harlow: Longman.
------ (2004) *Trust the Text. Language, Corpus and Discourse*, London & New York: Routledge.
------ (2005) 'Corpus and Text - Basic Principles', in Martin Wynne (ed.) *Developing Linguistic Corpora: a Guide to Good Practice*, Oxford: Oxbow Books: 1-16. Available at http://www.ahds.ac.uk/creating/guides/linguistic-corpora/chapter1.htm [Accessed on 10 February 2011].
------ (ed.) (1987) *Collins Cobuild English Language Dictionary*, London: HarperCollins.
Snell-Hornby, Mary (1988) *Translation Studies. An Integrated Approach*, Amsterdam & Philadelphia: John Benjamins.
------ (2006) *The Turns of Translation Studies: New Paradigms or Shifting Viewpoints?*, Amsterdam & Philadelphia: John Benjamins.
Somers, Harold (ed.) (2003a) *Computers and Translation: a Translator's Guide*, Amsterdam & Philadelphia: John Benjamins.
------ (2003b) 'The translator's workstation', in Harold Somers (ed.) *Computers and Translation: a Translator's Guide*, Amsterdam & Philadelphia: John Benjamins, 13–30.
Stefanowitsch, Anatol (2004-2005) *Quantitative Thinking for Corpus Linguists*. Available at http://www-user.uni-bremen.de/~anatol/qnt/qnt_dist.html [Accessed on 30 March 2011].
------ and Stefan Th. Gries (eds) (2006) *Corpus-Based Approaches to Metaphor and Metonymy*, Berlin & New York: Mouton de Gruyter.
Steinberger, Ralf, Bruno Pouliquen, Anna Widiger, Camelia Ignat, Tomaž Erjavec, Dan

Tufiş and Dániel Varga (2006) 'The JRC-Acquis: A multilingual aligned parallel corpus with 20+ languages', in *Proceedings of the Fifth International Conference on Language Resources and Evaluation, Genoa, Italy (LREC 2006),* Paris: ELRA, 2142-47. Available at http://arxiv.org/ftp/cs/papers/0609/0609058.pdf [Accessed on 30 March 2011].

Stewart, Dominic (2010) *Semantic Prosody. A critical evaluation*, New York & Oxon: Routledge.

Stubbs, Michael (1996) *Text and corpus analysis*, Oxford & Cambridge-MA: Blackwell.

------ (2001) *Words and Phrases: Corpus Studies in Lexical Semantics*, Oxford & Cambridge-MA: Blackwell.

TEI Consortium (2009) *P5: Guidelines for Electronic Text Encoding and Interchange.* Available at http://www.tei-c.org/release/doc/tei-p5-doc/en/html/index.html [Accessed on 31 March 2011].

TEI Stand-Off Markup Workgroup (2003) *Stand-off Markup.* Available at http://www.tei-c.org/Activities/Workgroups/SO/sow06.xml [Accessed on 31 March 2011].

Tengku Mahadi, Tengku Sepora, Helia Vaezian and Mahmoud Akbari (2010) *Corpora in Translation: A Pratical Guide*, Bern: Peter Lang.

Teuberg, Wofgang (1996) 'Comparable or Parallel Corpora?', *International Journal of Lexicography* 9(3): 238-64.

The Association for Computational Linguistics (2005) *What is Computational Linguistics?.* Available at http://www.aclweb.org/archive/misc/what.html [Accessed on 15 January 2011].

Tiedemann, Jörg (2003a) *Recycling Translations. Extraction of Lexical Data from Parallel Corpora and their Application in Natural Language Processing*, Doctoral Dissertation, Uppsala: ACTA UNIVERSITATIS UPSALIENSIS. Available at http://stp.ling.uu.se/~joerg/phd/html/thesis_html.html [Accessed on 31 March 2011].

------ (2003b) 'Combining Clues for Word Alignment', in *Proceedings of the 10th Conference of the European Chapter of the ACL (EACL03) Budapest, Hungary, April 12-17, 2003*, Stroudsburg, PA: ACL, 339-46. Available at http://portal.acm.org/ft_gateway.cfm?id=1067852&type=pdf&CFID=24136484&CFTOKEN=69308561 [Accessed on 31 March 2011].

------ (2004) 'Word to Word Alignment Strategies', in *Proceedings of the 20th International Conference on Computational Linguistics, Geneva, Switzerland (COLING 2004)*, 212-18. Available at http://aclweb.org/anthology-new/C/C04/C04-1031.pdf [Accessed on 30 March 2011].

------ (2006) 'ISA & ICA - Two Web Interfaces for Interactive Alignment of Bitexts', in *Proceedings of the Fifth International Conference on Language Resources and Evaluation, Genoa, Italy (LREC'2006),* Paris: ELRA. Available at http://www.let.rug.nl/tiedeman/paper/lrec2006_ica_isa.pdf [Accessed on 30 March 2011].

------ (2008) 'Synchronizing Translated Movie Subtitles', in *Proceedings of the Sixth International Conference on Language Resources and Evaluation, Marrakesh, Marocco (LREC 2008),* Paris: ELRA. Available at http://stp.lingfil.uu.se/~joerg/published/lrec08.pdf [Accessed on 23 February 2011].

------ (2009) 'News from OPUS - A Collection of Multilingual Parallel Corpora with Tools and Interfaces', in Nicolas Nicolov, Kalina Bontcheva, Galia Angelova and Ruslan Mitkov (eds) *Recent Advances in Natural Language Processing* (vol. V), Amsterdam & Philadelphia: John Benjamins, 237-48.

Tirkkonen-Condit, Sonja (2002) 'Translationese – A Myth or an Empirical Fact? A Study into the Linguistic Identifiability of Translated Language', *Target* 14(2): 207-20.

------ (2004) 'Unique Items – over- or Under-represented in Translated Language?' in Anna Mauranen and Pekka Kujamäki (eds) *Translation Universals: Do they exist?*, Amsterdam & Philadelphia: John Benjamins, 177-84.

Tognini-Bonelli, Elena (2001) *Corpus Linguistics at Work*, Amsterdam & Philadelphia: John Benjamins.

------ (2002) 'Functionally Complete Units of Meaning across English and Italian: Towards a Corpus-driven Approach', in Bengt Altenberg and Sylviane Granger (eds) *Lexis in Contrast. Corpus-based Approach*, Amsterdam & Philadelphia: John Benjamins, 73-95.

Toury, Gideon (1995) *Descriptive Translation Studies and Beyond*, Amsterdam & Philadelphia: John Benjamins.

------ (2004) 'Probabilistic Explanations in Translation Studies: Welcome as they are, would they Qualify as Universals?', in Anna Mauranen and Pekka Kujamäki (eds) *Translation Universals: Do they exist?*, Amsterdam and Philadelphia: John Benjamins, 15–32.

Trushkina, Julia, Lieve Macken and Hans Paulussen (2008) 'Sentence Alignment in DPC: Maximizing Precision, Minimizing Human Effort', in *Proceedings of the Sixth International Conference on Language Resources and Evaluation, Marrakesh, Marocco (LREC 2008)*, Paris: ELRA, 485-88. Available at http://www.lrec-conf.org/proceedings/lrec2008/pdf/126_paper.pdf [Accessed on 30 March 2011].

Tymoczko, Maria (1998) 'Computerized Corpora and the Future of Translation Studies', in Sara Laviosa (ed.) *L'Approche Basée sur le corpus/ The Corpus-Based Approach, Meta* 43(4): 452-59. Available at http://id.erudit.org/iderudit/004515ar [Accessed on 31 March 2011].

Ulrych, Margherita and Simona Anselmi (2008) 'Towards a Corpus-based Distinction between Language-specific and Universal Features of Mediated Discourse', in Aurelia Martelli and Virginia Pulcini (eds) *Investigating English with Corpora. Studies in Honour of Maria Teresa Prat*, Monza: Polimetrica, 257-73.

Utiyama, Masao, Daisuke Kawahara, Keiji Yasuda and Eiichiro Sumita (2009) 'Mining Parallel Texts from Mixed-Language Web Pages', in *Proceedings of the Twelfth Machine Translation Summit, August 26-30, 2009, Ottawa, Ontario, Canada.* Available at http://www.mt-archive.info/MTS-2009-Utiyama-1.pdf [Accessed on 31 March 2011].

Valentini, Cristina (2006) 'A Multimedia Database for the Training of Audiovisual Translators', *Jostrans* 06. Available at http://www.jostrans.org/issue06/art_valentini.php [Accessed on 31 March 2011].

Váradi, Tamás (2008) 'NP Modification Structures in Parallel Corpora', in *Incorporating Corpora: The Linguist and the Translator*, Clevedon, Buffalo & Toronto: Multilingual Matters, 168-87.

Varantola, Krista (2003) 'Translators and Disposable corpora', in Federico Zanettin, Silvia Bernardini and Dominic Stewart (eds) *Corpora in Translator Education,* Manchester: St Jerome, 55-70.

Varga, Dániel, László Németh, Péter Halácsy, András Kornai, Viktor Trón, and Viktor Nagy (2007) 'Parallel Corpora for Medium Density Languages', in Nicolas Nicolov, Kalina Bontcheva, Galia Angelova and Ruslan Mitkov (eds) *Recent Advances in*

Natural Language Processing IV. Selected papers from RANLP 2005, Amsterdam & Philadelphia: John Benjamins, 247-58.
Vela, Mihaela, Stella Neumann and Silvia Hansen-Schirra (2007) 'Querying Multi-layer Annotation and Alignment in Translation Corpora', in Matthew Davies, Paul Rayson, Susan Hunston, Pernilla Danielsson (eds) *Proceedings of Corpus Linguistics Conference (CL2007), University of Birmingham*. Available at http://ucrel.lancs.ac.uk/publications/CL2007/paper/97_Paper.pdf [Accessed on 25 March 2011].
Venuti, Lawrence (1995) *The Translator's Invisibility*, London & New York: Routledge.
Véronis, Jean (ed.) (2000) *Parallel Text Processing: Alignment and Use of Translation Corpora*, Dordrecht: Kluwer Academic Publishers.
Vigini, Luigi (1999) *Rapporto sull'editoria italiana*, Milano: Editrice bibliografica.
von Waldenfels, Ruprecht (2006) 'Compiling a Parallel Corpus of Slavic Languages', in Bernhard Brehmer, Vladislava Ždanova and Rafał Zimny (eds) *Beiträge der Europäischen Slavistischen Linguistik (POLYSLAV) 9*, München: Otto Sagner, 123-38.
Wales, Katie (1989) *A Dictionary of Stylistics*, London & New York: Longman.
Wallmach, Kim (2000) 'Examining Simultaneous Interpreting Norms and Strategies in a South African Legislative Context: A Pilot Corpus Analysis', in *Translation Studies in South Africa, Language Matters: Studies in the Languages of Africa* 31(1): 198-221.
Wang, Kefei and Hongwu Qin (2008) 'A Parallel Corpus-based Study of Translational Chinese', in Richard Xiao, Lianzhen He and Ming Yue (eds) *Proceedings of The International Symposium on Using Corpora in Contrastive and Translation Studies (UCCTS 2008), Zhejiang University, Hangzhou*. Available at http://www.lancs.ac.uk/fass/projects/corpus/UCCTS2008Proceedings/papers/Wang_and_Qin.pdf [Accessed on 31 March 2011].
Warren, Martin (2009) 'Introduction', in Chris Graves, *ConcGram 1.0 Manual*, Amsterdam & Philadelphia: John Benjamins, 1-11.
Wechsler, Robert (1998) *Performing Without A Stage. The Art of Literary Translation*, North Haven, CT: Catbird Press.
Wiechmann, Daniel and Stefan Fuhs (2006) 'Corpus Linguistics Resources. Concordancing Software', *Corpus Linguistics and Linguistic Theory* 2(1): 109-30.
Wilkinson, Michael (2006) 'Compiling Corpora for Use as Translation Resources', *Translation Journal* 10(1). Available at http://accurapid.com/journal/35corpus.htm [Accessed on 31 March 2011].
Williams, Geoffrey C. (2008) 'The Good Lord and His Works: A Corpus-driven Study of Collocational Resonance', in Sylviane Granger and Fanny Meunier (eds) *Phraseology: An Interdisciplinary Perspective*, Amsterdam & Philadelphia, John Benjamins, 159-73.
Williams, Ian A. (2009a) 'Discourse Style and Theme-Rheme Progression in Biomedical Research Article Discussions: A Corpus-based Contrastive Study of Translational and Non-translational Spanish', *Languages in Contrast* 9(2): 225-66.
------ (2009b) 'A Corpus-based Study of Spanish Translations of the Verb 'report' in Biomedical Research Articles', *Meta* 54(1): 146-60. Available at http://id.erudit.org/iderudit/029798ar [Accessed on 3 March 2011].
Winters, Marion (2004) 'F. Scott Fitzgerald's *Die Schönen und Verdammten*: A Corpus-based Study of Loan Words and Code Switches as Features of Translators' Style', *Language Matters* 35(1): 248-58.

------ (2007) 'F. Scott Fitzgerald's *Die Schönen und Verdammten*: A Corpus-based Study of Speech-act Report Verbs as a Feature of Translators' Styles', *Meta* 52(3): 412-25. Available at http://id.erudit.org/iderudit/016728ar [Accessed on 31 March 2011].

------ (2009) 'Modal Particles Explained. How Modal Particles Creep into Translations and Reveal Translators' Styles', *Target* 21(1): 74-97.

Woolls, David (1995) *Multiconcord: The Lingua Multilingual Parallel Concordancer for Windows*, CFL Software Development.

------ (2000) 'From Purity to Pragmatism; User-driven Developments of a Multilingual Parallel Concordancer', in Simon Philip Botley, Tony McEnery and Andrew Wilson (eds) *Multilingual Corpora in Teaching and Research*, Amsterdam & Atlanta, GA: Rodopi, 116-33.

Wynne, Martin (2005) *Developing Linguistic Corpora: A Guide to Good Practice*, Oxford: Oxbow Books. Available at http://www.ahds.ac.uk/creating/guides/linguistic-corpora/index.htm [Accessed on 30 March 2011].

------ (2008) 'Building Corpora', Online posting. 24 January 2008, *Corpora-List*. Available at http://mailman.uib.no/public/corpora/2008-January/005805.html [Accessed on 30 March 2011].

Xia, Yun and Defeng Li (2010) 'Specialized Comparable Corpora in Translation Evaluation: A Case Study of English Translations of Chinese Law Firm Adverts', in Richard Xiao (ed.) *Using Corpora in Contrastive and Translation Studies*, Newcastle upon Tyne: Cambridge Scholars Publishing, 62-78.

Xiao, Richard (ed.) (2010) *Using Corpora in Contrastive and Translation Studies*, Newcastle upon Tyne: Cambridge Scholars Publishing.

Yuste Rodrigo, Elia (ed.) (2008) *Topics in Language Resources for Translation and Localisation*, Amsterdam & Philadelphia: John Benjamins.

Zanettin, Federico (1998) 'Bilingual Comparable Corpora and the Training of Translators', in Sara Laviosa (ed.) *L'Approche Basée sur le corpus/The Corpus-Based Approach, Meta* 43(4): 616-30. Available at http://id.erudit.org/iderudit/004638ar [Accessed on 31 March 2011].

------ (2000) 'Parallel Corpora in Translation Studies', in Maeve Olohan (ed.) *Intercultural Faultlines*, Manchester: St Jerome Publishing, 105-18.

------ (2001a) 'Swimming in Words: Corpora, Language Learning and Translation', in Guy Aston (ed.) *Learning with Corpora,* Houstox,TX: Athelstan, 177-97.

------ (2001b) *IperGrimus*, in *inTRAlinea.* Available at http://www.intralinea.it/intra/ipermedia/IperGrimus/ [Accessed on 31 March 2011].

------ (2002a) 'CEXI. Designing an English Italian Translational Corpus', in Bernhard Ketteman and Georg Marko (eds) *Teaching and Learning by Doing Corpus Analysis*, Amsterdam: Rodopi, 329-43.

------ (2002b) 'DIY Corpora: The WWW and the Translator', in Belinda Maia, Johann Haller and Margherita Ulrych (eds) *Training the Language Services Provider for the New Millennium*, Porto: Faculdade de Letras da Universidade do Porto, 239-48.

------ (2009a) 'Corpus-based Translation Activities for Language Learners', *The Interpreter and Translator Trainer (ITT)* 3(2): 209-224.

------ (2009b) 'Corpora multimediali e analisi dell'interazione. Osservazioni su strumenti e metodologie', in Laura Gavioli (ed.) *La mediazione linguistico-culturale: una prospettiva interazionista*, Perugia: Guerra, 210-31.

------ (2011) 'Hardwiring Translation Studies: Corpus Encoding', in Alet Kruger, Kim Walmach and Jeremy Munday (eds) *Corpus-based translation studies. Research and Applications*, London & New York: Continuum.

------, Silvia Bernardini and Dominic Stewart (eds) (2003) *Corpora in Translator Education*, Manchester: St Jerome.

Zweigenbaum, Pierre, Pierre Jacquemart, Natalia Grabar and Benoît Habert (2001) 'Building a Text Corpus for Representing the Variety of Medical Language', in Vimla L. Patel, Ray Rogers and Reinhod Haux (eds) *Medinfo 2001: Proceedings of the 10th World Congress on Medical Informatics*, Amsterdam: IOS Press, 290-98.

------, Éric Gaussier and Pascale Fung (eds) (2008) *Proceedings of the Workshop on Building and using parallel corpora, in Proceedings of the Sixth International Conference on Language Resources and Evaluation (LREC 2008)*, Marrakech, Morocco. Available at http://www.fb06.uni-mainz.de/lk/bucc2010/documents/Proceedings-BUCC-2008.pdf [Accessed on 28 February 2011].

Index

U

V

W